Travels with Ernest

ETHNOGRAPHIC ALTERNATIVES BOOK SERIES

Series Editors
Carolyn Ellis
Arthur P. Bochner
(both at the University of South Florida)

About the Series:

Ethnographic Alternatives emphasizes experimental forms of qualitative writing that blur the boundaries between social sciences and humanities. The editors encourage submissions that experiment with novel forms of expressing lived experience, including literary, poetic, autobiographical, multi-voiced, conversational, critical, visual, performative, and co-constructed representations. Emphasis should be on expressing concrete lived experience through narrative modes of writing.

We are interested in ethnographic alternatives that promote narration of local stories; literary modes of descriptive scene setting, dialogue, and un-folding action; and inclusion of the author's subjective reactions, involvement in the research process, and strategies for practicing reflexive fieldwork.

Please send proposals to:
Carolyn Ellis and Arthur P. Bochner
Department of Communication
University of South Florida
4202 East Fowler Avenue, CIS 1040
Tampa, FL 33620-7800
E-mail: cellis@cas.usf.edu

Books in the Series:

Travels with Ernest
Crossing the
Literary/Sociological Divide

Laurel Richardson and Ernest Lockridge

ALTAMIRA
PRESS

A Division of Rowman & Littlefield Publishers, Inc.
Walnut Creek • Lanham • New York • Toronto • Oxford

ALTAMIRA PRESS
A Division of Rowman & Littlefield Publishers, Inc.
1630 North Main Street, #367
Walnut Creek, CA 94596
www.altamirapress.com

Rowman & Littlefield Publishers, Inc.
A Member of the The Rowman & Littlefield Publishing Group, Inc.
4501 Forbes Boulevard, Suite 200
Lanham, Maryland 20706

PO Box 317
Oxford
OX2 9RU, UK

British Library Cataloguing in Publication Information Available

Library of Congress Cataloging-in-Publication Data
Richardson, Laurel.
    Travels with Ernest : crossing the literary/sociological divide /
    Laurel Richardson and Ernest Lockridge.
        p. cm. — (Ethnographic alternatives book series ; v. 16)
    Includes index.
    ISBN 0-7591-0596-0 (alk. paper) — ISBN 0-7591-0597-9 (pbk. : alk.
paper)
        1. Lockridge, Ernest, 1938– Travel. 2. Novelists, American—20th
century—Biography. 3. College teachers—United States—Biography. 4.
Married people—United States—Biography. 5. Sociologists—United
States—Biography. 6. Lockridge, Ernest, 1938– Marriage. 7.
Richardson, Laurel—Marriage. 8. Richardson, Laurel—Travel. I.
Lockridge, Ernest, 1938– II. Title. III. Series.

PS3562.O27Z88 2004
813'.54—dc22   2003022898

Printed in the United States of America

∞™ The paper used in this publication meets the minimum requirements of American
National Standard for Information Sciences—Permanence of Paper for Printed Library
Materials, ANSI/NISO Z39.48–1992.

CONTENTS

CONTENTS

ACKNOWLEDGMENTS

We thank the AltaMira Press editor, Mitch Allen, and the Alternative Ethnographic series editors, Carolyn Ellis and Arthur Bochner, for their general support of alternative writing, and for their specific support for and contributions to this project. The editorial staff—Melissa McNitt, Brigitte Scott, and Kristina van Niekerk—has been generous, and we appreciate their contributions. Elizabeth St. Pierre, Betty Kirschner, Bob Canzoneri, Belinda Gore, Gordon Grigsby, Barbara Bergmann, Maggie Kast, Susan Knox, Stuart Mitchner, and Merry Norris have graciously given us their thoughts on various parts of this manuscript. The members of the Memoir Writing Group (Beverly Davis, Nancy Lee, Diana Newman, Linda Royalty, Linda Thompson, and Deanne Witiak), the members of the Woman's Poetry Workshop (Ellin Carter, Molly Davis, Meg Hoskins, Elizabeth Ann James, Micki Seltzer, Anne Sostrom, Kezia Sproat, Cathy Tucker, and Kay Wolf), and the members of the Postmodernist Theory Reading Group (Patti Lather, Patricia Stuhr, Marilyn Johnstone, Suzanne Damarin, Amy Shuman, Nancy Johnson, Mary Margaret Fonow, and Linda Meadows) have been steadfast in their support of Laurel's writing, and have given good counsel along the way. We are appreciative of their input. We thank the hosts in the places we visited. And we thank our grandchildren for being in our lives: the grown-up Shana, who can read this book now; and the young ones—Akiva, Maxwell, Natasha, Katya, Alex, Caroline, and Christopher—may they enjoy this book when they are old enough to read it!

TRAIL GUIDE: AN INTRODUCTION

Hope is the thing with feathers
That perches in the soul,
    And sings the tune without the words
And never stops at all.

                                    —Emily Dickinson

I am a sociologist; my husband, Ernest Lockridge is a novelist. We've been traveling together for a quarter of a century, seeing the world through different professional eyes, biographies, spiritual and emotional longings. We wanted to collaborate on a book about our travels that would simultaneously honor our distinct voices, deepen our understandings of ourselves and our relationship, and offer some new writing ideas to others.

We decided to each write a personal narrative inspired by our shared travel, to read each other's narrative, and to have a freewheeling conversation (tape-recorded and transcribed) about the narratives. We talked about writing issues—ethics, authorship, collaboration, witnessing, genre, audiences, memory, observation, and imagination; and we talked about our relationship, our blended family, our biographies, and the world at large. (For those with interests in how this book was made, please see the appendix.)

Because we crisscrossed personal and professional boundaries, our "travels" have been more than geographical; they have been intellectual, emotional, and spiritual. The result is *Travels with Ernest*—the contemporary love story of two people who love each other, their work, and their lives.

Both Ernest and I think of writing as a method of discovery—a way to learn about one's self and one's world. In *Travels*, our discoveries build on

each other. Ernest writes a meta-narrative, beginning with the mystery—
"Why is this guy so edgy?"—and ending with the mystery solved. He re-
tains his novelistic perspective. In my narratives, I engage cultural themes,
identity issues, and social processes; I do not have a novelist's perspective.

Ernest joins me in inviting you to travel with us—to Death Valley,
Ireland, Beirut, Copenhagen, Russia, and to St. Petersburg, Florida, and
Sedona, Arizona. And we invite you to join us in a summing-up of sorts,
direct from our hometown of Worthington, Ohio, the location of our final section, "Happy Trail—The Movie."

Laurel Richardson

CHAPTER I
DEATH VALLEY
March 5–12, 1993

And if you're lost enough to find yourself
By now. . . .

—Robert Frost

Death Valley Day

Sunday, March 7, 1993

Ernest Lockridge

"**D**oesn't look much wider than a football field," I observe, climbing from the driver's side of our bright red rental car, a Pontiac Grand Prix. "Really makes you wonder why those old pioneers in their covered wagons didn't cross the valley right here."

Our gear's stowed in the car trunk—wide-brimmed hats, multipocketed hiking vests, push-here-dummy camera, Power Bars, matching pair of aluminum Cub Scout canteens encased in navy-blue canvas that we filled and wet down in our room at Furnace Creek Ranch. It's mid-morning. The sky is clear, the air utterly transparent and heating up in the blazing white sun. I've parked alongside Route 190 skirting the east side of Death Valley, which isn't a "valley" but something called a graben, its floor sinking into a fault in the earth's crust. Death Valley's the hottest spot on the planet. There's some hellish sand-hole in the Libyan Desert that once or twice has received a higher scorecard, but no place holds a candle to Death Valley for sheer consistency. Badwater Basin near the valley's southern boundary is the lowest place on the earth's surface—282 feet below sea level. Ten thousand years ago an inland sea covered the entire area to a depth of six hundred feet.

Our plan is to hike due west across Mesquite Flat. We selected the jumping-off point yesterday during a foray of driving about. The terrain looked friendly here, the crossing itself almost unbelievably narrow. West across Death Valley loom the Cottonwood Mountains, gray and white. Behind us are the Funeral Mountains. The story goes that back in 1850, when those who stayed behind in the Valley were finally rescued, one of their number, a woman, looked back over her shoulder and said, "Goodbye, Death Valley." In Death Valley death is a serious business.

"Let's look at the map," says Laurel.

I rummage through my vest pockets for the green circular handed to us by the park ranger who took our entrance fee the day before yesterday when we arrived at Death Valley National Monument, driving here from Las Vegas. "Guess it's still in the room," I say. "We were going to pick up a topographical map at the Visitor Center, remember?"

"I do."

"Can't trust those flimsy hand-outs, you know. The proportions are way the heck off."

"Should we go back?"

"That lucky old sun's not gonna get any lower, Laurel. And look at . . . whatever they call those things. . . ."

"Alluvial fans?"

"Yeah, that alluvial fan." An upside down V flowing out from between two of the Cottonwoods, the alluvial fan, composed of mud and boulders washed down from the mountains during the infrequent torrential bouts of rain that strike Death Valley, resembles a vast mons veneris. "You can practically reach out across the valley and touch it."

"I know," says Laurel. "Still, something doesn't feel quite right."

"Let's set off and see what happens."

"You did remember to bring the compass?"

"Of course. Why?"

"Better make sure."

I explore a number of the Velcro-sealed vest pockets. "Aha! Told you." I wave the plastic wafer over my head. "And we remembered our canteens."

"Why is this reminding me of Shenandoah?"

Three years earlier we'd set off from Milam Gap to Camp Hoover in Shenandoah National Park, Virginia. I'd forgotten to bring along our detailed topographical map. The trail map—a mimeographed sheet of paper from the ranger station at Big Meadows—showed a loop-shaped walk significantly less complicated than the little Worthington, Ohio, square block on which our house stands: Prong Trail down to Camp Hoover, then Laurel (!) Trail to Hazeltop Trail returning us to the parking lot at Milam Gap. An easy day-walk, easy as pie, except that a mile or so south of Camp Hoover we missed the Laurel Trail and (as we later learned) I got us off onto Fork Mountain Trail, to Staunton River Trail, which we followed for several miles to where the Staunton River meets the Rapidan— though we did not know their names. We forded the Rapidan, then followed the Rapidan River Trail into the heart of the wilderness where the Battle of the Wilderness, among the fiercest slaughters of the Civil War, was fought in 1864. Fighting panic, we began retracing our steps. Our food was gone, our water low. We knew that giardia, a deadly intestinal parasite, made the river water undrinkable. The sun was going down. We had no flashlight. Poison ivy sprouted everywhere along the trail. With darkness descending we could scarcely see the ground in front of our feet as the trail grew increasingly rocky and steep. Seconds before night fell upon us like a shroud I spotted an open space off to our left—flat and devoid of rocks or poison ivy. We passed the night at the foot of twin pin oaks whose trunks forked from one another at ground level. We covered ourselves with a flimsy windbreaker. Throughout the night I kept my camera handy. In the event we were set upon by one of the many hundreds of brown bears and grizzlies prowling the park at night I could pop the flash into its feral inhuman eyes. Our sole defense. I spent the night observing a full moon as it veered across a sky bristling with stars. . . . Later, discussing our ordeal with a park ranger and consulting a detailed map of the region, we learned that we had hiked more than thirty miles. . . . After such knowledge what forgiveness?

"Shenandoah, oh boy," I sigh, looking out across Death Valley. "Well, you know what, Laurel? This is entirely different. For one thing you can see exactly where you're going and where you're coming from. I mean, no hills or forests or anything. And for another, we don't have to go any farther than we're comfortable with. Here, I'll take a compass reading. We can sight up with our Grand Prix—I mean, it looks like a stop light, or some kind of beacon you can spot for miles . . . and, uh, I guess that's it."

"And when our car's still sitting here after a few weeks someone may come looking for us." So far no cars have gone by us on the road.

"I like it when people put the Power of Positive Thinking to work," I say, taking our first step out onto Mesquite Flat, its hard-baked clay surface strewn with fist-sized rocks. "One small step for a man—oops, I mean 'person.'"

Here and there rise gnarled stands of the eponymous mesquite. There's also a sparse scattering of some pint-sized shrub I can't name or identify, having been a lazy, good-for-nothing Cub Scout (my Den Mother was my mother) and Boy Scout who never learned his vegetation beyond the rudiments of oak, maple, catalpa, beech, and poison ivy. Several inches of rain have fallen during recent weeks. Portions of Death Valley are alive with wild flowers, but not Mesquite Flat.

"How long have we been walking?" asks Laurel, who prefers to hike out in front, imagining herself in the role of trailblazer. Now she's trailing me like an Oriental wife of yore.

"Maybe about a half hour is all. Why?"

"Well, for one thing that alluvial fan doesn't look an inch nearer than it did when we first started out. And for another. . . . Please, just turn around for a moment."

I turn to face the direction we've been coming from. In the blazing sun the Grand Prix appears to my eyes as a burst of unripe apple green before resolving back to red.

"Our car looks like we could get back to it in about five minutes," Laurel observes.

"Or less," I agree. "Jeez, what's that odor? Some kind of spice?" There's a musky, tangy aroma I don't recognize—pine and juniper and some vaguely familiar but unidentifiable perfume, an invisible spirit floating like a vapor in the hot dry air of March. It's almost as though I can *hear* it—a low subliminal whirring like the Flying Saucer in *The Day the Earth Stood Still*, but a mere shade shy of complete and utter silence. "God, it's delicious!"

"Maybe that's the mesquite," Laurel suggests.

"Don't you wish we could bottle whatever it is and take it home? Wait . . . look, Laurel! Up in the sky!"

"It's a bird . . . no, it's a *plane!*"

Two or three thousand feet directly overhead an enormous bat-winged aircraft is floating southward. A smaller bat-winged aircraft coasts alongside it like one of those sparrow-sized birds that buddy up to ravens in flight. They make a noise like feathers. "What is it, Ernest? What are they?"

"The little one's an F-111 Stealth Fighter. But, wow! The big one's the B-2 Stealth Bomber! There's still a debate about whether it even exists, the whole project's supposed to be such a hotshot top secret. And there it is!"

"What's it doing *here?*"

"Well, Nellis Air Force Base is just north of where we are. I think there's a bombing range. . . ."

"Could they have flown off track?"

"Bombing Death Valley!"

"There's a thought," says Laurel.

"B-2 or not B-2, that is the question. And there, up in the sky, is the answer!"

"Did you make that up, Ernest?"

"Afraid not. Some Senate staffer did, back when they were debating whether or not to fund the thing at two billion a pop."

B-2 and little buddy F-111 vanish over the southern horizon of Death Valley.

"Wow! And they seemed to be just floating up there like blimps."

"Ernest?"

"Uh-huh?"

"How long have you been retired?"

"Uh . . . let me think . . . one year, six months, twenty-one and one-half days, sixteen hours and," I glance at my wristwatch, "forty-seven seconds. About."

"Don't you miss all those day-in, day-out conversations and discussions concerning literature?"

"No."

"You're always quoting stuff, making literary references. . . ."

We're stepping through a minefield of waist-high boulders. "Where'd these come from?" I ask. "They sure as heck weren't visible from the road. . . . So, did I tell you my latest teaching dream?"

"I don't know," Laurel says. "Did you?"

7

CHAPTER 1

"Let's see. . . . As usual, here I am back on campus thinking classes are supposed to start in a week, but the walkways are chock-a-block with students, and I see one of my colleagues, some faceless Entity, and I say, 'Hi there, So-and-so, how come there are these students all over the place?' And Entity responds that it's the first day of classes. And my heart drops, and I ask, 'Where am I teaching?' And Entity answers with the name of some building I've never heard of, that isn't even on the map, and Entity informs me that it's somewhere way the hell clear over on the other side of the university. So I ask, 'What time am I supposed to be teaching?' And Entity answers that my first class began five minutes ago. And I ask frantically, 'What precisely is it that I'm supposed to teach?'"

"So far, it's the old familiar dream," says Laurel.

"Right, the one that's afflicted me ever since the night preceding my maiden voyage into the classroom. But here's the part that's new. So Entity answers that the name of my course is 'Food Good for Women!' And I ask, 'What in God's name are the books I've assigned for the course?' And Entity vanishes. And the sole, the one and only title that comes to mind is *Looking for Mister Goodbar!*"

"No, you didn't tell me," laughs Laurel.

"Do I miss teaching? Do I, Laurel?"

"You were so good at it."

"But do you think I could actually miss twenty-eight years of something I never wanted to do in the first place?"

"I've never quite understood it," Laurel says. "Was it wanting to be a novelist, or—?

"Honey, I'm a coward in front of groups—terminally shy."

"*You?*"

"True Confession time, Laurel. I've battled stage fright most of my life. I'd pathologically overprepare the classes I taught. There were mornings I'd sooner enter an execution chamber than a classroom where I had to teach. I've had panic attacks that forced me to dismiss class. Far safer, less stressful to hunker down in some monastic bunker and make things up on the typewriter, don't you agree?"

"Golly, Ernest. . . ."

The field of boulders ends abruptly. Before us lies a sandy maze of ravines—and we are teetering at the lip of a gaping slit fifty feet deep.

"What are you thinking, Ernest?"

"Oh, this? Well, the banks look a little steep, but it's sand."

I'm puzzled, though. Where did this formation come from?

"How long have we been walking?" Laurel asks.

I glance at my wristwatch. "I forget when we started out. Why?"

"Because I no longer see the car."

"See that mountain?"

"I see dozens."

"The really tall kind of peaky one?" I wave at one of the distant Funerals, a sharp-pointed shadow against a sky of periwinkle blue where clouds are now forming.

"I think maybe—"

"Well that baby ought to line up with our Grand Prix."

"Less than half my water's left."

"You can have mine if you run out. Hell, I'm not even remotely thirsty."

I rush headlong down the embankment and vigorously forge my way across the sandy bottom, Laurel following, our feet sinking to the ankles in the moist, powdery sand. We mount the far embankment's summit to discover another, deeper ravine awaiting us a few yards beyond the first.

"Let me . . . catch my breath, Ernest. . . . That . . . alluvial fan doesn't look . . . any closer . . . than when we started."

"Like some weird illusion."

"Maybe . . . we ought to consider . . . heading back," Laurel says, panting.

"Let's see what's on the other side of this ravine." And down I go.

Reaching bottom several seconds behind me Laurel gasps out, "I don't . . . envy how you . . . must have felt . . . during all those years of teaching. . . . A little like . . . I feel now."

"Like the laborers they shipped over from China to mine borax." Yesterday we visited the Harmony Borax Works Interpretive Trail near Furnace Creek Ranch. We learned that Zabriskie Point is named for an undertaker who made his first fortune burying Chinese laborers before he scaled the Harmony ladder and acquired a second fortune in borax. The museum's photo of Zabriskie sports the coldest, meanest eyes I've seen. "My current ambition is to live twenty-eight years as a retired person. At the present moment, I have another twenty-six years, six months—"

"But who's counting? . . . up we go again?"

"When he hosted 'Death Valley Days' didn't they pronounce Ronnie's name 'R*ee*gan'?" I ask.

"That's . . . what I remember. . . ."

"Must've recalled it was the name of Lear's evil daughter," I say. "Not a proper handle for the president."

"I'm . . . sure that's . . . the reason . . . they changed the . . . pronunciation."

"Ree-gun . . . Ray-gun. . . . It's a Horatio Alger success story either way." We're cresting the rise.

"Here's . . . another . . . one," says Laurel, laboring to breathe.

Confronting us now is a chaotic fast-moving body of water with innumerable rushing, gurgling rivulets and streams bulging with boulders. Jutting islets bristle with coarse vegetation. Birds flit and dart through the saturated air.

"Wouldn't you love fording this mess in a covered wagon, Laurel?"

"I won't even do it . . . on foot. . . . Now can we . . . head back?"

"But we're nearly there." The Great American Alluvial Fan now looms larger by perhaps a third than when we set out. Beyond the water hazard, power lines sag between towering erector-sets. Civilization has preceded us.

"Where did all this come from?" I ask. "I sure didn't see it from the road."

"Isn't there a phenomenon called 'telescoping'? When the air is heavy and completely clear it acts as a giant lens. Objects miles away look like they're in your back yard."

"Oh. Beware, objects are *farther* than they seem?"

"That might explain it," Laurel says.

"I guess."

"How far do you think we've come?"

"Miles and miles. . . . Wow! Now the sky looks like that ceiling in Caesar's Palace!" The casino shopping mall creates an illusion of blue sky full of white clouds. There's a fountain whose statuary comes to life on the half hour. Gods and goddesses. Bacchus. . . . Now the sun's a blast furnace in spite of proliferating clouds. "Sure could do with a couple of ice cold beers," I remark.

"Remember Grand Canyon, Ernest?" Laurel almost suffered heat stroke during our climb back from the bottom of the Canyon to its North Rim.

"Uh-huh."

"We didn't bring enough water," Laurel says.

"Here." I hand her my Cub Scout canteen, purchased in Graceland Shopping Center right before we flew to Las Vegas.

"This feels full," Laurel says.

"I told you," I say. "I'm not thirsty."

"You're sweating like crazy, Ernest."

I'm looking at the sky. "Hmm. . . . Maybe we'll have some flooding after all."

"Drink your water, Ernest."

"I'm keeping it in reserve. For you."

"Who do you think you are?" asks Laurel. "Superman?"

"Hardly."

"Ernest, why are you trying to kill yourself? Would you kindly tell me that?"

"Ready to head on back?" I ask her.

We're reentering the boulder field after traversing the two sandy ravines. Slow going. We lean against a boulder and Laurel makes me drink some water.

"Ernest?"

"Uh-huh?"

"Is this about your mother?"

"Mom's a fighter. I told you her dream, didn't I?"

"Would you like to tell me again?"

"Well, this naked intruder attacks her while she's taking a shower. And she realizes that he's Cancer and she decides rather than giving in she's going to fight him tooth and nail and she does. And she ends up beating him senseless and bloody on the bathroom floor."

"Do you think she'll make it?" asks Laurel.

"She does." The last time I visited my mother in Bloomington I took her to be fitted for a wig. She recently told me over the phone her hair's all fallen out now. "Hell, they cured my brother using pretty much the same treatment, and he's been in remission now for—what—twenty-five years? Mom's seventy-eight . . . seventy-nine in what is it, twelve days? And her mother lived to ninety-three."

Non-Hodgkin's lymphoma. My youngest brother came down with it at twenty-five, but he did drugs. My mother's a lifelong nonsmoking teetotaler. During the fifties and sixties, however, a number of electronics plants began discharging toxins into Bloomington's air and water. And the atom bomb tests in Nevada sent tons of radioactive debris drifting directly over us.

"Can't be genetic, can it?" I ask. "Look at the age difference when Mom and Ross came down with it."

"Just an odd coincidence."

"Well. . . . Ready?"

"If you are," says Laurel.

The sun's against our backs now, casting broken shadows among the boulders. "I'm kind of looking forward to Las Vegas again," I say. Laurel calls Las Vegas "a Great Big International Block Party." Before coming to Death Valley we spent three days at the Tropicana. We have a stay-over of a couple of days on our return. "Maybe we'll take in that albino tiger act."

"If you like."

"You're playing poker, Laurel. You're holding a Siegfried and Roy. What do you have?"

"What do you mean?"

"In your hand."

"Hand?" Laurel asks.

"Your *poker* hand."

"Oh . . . I don't know."

"A pair of queens!" I say.

"I don't get it," says Laurel.

"The magicians, for God's sake. Everyone knows they're lovers."

"Not me," says Laurel.

"What's wrong with you?" I ask.

"What's wrong with *you*?"

"What do you mean?"

"You've been acting strange for days, Ernest. You can't remember from one minute to the next. You take out across the desert without a map. I practically have to twist your arm to turn back. Sweat's pouring off you in sheets. You won't drink."

"There's our car!" It's green, then red, then green. But it's the Grand Prix. "See? I told you so."

"I feel better just seeing it. Ernest?"

"Yes?" I'm frantically patting my multipocketed vest with both hands.

"Did you forget the car keys?" Laurel asks.

"Ah . . . they're . . . *here!*"

"Whew!"

"We have a ways to go yet."

"Will the rain catch us?" Laurel asks.

Downpours cause instantaneous catastrophic flooding in Death Valley, washing hikers down abandoned mine shafts. Downpours grind the mountains into alluvial fans. In a few million years downpours will have washed the mountains away. "Not a chance," I answer.

We hike awhile in silence. My eyes are on the mountains, calm and lovely. Finally I say, "I am bothered by Mom."

"I know."

"Did you know that I've never loved her enough?"

"Has she loved you enough?" asks Laurel.

We're nearing the Grand Prix. The sun is casting long shadows. "There're other things, but I can't remember what. Or get my mind around them. Something's coming up, but what it is . . . has slipped my mind."

"It'll come to you," Laurel says.

"It's as though I can see its footprints." I'm pointing toward the hard-baked rocky ground between us and the Grand Prix. "Coming toward me. Just about . . . *there*. But I can't make out what it is."

"What are you seeing?" Laurel asks me.

"Don't know. I just don't know."

Ah, Wilderness!

Laurel Richardson

Death Valley—three million acres of wilderness in which all the great divisions, and subdivisions, of geological time are represented. Lavender, pink, white, marble cream, black mountains, contortions, alluvial fans, craters, mosaic floors, tiltings, dunes. Deep blue sky, hints of pale green, ravens, locoweeds, eyeless fish. It is the driest, hottest, lowest spot in the Western Hemisphere. Never have I been anywhere more beautiful than Death Valley.

CHAPTER 1

"Before us lay a splendid scene of grand desolation," William Manley wrote as the party he led entered Death Valley on Christmas Day, 1849. They had already abandoned most of their belongings and slaughtered most of their oxen for food. Routes north and west out of the valley proved futile. Exhausted from their journey, unprepared for the harsh desert, and with provisions severely depleted, the clutch of pioneers encamped by a spring, while the two "ablest" men headed south by foot. If they could find a passage through the Panamint Mountains, they reckoned they could quickly reach the little village of Los Angeles. They did not know that to get there they would have to traverse two hundred miles, one hundred of it in the desert.

Days passed. I cannot imagine the fear and anguish of the little party of women, children, and less-abled men in the desert nights that they shared with the hairy scorpion, tarantula, rattlesnake, and centipede. But nights were probably easier than days, hungry, anxious, day after day— some certainly losing faith that they would ever be found alive.

More than three weeks passed before "the boys" returned with provisions. As one of the women, weak and weary, ascended the last ridge, she looked back and said, "Goodbye, Death Valley."

For years, I refused to go to Death Valley. I was frightened by its name, fearful that it might have some metaphoric hold on me. I wasn't ready to "Walk through the Valley of . . . Death. . . ." The Panamint Indians who survived this lowest, hottest place on earth are now extinct. The forty-niners seeking a shortcut to gold did not find it here. The Chinese brought here to mine borax, dead, too, after enduring unspeakable working and living conditions; their lives undisclosed in guidebooks, their graves unmarked.

But, now, although still not ready for that final "walk," I long to be again in Death Valley for both its beauty and it's history call to me. Why? To answer that I turn to another beautiful place where I have my own familial history: Shenandoah.

On the third day of our second trip to Shenandoah, early September 1990, Ernest and I plan an easy day-hike, the 7.5-mile Hoover–Laurel Loop. During the hike out, I think and talk about death, about how quickly and unexpectedly death can happen, just one wrong turn. We do not know, I muse, how things are going to turn out, only that they will.

Therefore, I reason, this is the time in our lives—as in any time in any life—to "follow our bliss."

We reach Laurel Prong, but a new trail has been blazed with the old color, which we guilelessly follow. We're hiking too long, I think.

"Let's turn back, Ernest. Let's retrace our steps," I say.

"It'll be much longer if we do that," he counters. "Just ahead we'll be finishing the loop."

"But, what if you're wrong?"

Knowing I can't trust my judgment in these matters, I give in. The trail becomes rough, overgrown; the blazes disappear, along with signs of any other hikers—ever. The remnant of our trail runs into the tailings of a gravel road.

"See," Ernest says. "We'll just follow this gravel road back."

I feel relief.

We turn down the gravel road, but it dead-ends at groves of trees a half century high. How can there be a gravel road that goes nowhere in the middle of a forest? Nothing makes sense.

"Let's retrace our steps, now," I say, and under my breath, "if it's not too late."

"None of these forest openings," Ernest says, as we go in and out of the forest, "get us anywhere. It'll be dark soon. We'd better find a place to sleep," and I hear him saying, under his breath, "before we break our necks."

"Here, under this large tree. This will be good," he says. We curl together. Dark falls. We "sleep" that night with one windbreaker jacket between us, a full moon, six ounces of water, no guarantee of finding our way back, and visions of Laughing Wolf gently pulling the blanket, Night, over us.

When daylight breaks, we begin our search again. It feels futile. I am certain that we will die here. No one will come looking for us. Our car is properly parked; we didn't sign the trail book, and the room we've rented for the week has a sign on its door—"Do Not Disturb."

"I love you, Ernest," I say.

"I love you, too, Laurel," he says.

We laugh over our tacit agreement that if either of us should utter those little three words, the other must respond in kind. Thinking I will be dying soon, I don't lament or feel angry or cry. I simply give in to what I think is to be my fate. Our fate.

Too exhausted to continue our hike—now uphill on the gravel road that leads nowhere—I lie down on my back and close my eyes. Far away, it seems, I can hear Ernest yelling, and I think he is hurt, but I am unable to rouse myself.

"I have found the marker for our trail back! It's written on a gray metal strip on a concrete post!" Ernest is standing over me. "Get up, Laurel." He gives me a sip of his water. We survive. Our marriage survives.

We learn the next day that when Shenandoah became a National Park, fifty years earlier, groves of trees were planted across the gravel roads to keep the displaced mountain families from returning to the homes they were forced to abandon.

And, our hike? We had nearly twenty-two miles of wilderness hiking under our boots and twelve more to go before we left the area—called since before the Civil War and to this day "the Wilderness"—inhabited, now, by some four hundred bears, each a night roamer with a twenty-square mile territory.

The next year, Ernest and I return to Shenandoah. Prepared for a long hike, we retrace our steps to where we had spent the night. The giardia-filled river is rolling along below the arc of the hillside. We have seen no other clearing.

"We were really lucky that we found this. We only had a few seconds before dark," Ernest comments.

"You found it," I say. "I would have just crashed on the trail and rolled into that rolling river."

We spread out our lunch. "Look," I say, "we didn't camp under one tree. It's two of them, intertwined at the trunks, independent in their branches. What a metaphor for our lives!"

"If I put that in a novel," Ernest comments, "it would be too literary to be believable."

After lunch we build a dolman. Stone upon stone. We give thanks.

"Those are bear tracks, aren't they?" I ask, seeing fresh paw prints in our clearing.

"Yep," Ernest says, adjusting his pack.

Ernest and I both have ancestral roots in the Shenandoah. My father's ancestors and Ernest's father's ancestors had lived there in the Wilderness at the same time a way before the Civil War. Some of them died there. On the third day of our fourth trip to Shenandoah, we are again hiking the Laurel Prong trail.

"Can you feel it?" I ask him. In the air I feel stories, lives, deaths.

"Yes," he says.

We veer off the hiking trail into an overgrown clearing. Fallen, scattered, are gravestones, plain, uncarved. No need to carve the names of the dead on stones for family knows who is buried where. Oral tradition passes on the history. And I, who have spent my lifetime writing, mourn for the passing of the oral tradition—and, yes, for my forgotten people. No one knows the names of the dead, the stories of their lives. I am crying. We set the stones upright and return to our hike.

"Ernest," I say as I finish writing, "let's go back to Death Valley. I want to look for gravestones."

"How about early April?" he says.

"Perfect!"

Conversation: Death Valley

February 20, 2003

Morning. The Great American Kitchen in Middle America. Laurel and Ernest are sitting by one another at their round table. The Great American Back Yard, visible through the French Doors, lies buried beneath two feet of new-fallen snow. There's a speckled crinoline of seed-husks surrounding the tall bird feeder that juts eight feet high out of the yard's southwest quadrant. A roiling red-gray throng crowds the glass-walled feeder: cardinals, top of the pecking order. An electric birdbath brims with liquid water and a bobbing of finches. Winter has cancelled their brightness. A segment of orange electrical cord coils upward from the whiteness. Possum and Blue, beloved felines, rest in peace beneath a comforter of earth and snow. Ernest turns on the Radio Shack tape recorder.

Laurel: That is the idea; let's make a little conversation.

Ernest: There's a Frost poem where he talks about getting lost in order to find yourself. In some ways our narratives are also about that. Or

17

they're angled in that direction. We didn't exactly get lost in Death Valley but we made a pretty good stab at it. And we certainly did get lost in Shenandoah, and I think you were a good bit more generous to me than I would be to myself because, as I recall, I actually panicked. We should've retraced our steps much earlier, but I irrationally insisted on forging ahead, and we ended up walking in circles. One thing I discovered about myself is that I could do with more presence of mind, to say the least.

Laurel: I discovered things about myself as well in Shenandoah. I had recently finished the poem based on my interview with "Louisa May." Her philosophy that "things just turn out" was in my mind. Rather than panicking, I went into a stillness. I became somewhat fatalistic, accepting of my fate.

Ernest: Yes. You did.

Laurel: While working on my Death Valley narrative, I had a dream whose theme was my unwillingness to fight to stay alive. On waking, I decided that it was okay to accept the inevitable—or what one feels is the inevitable.

Ernest: It never even occurred to me that we wouldn't be able to get out of Shenandoah. I knew we could retrace our steps. I had a clear enough memory of how to do that—

Laurel: [*Laughs.*] Excuse me for laughing.

Ernest: Really, I knew we were going to find our way out. But also that we were doomed to rough it, in the Babes-in-the-Woods Motel.

Laurel: It was the only night that whole month that wasn't touched with frost.

Ernest: The old nursery song was floating through my mind that night. "They sobbed and they sighed, they bitterly cried, those poor little babes, they lay down and died." I had enough presence of mind not to sing it out loud.

Laurel: I thank you for that!

Ernest: You're welcome.

Laurel: We've never talked about this—this difference in perception— I didn't know until now that you thought we would get back. Did you know I thought we were going to die?

Ernest: When did you think that?

Laurel: In the morning, when I collapsed.

Ernest: Okay. When I came back to where you were lying on the ground, after I'd found the way back, you told me you'd given up. That's when I knew. But not until then, and not until I absolutely knew for a fact that we were getting out in one piece.

Laurel: And gratefully we did. So, even when I think I don't have the energy or the stamina to go on, I do.

Ernest: You do, yes.

Laurel: There is a reserve. Although sometimes I think I run on near empty. But I do have this coping mechanism. I imagine the worst possible outcome. So when whatever happens isn't that bad, it's okay. So, the worst possible outcome was that we were going to die out there. And well, that's how it is.

Ernest: And we didn't get into recriminations or arguments. We focused our energies on rescuing ourselves.

Laurel: We were in it together, we were complicit in it, and I wouldn't have been found again if you hadn't found a path.

Ernest: And no one did this on purpose.

Laurel: There was no malice aforethought.

Ernest: None.

Laurel: And you were generous in terms of sharing your water and in believing that I could get back out.

Ernest: I knew we could get out, even if one of us became incapacitated. You said you thought I'd broken my leg when you heard me yelling. I'd walked a mile up the road, found the way back and was hollering— hoping I wouldn't have to retrace my steps completely, that maybe you'd head toward me. But you were lying in the road, thinking it was all over, when in fact I was bringing you the news we were saved.

Laurel: Do you think that we often have such different interpretations?

Ernest: Would our marriage survive the "often"? On the whole, you tend to be positive about things, with a philosophy of "let's wait and see" instead of giving into the crisis of the moment. We don't live from crisis to crisis by any means.

Laurel: No.

Ernest: Nor do I consider you a fatalist. Or myself as someone who's always panicking.

Laurel: But when circumstances are really outside of my control, I do accept them. I'm not a Don Quixote tilting at windmills.

19

Ernest: There've been times in your professional life when maybe you have. But, no, generally you don't. . . . Of course, there's always The Big Windmill. You had a closer brush with it in Shenandoah than I did, but we both know where we're headed in the end. We know in our bones that it's only a matter of when. We don't want to be collaborators, you know—throwing ourselves into the blades. But when the time comes, it comes, not tonight maybe. . . . Not that night in Shenandoah, anyway. I knew from my Boy Scout days that there are worse things than an overnight in the woods.

Laurel: We seem to feel the need to tell of this experience often, as we are doing now. It's like a bone-deep memory that binds us deeply to each other. . . .

Ernest: Yes, it does.

Laurel: And our later experience in Shenandoah, too, where we felt the presence of our ancestors, the land alive with their deaths.

Ernest: And their continuity with the living, with ourselves.

Laurel: Yes, the continuity with the living, with ourselves, and that our families were neighbors in Ireland, too.

Ernest: If we're cousins, we're probably not close enough to be illegal.

Laurel: Kissing cousins?

Ernest: You know, the place where we stayed the night in Shenandoah just cropped up fortuitously . . . really the only place like it—level, soft, devoid of poison ivy. And we regard it as a kind of holy place and shrine and have returned to it several times. We've found our dolman mostly intact, with fresh bear paw prints crossing where we slept. So our experience there has given us quite a few reasons to feel blessed—and connected. Maybe our ancestors were watching over us.

Laurel: A couple of years later, Hurricane Andrew came right through there.

Ernest: But we wouldn't have gone trail hiking with Andrew approaching.

Laurel: Oh, I don't know about you.

Ernest: Am I that reckless?

Laurel: No, you're not. And I'm not that reckless either!

Ernest: We've chosen these valleys of the shadow of death to start this book. Facing death, coping with it. My mother's cancer took her a year later, and, though it's not stated in the piece—something to do with the date, March 7—well maybe I won't say anything here and let it remain—

Laurel: For the reader—

Ernest: To discover later. I didn't know at the time that I was being pulled along by unconscious forces in Death Valley. Driven.

Laurel: Your description of Death Valley brought me back there again. I was thirsty, tired, scared. Angry. I was enmeshed in the beauty. All those feelings were back again. You know, I didn't know what was going on with you then, and I haven't known until now, when I read your piece.

Ernest: I put myself back there in memory as much as I possibly can, so that I'm back among all the sensations and the feelings.

Laurel: I've never asked you this—but did you think you might get cancer, too? Or, do you?

Ernest: I'm in denial.

Laurel: When I read your story to my friend Betty, she thought you made me sound very negative, not at all like my usual positive self.

Ernest: I know I have you sounding cautionary notes in my narrative. With plenty of reason, lord knows. Shenandoah . . . and, too, our descent from the North Rim of the Grand Canyon without sufficient water, and when we reached the canyon floor your knee felt so bad you felt you couldn't make it back up to the rim.

Laurel: I never thought I was going to die in the Grand Canyon, though, just that I was going to be miserable until someone came down with a mule to get me.

Ernest: Yet you were much nearer to death than you ever were at Shenandoah.

Laurel: Because during the climb I almost went into heat stroke—

Ernest: Which we didn't realize at the time. Fortunately we were only a few feet from the water source, though we didn't know it. I went on ahead—

Laurel: Like you did in Shenandoah—

Ernest: And brought water back to you. And, I suppose, life. This is not a behavioral pattern that I would recommend.

Laurel: And we did break the pattern in Death Valley. Still, that place speaks to me metaphorically. The ablest men in 1850 went ahead to find a path to save the others. You went ahead on our adventures, too.

Ernest: Ah, yes. Though I do not exactly hold myself up as a Role Model for survival.

Laurel: And the Chinese died here, misused in labor camps by people who considered themselves superior beings, which was of course the experience of my mother's Jewish kin, and to some extent my father's Irish family.

Ernest: It's hard to find truly factual things about how the Chinese were treated. What you turn up at the site and on the Web is a much more benign vision than what I suspect is the truth.

Laurel: The Chinese buried in unmarked graves, our people buried there in Shenandoah with their gravestones uncarved. Nobody knows who or which or where. But there they are. Dead and gone and unmarked.

Ernest: Yes.

Laurel: My first draft about Death Valley began with a long introduction about my mother coming from Russia, traveling westward. I deleted it from the later drafts, but it focused my thinking. Her father, too, came ahead before his family. It's a gendered thing. The men go ahead and if they are successful in their forays, the women might be saved. The rest of my mother's family—those who did not go westward—lie in unmarked graves in Russia. Irish, English, Chinese, Russian. I am confusing myself.

Ernest: Look at our narratives as grave-markers. Legends carved into our headstones. Who we were, what we were to one another.

Laurel: I like that.

Ernest: Back when we were first together you expressed concern that we didn't have a "history" with one another. We sure have one now. And here we are writing it down.

Laurel: We "got lost enough to find" ourselves—as individuals and as partners. One more thing. You edited my sentence about walking through the "Valley of Death" to the "Valley of the Shadow of Death," which is the correct biblical passage, I know. But to me the idea of death is concrete. It is not a shadow. It's not the fear that Death is going to darken my way, it's more that Death is a real experience that I will be in, materially, physically.

Ernest: It's coming toward us, all right. Its footprints are almost visible there in front of us on the valley floor. And I have us walking to meet it, I guess. . . . Shenandoah. Grand Canyon. Death Valley. The Valley of the Shadow of Death deepens the . . . *mythology* of our time spent together.

Laurel: You descend into death.

Ernest: We haven't exactly had our near-death experiences on mountaintops.

Laurel: Well, you had one in Ireland.

Ernest: Whoops! Forgot that one.

Laurel: We should write about our travels in Ireland.

Ernest: We've got the photographs, the receipts, the ticket stubs. And, now, the memory.

Laurel: Why don't we write about Ireland?

Ernest: Begorra!

CHAPTER 2
IRELAND
July 5–26, 1987

Only connect.

—E. M. Forster

All in the Family

Laurel Richardson

Sixteen years have passed since Ernest and I went to Ireland, and a dozen since I've looked at our photo album. We went to Ireland to present papers for the Third International Interdisciplinary Congress on Women, July 1987, to sightsee, and to visit the town from whence my father's family came centuries ago.

Opening the photo album unlocks my memories.

"Is this really where we have to stay?" I whine. To Ernest's chagrin, I will often request a room-change several times before accepting the inevitable.

"This is as good as it gets," Ernest says. "Get used to it."

Jet-lagged and tired, we register at the Clarence Hotel, built in 1852 on the left bank of the river Liffey in the heart of Dublin. Our European double bed—a whit wider than a single and shorter than the same—consumes most of the splintered floor and nearly grazes the soiled windowsill.

"We have our own toilet," Ernest continues. "Be glad."

A stench arises from the streetside—garbage, ale, diesel fuel, and sweat. Raucous laughter, clanking, and shouting waft into our room from the street and the hotel's "famous" Octagon Bar.

"How can I possibly give my speech tomorrow without enough sleep," I whine as I fall asleep.

I had recently completed a sporadic two-year book tour to promote my trade book, *The New Other Woman*. Because of my participant-observation in television and radio talk shows and my smart analysis of the same, I thought myself pretty savvy about the ways of the fork-tongued serpents that produced and hosted those shows. I knew how feminists could co-opt the media. I was eager to share my knowledge with the worldwide family of feminists. My paper held such universal promise: "Disseminating the feminist Vision: Media Strategies." Oh, how wonderful, I thought, to do something important in something this big: International! Interdisciplinary! Congress!

"This is the right room, I think," I say to Ernest, finding again the page I've dog-eared on our thousand-page conference program. The modern auditorium in a newish building at Trinity College is packed. Six people will present in ten-minute intervals. English, French, and Gaelic are the official languages. I have trouble understanding the accented English of the first three speakers.

My speech is divided into two parts and twelve points: (1) Strategies for keeping your power—eight points, and (2) techniques for handling the misconstruing of your research—four points. I am very well organized and disciplined. I speak for my allotted minutes, accept the applause, and sit down. I don't understand the next two papers delivered in French—or maybe Gaelic—I'm not sure.

"You were great," Ernest says. He is always and unequivocally my staunch supporter.

As we walk across the ancient cobbled paving stones into the bleak day, I feel bloated with success and shame. I spoke well, I know, but oh, the presumptiveness. I had assumed that my ideas about the media in the United States had direct application worldwide. What arrogance! What ignorance! I make a mental note to delve more deeply into deconstruction.

"I'm hungry," I say. We make our way, coughing from the leaded gas fumes, to a stone building's second-floor cafeteria jammed with women speaking Indo-European languages.

"Hmm. Corned beef and cabbage and boiled potatoes," Ernest says.

"Yum. My father used to make it in our Nesco," I say. "Comfort food!" I am thinking a lot about my father, and with the smell of the cabbage under my nose, of the potlucks we'd have with his relatives and "fictive-kin."

The red-haired cafeteria worker heaps our plates.

That night Ernest and I join the throngs for the keynote lecture by Mary Daly, radical feminist theologian and philosopher.

"This should be fun. She's so wickedly clever," I comment to Ernest, thinking about her *Wickedary*, an outrageous feminist dictionary, a copy of which Ernest gave me one year for Christmas and which I bring to my Sociology of Women's classes for their edification and amusement. "But," I continue, "these convention women all look rather sour and heavy, weighted down with bookbags, glasses, hiking boots."

Quoting from his memory of *Wickedary*, Ernest says, "Academentia— the normal state of persons in academia, marked by varying and progressive degrees; irreversible deterioration of faculties of intellectuals."

"Do you think we're doomed?" I say, laughing. "We still have twenty more years, more or less, of professing?"

"God, don't say that!"

We wind our way through scores of protestors, dressed in black, standing mute and still on the building's steps. They represent dead babies.

"I suppose the protestors are here because Mary Daly is a pro-choice Irish American, raised Catholic, and teaching in a Catholic university," I say. I like showing off my knowledge.

"No, I think it's just because this is Ireland," Ernest responds.

We locate two seats on the aisle toward the rear of the packed auditorium.

"Do you see any other men?" I ask Ernest.

"Nope! I see the emergency exit though."

Mary Daly's keynote focuses on Mary Daly's troubles with Boston College, brought on by her refusal to allow men to take her classes. Ad-libbing her keynote, she rants on about how men poison women's spaces, and how her "college family" is defiling her. She talks over an hour and shows no sign of stopping.

"Maybe you'd better duck and cover," I whisper to Ernest as we escape.

Mary Daly's keynote sets a "victim" tone for the conference, and I feel molten anger seeping out around me in the claques. I cannot condone the anti-male sentiments, engage in proposed radical street politics, or join the fomenting Marxist brigades. I have trouble understanding the words, concerns, and purposes of the presenters. The internecine Marxist wars are not my turf. I am not a socialist, communist, female separatist, or linguist! My feelings fluctuate between alienation, boredom, anger, and sorrow that I am incapable of being a member of the International Feminist Family. As if I have joined a dysfunctional family, I am blaming myself—and finding fault with *them*. Best to spend my time exploring Dublin with Ernest.

Dublin is one of the dreariest places I've ever been. This is July and I am wearing a wool sweater and rain jacket. Museums are lackluster, Irish treasures having been pilfered over the centuries by the English. James Joyce sites have no visitors, sans Ernest and me, but I find them of little interest. Store windows display large red "SALE" banners, dresses on hangers with oversized red sale tags hanging from their sleeves, scrunched red-tissue paper for heads in one window, rubber animal masks as heads in another, and in two others creamy mannequins, naked. Odious smells arise from the street-grills; street noises are incessant; buses skirt the bombed-out Trafalgar Square; people look worn. They are at war with Northern Ireland. Their economy is broken. Unemployment staggering. Bars fill early in the day. Drunk men and women weave in and out. Parents hold their infants close; spank their toddlers, jerk them by their arms; slap their older children and call them awful names; and, then, they send their near-adult children to America to get jobs and send some money back home. Young people are Ireland's major export. I feel the depth of the depressions—economic and psychological—as I walk about Dublin this July week in 1987. I want to leave. I don't want to connect to their suffering.

I take a break from my writing, unhappy with my negativity. Turning past the Dublin pages in the photo album, I come to the pictures of that which did call to my spirit in Ireland. That call, primitive and demanding, has stayed deep in my psyche, unconsciously driving what I have looked for, seen, and resonated with in subsequent travels. It is not the Dubliners or the conventioneers; it is not the famous writers, their sites, or their books; it is not the shop windows or museum shelves. No, it is the *stones*!

Throughout Ireland—and throughout the pages of our album—are wondrous examples of the stones of Ireland. As long ago as 3,000 BCE, farmers, using stone tools, deforested and tilled the land, built themselves mortarless stone huts and, from massive stone blocks, megalithic tombs decorated with spirals, triangles, zigzags. We have a picture of ourselves in the burial chamber of a megalithic passage tomb, the ceiling high enough for us to stand upright. We have a picture of a stone dolmen, five long stones supporting a capstone, marking a grave. Other long stones mark tombs and boundaries. Vikings entered Ireland and built stone ring forts, cashels enclosed by stonewalls, and crannogs—the artificial islands built on wood and stones. We have pictures of all of these, too. And of gravestones, high crosses, stonewalls, battlements. Some of the artifacts in ruins; some not.

The Vikings split Ireland into many different kingdoms. The rulers stayed behind their fortifications while their "kin-folk" wandered the fiefdom. No one could cross a kingdom's borders except for people like Ernest and myself—doctors and poets and bards. And Druids—followers of the "Wisdom of the Oak."

I find myself back in Ireland, crossing into Dingle.

"Oh my goodness," I say to Ernest as we come upon what appears to be a little town of beehives, made of stones.

"Built twelve hundred years ago," Ernest says, reading the guidebook. "By Vikings—without any mortar."

"They're so inviting."

"Monks still use them for retreats."

"Yes, they feel—I don't know—loved, I guess."

We walk in and out of the beehives. I am enchanted.

"We'll stay out of that one," Ernest says, pointing to a bright red tent. "A monk's in there."

It's amazing to me that these structures—unmortared piles of stones—have lasted for twelve centuries despite wars, famines, plagues, and weather. I feel humbled. "If you pay attention to how you pile up your stones," I muse to myself, "you can walk humbly and justly. . . ."

"You're more moved, Laurel, by these humble dwellings—"

"How did you know I was feeling humble, myself. . . ?"

"Than you are by the monasteries and churches and round towers that dot this land," Ernest says.

"You're right. The modest, the small, the picturesque call to my heart," I say, pocketing three small, undistinguished gray stones, shards neither sharp nor smooth—but both depending upon how I hold them; touch them.

I am ready to find my heritage—Tyrrellspass.

Canopied by a roiling Constable sky, 180 degrees of horizon, we drive inland. I watch the cloud formations and think about my father, dead so many years, and my heart fills with gladness and my eyes begin to tear. I accept my clichéd language, for it is the language of my childhood, and that's where the clouds have taken me.

At bedtime, my father, Tyrrell Alexander Richardson, would often sit at the foot of my bed and sing Irish lullabies in his scratchy Irish tenor voice, while my dog Happy howled along. Father had personally seen elves and leprechauns and he told me the stories of their lives. His leprechauns were neither evil nor capricious, but clever, smart, and lucky, just like me, he said, especially the "lucky" part. Because of his stories, I would imagine myself very small and safe, living under the pansies that hemmed the fence.

Some years, Father took the kids downtown for the humungous St. Patrick's Day parade on Chicago's State Street. Some years we'd even march in it, Father wearing a green bowtie, and the kids with shamrocks pinned to their green clothes, waving little green flags. When we got home, Father would magically make us green milk, which even more magically tasted just like white milk.

"Tyrrell, you're a happy-go-lucky Irishman," Mother would say.

"We're lucky," he'd say. And then maybe he would do some sleight-of-hand card tricks, false shuffles, and tell us about his childhood and the signs in the shop windows: "HELP WANTED: NO IRISH NEED APPLY."

Mother was a Russian-Jewish immigrant who seemed to like the Irish connection. It gave her an American identity and protected her children from pogroms—and worse. She especially liked that I had my father's strawberry blond hair. Father told me he was a Druid; he believed in the wisdom of nature, the value of learning, the importance of memorization, and that souls never died. He revered the lives of creatures great and small and had a photographic memory. He was a walking encyclopedia, and wanted me to be one, too, a goal that is beyond me. Maybe that's another reason I so admire Ernest's prodigious memory. Father would have liked Ernest.

Father's ancestors have been in America since the American Revolution. One, Frank Tyrrell, was a drummer boy in the Civil War; another, James Tyrrell, a Union officer, a famous escapee from the Confederate's Libby Prison. Another Tyrrell was in the secret service during the Civil War and later exposed and prevented the plot to kidnap and hold for ransom Lincoln's body from the tomb in Springfield. Todd Lincoln sent a letter of appreciation.

The Tyrrell family has an ancient motto: "Truth is the Way of Life." So, it is not surprising that Father became an ACLU Republican, an Illinois states attorney, a horse-racing tout, a manager of Senator Dirksen's campaigns, a real estate mogul (who rented below his costs to "deserving" families), an amateur magician, ex-Cavalryman, champion amateur boxer, horse-trainer, champion backstroker, lady's man, family man, and a criminal lawyer, serving some of Chicago's finest—like Al Capone—and never, ever told a lie. Blarney, well. . . .

On the backside of a genealogical tree, my father had written about our heritage. I learned that I am of Viking stock, "a direct descendant of Tyrrell the Red, who hacked out a kingdom for himself in Ireland. On early maps it is called Thorwald—Thor's Forest." My ancestors lived in stone forts and in crannogs on the edges of lakes and marshes in what is now called the Midlands. I check my pocket to make sure I still have my "touchstones."

"This is beautiful. Green, green, green," I say as we drive into the Midlands toward Tyrrellspass. The sky is like an upside-down blue stoneware bowl with its rim dipping into salad greens.

"The green reminds me of Ohio in the spring," Ernest says. "Like our own backyard!"

"It does, indeed! I wonder why people say we shouldn't bother to come to the Midlands? That there's nothing here," I say, not at all in jest, but taking in the glories of the Irish landscape and skyscape. I think I can see Forever—as if Forever is a place all around me.

"Look at that sign!" Ernest says, slowing down the car. "Loughrea. That must be the Irish version of Lockridge."

We drive into the medieval town of Loughrea, walk about its stone arched walkways, town moat, and enter its Church of Ireland. Instructions behind the glassed-in bulletin board tell the parishioners to "BE IN CHURCH BEFORE MASS BEGINS," "Take a Seat . . . Don't Stand near Door . . . Be Reverent during MASS . . . Remain in Your Place until MASS Is Finished."

"Fortunately, there's no mass going on now," Ernest comments. "We'd be heckled. Shackled."

A cross-emblazoned flyer offers "A Marriage Introductions Bureau" for "persons wishing to be introduced to suitable prospective marriage partners." A "PREPARING FOR MARRIAGE" official document depicts hands partially entwined, and the announcement that "All couples must give at least THREE MONTHS ADVANCE NOTICE of their marriage to one of the priests in their parish."

"Do they have to wait three months if they marry a priest from another parish?" Ernest comments.

I'm wondering why all these admonitions, rules, and strictures are deemed necessary. Has the Catholic population become totally unruly? The "three month" rule guarantees a shame to fall upon a pregnant woman, and her born-too-soon child, too. Abortion is completely outlawed. Are they trying to prevent premarital sex? My sympathies for the Irish women at the conference in Dublin increase.

"We're less than twenty kilometers from Tyrrellspass," I say. "Surely our ancestors knew each other. Maybe they intermarried."

"After waiting their three months, of course."

"Maybe we're quadzillion cousins." I touch my touchstones.

"Tyrrellspass—Overall Winner—Bord Falite Tidy Town Competition," says the sign as we enter the village. Surrounded by tree-crowned hillocks, Tyrrellspass is a pleasing little town with tidy lawns, tidy hedgerows, tidy oak trees. Unlike the linear layout of other Irish towns, Tyrrellspass is built around a village green.

"This is totally charming," I say, surveying "my" village.

Small businesses, a crescent of Georgian houses, the Belvedere Orphanage, a church, and the Village Inn Hotel encircle the expansive green, which boasts newly planted trees, shaped shrubs, a tribute to World War I soldiers—a statue of three school children, grim but walking forth—and a freshly painted serviceable red water pump, in place since the mid-1800s.

"Let's look at that," I say, pointing to a castle at the edge of the village. It is a square-shaped stone tower, with battlements around its roof, flanked by a shorter round building and a shorter still rectangular one. Between those two a carport—with a car parked in it.

"Winner of the Project-Village, European Architectural Heritage Award, 1975," the sign says. "Built circa 1410, the castle occupied a strategic pass between two vast areas of bog, swamp, and lake—water level, then, being much higher than it is now. The Castle is the last one standing from the five hundred-year reign of the powerful Tyrrell family."

"This castle is my ancestral home!" I shout. Or maybe, just gasp.

"Yup," says Ernest. "You're my Jewish-princess."

"Hello," I say to the sweet-faced older man who answers the door. "I'm Laurel Tyrrell." Truth being a way of life for us Tyrrells, I say this without a whit of guilt, and in a faux Irish accent, which I developed for a Synge play. But, honestly, if the truth be told, Tyrrell would be my last name if my father's childhood had taken a different turn, but that's another story.

"Well, it wouldn't be a good idea not to let a Tyrrell in, now would it?" the sweet-faced man says in his Irish cadenced voice. "I'm Phillip Ginnell— architect, restorer, resident, and current owner of 'your' castle."

"How did this castle survive the Cromwellian Wars?" Ernest (who knows most everything and who wants to know what he doesn't know) asks.

"After negotiations to save the village, the defenders surrendered to Colonel Green," Mr. Ginnell tells us.

"Who had the defenders shot. Right?" asks Ernest.

"Regrettably."

Mr. Ginnell tells us the history of the castle, which, although I am averse to historical facts, I find fascinating. This is not History—this is my family's history. The castle passed into the hands of the Earl of Belvedere, whose wife Jane imagined and supervised the village's plantings, buildings, and social welfare. In its lifetime, the castle had been a garrison, secondary school, family home, and a near ruin until Philip Ginnell restored and modernized it in the 1970s.

I brush a stone wall inside the castle, which seems to respond to my touch. The arched ceilings and doorways in the "first floor reception" encircle my spirit; the "banquet room with seating for thirty-two persons" elicits visions of medieval feasts; climbing the worn stone steps to the fourth floor of the tower, I am literally stepping in the footsteps of family who came before me; and the "scullery" and "hot press" remind me that in every castle, except for those one makes in the sky, some woman's work was hard and hot. My mind returns briefly to the International Woman's Conference. Why didn't we talk about the actual plights of poor women—rather than academic theories?

"My wife has died," Mr. Ginnell tells us. "The castle will be on sale. It's listed with Sotheby's." He hands us several large elegant brochures, we commiserate with him, thank him, and take our leave. I place one of my touchstones by the castle's entryway, a Jewish tradition for commemorating the dead.

"Wasn't this lucky?" I say to Ernest. "That we got to see the castle and even have these great souvenirs?"

Ernest looks at the backside of a brochure. It has an architectural drawing and specifications of the castle's floor plan. "Lookey here," he says, "your castle is for sale for only $350,000. Shall we buy it?"

"Thanks, but no thanks," I answer. "I don't think we want to live in Ireland. We have no family living here. They're all gone or dead."

"Ah, the Tyrrells are back," the jolly man behind the desk at the Village Hotel Inn, says.

I wonder if I look that much like a Tyrrell. I look confused.

"Ah, the wee leprechauns, they told me," he says grinning.

"And a shefro, too?" I ask.

"So, you caught me out with my blarney, eh? Well, Mr. Ginnell called me to look out for you," the jolly man says, enjoying his little joke. "And here you are. Enjoy your stay—and please, join us for dinner. On the house."

"What's a shefro?" Ernest asks as we climb the stairs.

"A cheerful little being alive and well in Irish legends," I say.

We enter a lovely large room with a door that leads to our own private roof garden replete with comfy chairs, a profusion of flowering plants, and a view of the village green. Everything is peaceful and quiet.

"From up here," Ernest says, "Laurel Tyrrell can survey the kingdom her relatives gave their lives to preserve."

"Ernest, do you remember when you said that our hotel room in Dublin was as good as it gets?" I ask.

"Yup."

"Well, you were wrong."

"For the first time in me life."

"*This* is as good as it gets."

In the morning, we visit the cemetery at Castlelost Church. Girls have written out their names in little stones—"Deirdre," "Bridget," "Mona"— on a gravesite. A lanceman, it would appear, has beheaded a stone tombstone carving of a medieval warrior. Ernest, who has an uncanny ability to identify faces in paintings, sculptures—and now, tombstones—says, "He resembles your father. He's definitely a Tyrrell." I place another of my little gray stones on the broken stone effigy.

After writing a draft of this piece, I decide to visit my older son, Ben, and bring him some photos of the castle. When Ben was nine, in mid-June 1971, he flew to Miami to see my father—his grandfather. By Ben's accounts, Father cooked "bacon-fried-fried-potatoes," did "magic tricks with cards and mirrors," and told stories of his childhood. Father died three weeks later; Ben says the timing of his visit was lucky.

"I see you've framed the castle brochure," I say to Ben. It's on the wall by his computer.

"It's my family's history," he says. "It's there with the other family pictures."

I look at the collection of framed photos of Ben, his wife Tami, and his stepdaughter Shana, who is a joy in my life. They are a family; and they look like a family. Shana's "Walum-West Family," drawn when she was eight, is framed and hanging there, too.

Ben is blond, blue-eyed, square-faced, tall, strong, Nordic. Up to this time, I have assumed that he had inherited all this from his Norwegian father. Now, for the first time, I see that he is a Tyrrell.

"How's my Viking son, today?" I ask.

"Taking care of my family!" he says.

"I have something to give you," I say, remembering the last of the little gray stones, sharp and smooth, tucked away in a drawer these past sixteen years.

Unquiet American

Ernest Lockridge

"I don't know when I've seen you this excited," Laurel says.

"Oh, there must've been a few times," I say, surreptitiously touching my left groin through the gray corduroy cloth of my trousers, not wanting to worry my wife. Unreassuringly, the lump—tender and rubbery—is still there, oblong and about the size and consistency of an art student's gutta-percha eraser. Last night when I discovered it in the oubliette of the shower stall adjoining our Lilliputian room at the Hotel Clarence, an image flashed into my mind of the Duke of Clarence upside down in the malmsey-butt, naked bony ankles struggling in the iron grip of his murderers in the Olivier movie of *Richard III.*

"What about a few thousand times?" I venture in jest.

"I am not referring to that sort of thing, Ernest."

We've just scaled a stand of granite steps, edged sideways through a narrow passageway in the thick granite wall, and emerged atop the Martello tower where the opening pages of *Ulysses* take place. I've taught The Great Irish Novel at least a dozen times over the years, in seminar rooms and in lecture halls, to undergraduate and graduate students. And to the four winds. Round and forty feet high, with walls eight feet thick, Martello towers ring the Irish coast. The English built them in 1804 to defend Ireland against Napoleon before early retirement dropped him beneath a parachute of solid lead onto the rat-infested island of St. Helena. James Joyce briefly occupied this tower during 1904. It now functions as his shrine.

Ulysses was published in 1922, in Paris, and is set in Dublin on Thursday, June 16, 1904. Now, early afternoon of Thursday, July 9, 1987, Laurel and I are in Sandycove on the outskirts of Dublin, having taken a train to come here. At nine this morning I got up on my hind legs in a cramped lecture room and held forth for exactly fifteen minutes to a diminutive odds-and-ends session of the Third International Interdisciplinary Congress on Women at Trinity College. I held forth on Ernest Hemingway(!), my presentation a spin-off of the essay-writing binge I embarked on recently to get onto paper and into print "Lockridge's Greatest Hits" from among the numerous literary interpretations— "too numerous," in words from the pen of the immortal Joyce, "to be enumerated"—that I derived, or concocted, during my twenty-four years of university teaching. The project possesses the urgency (hypothetically speaking) of an orgy. Why, I'm uncertain. Having delivered my little Hemingway paper, I am now duty-free, as is Laurel, who gave her own presentation yesterday. "Free," that is, to trail along behind me on *my* literary pilgrimage.

"I wish you could see yourself," Laurel says. "You're surrounded by a sort of . . . halo."

"*Introibo ad altare Dei*," I intone.

"What's that?"

"First line of dialogue in *Ulysses*. 'I approach the altar of God.' From the Roman Catholic Mass."

"Stephen Dedalus?"

"Nope, Buck Mulligan intones the line, false friend acting as false priest. Here." I hand Laurel the camera. "Immortalize me, *s'il vous plaît*."

I strike a pose. She shoots my picture and hands back the camera.

"It's so incredible!" I say. "Just being here on the actual site. . . ." I take in the thick, gray parapets, inlaid iron rails on which cannons once were wheeled, the tall iron cannon-pivot rising from the granite floor's center, the iron rings set at ten-foot intervals into the granite walls, the gray sky, the snotgreen sea with nary a ship in sight. "This must be how it looked to Joyce. . . . Lord God! I can almost see Stephen Dedalus coming through our portal there. . . . And Mulligan in his bathrobe, his plump belly, the straight razor, the nickel shaving bowl as a profane chalice. . . . It's an epiphany!"

"Didn't they film *Ulysses* on location here? When was that?"

"Back in the mid-sixties."

"I recall where we're standing now from the movie. Vaguely."

"Terrible movie."

"I liked it," Laurel says.

"Censors wouldn't even allow the thing into New Haven, so I drove to Waterford. 1967. Must've been a dozen cops inside ringing the seats, like later when I watched *Barbarella*. *Last Tango in Paris*, too. Absent the police presence audiences might've lost control and exploded into a mass orgy. Alas, no such luck."

"Times have changed," says Laurel.

"Now it's an around-the-clock orgy."

The afternoon air is crisp and clear, with a salt tang. It is almost warm. There's a distant scrawing of gulls as we head back down the crepuscular stairwell.

The tower's interior is a travesty: cobbled into a sterile, anonymous maze of cubicles and displays. You could be inside any small museum anywhere. We exit Joyce's Martello tower through this space, passing

Joyce's bronze death mask, which hangs against a wall, lips pressed together, eyes clamped shut, hair all greasy and plastered down, like fresh
manure. The Congress on Women is swamped with people, but today—
judging from the register where we sign our names on leaving—we are the
Martello tower's sole pilgrims. "If only they'd turned it into a pub."

"Why?" Laurel asks.

"The James Joyce Tavern! It'd be crammed wall-to-wall with wor-
shippers."

Outside, she says, "Watching you back there almost makes me wish
I'd been able to read *Ulysses*."

"You tried?"

"Not really. I delivered Molly Bloom's soliloquy onstage in Chicago,
years ago when I was with the Compass Players."

"All of it?"

"The last page or so. But plowing through seven or eight hundred un-
punctuated, unreadable pages. . . ."

"The first chapter's just incredibly good."

"What's it about?"

"You mean—?"

"What happens?"

"Well, Stephen Dedalus—he's pretty much Joyce, himself—has been
kept up most of the night by some deadbeat English lunatic named
Haines. The guy has screaming nightmares that he's being attacked by a
black panther . . . ?"

"Which stands for something?"

"Who the hell knows? There must be a thousand interpretations
floating out there. For example, Christ's true father, according to someone's blasphemous account, was a Roman Centurion named Pantherus.
So, here's Haines, who 'represents England,' having nightmares about
Christ's father, to the extreme annoyance of Stephen Dedalus, who 'represents Ireland'—and so on. Which is how one goes about 'understanding'
Ulysses. Go figure."

"Thanks all the same, but no thanks."

"Anyway, Stephen is terrified of Haines, and for good reason because
not only is Haines a violent paranoiac in his sleep, he's brought his
firearms into the tower where he's staying rent-free because Stephen's
snake-in-the-grass roommate Buck Mulligan is trying to hit Haines up

for money, thus far without success—if you can follow any of this, or want to."

"No, go on."

"Mulligan's pissed off at Stephen and trying to get rid of him because he won't play along, won't suck up to Haines. In addition to which Stephen's in deep mourning, still wearing black though it's been a year since his mother's death. And Mulligan mocks Stephen mercilessly because he won't give up grieving for his mother."

"Nice guy."

"Even worse, Mulligan mocks Stephen for *killing* his mother."

"What?"

"With her dying breath Stephen's mother begged him to pray for her soul and he refused. Stephen's abandoned Catholicism, you see. He's a 'free thinker,' a devout atheist sticking to his principles even in the face of his dying mother. In addition to grief he's being eaten alive by guilt. So that morning when Stephen departs from the Martello tower he realizes that he won't be returning. He gives up his key to Mulligan. By the end of chapter one Stephen Dedalus is grieving, guilty, depressed, and homeless."

"I've always heard of *Ulysses* being a novel where nothing happens."

"Well, you still hear it."

"That it consists of myth, symbols, philosophy, but little or no story."

"That, too."

"You hear it from your students?"

"It's how they've been taught to read literature. The most highly respected academic critics of modern literature take precisely that approach, so it pretty much comprises the canon of received wisdom. And not only regarding Joyce."

"Hemingway, too?"

"All writers are fair game. According to the Critical Canon, characters and their stories serve as springboards into symbolism and myth. It's an approach that reverses what novelists like Joyce and Hemingway are really all about—reads them backward, at least to my eyes. Myth and symbolism serve a secondary function, helping us understand the characters and their world—triptik simplifications of the actual journey at best. And now here comes the creeping mustard gas of Theory smothering literature beneath a comforter of yellow smog. A university course in modern literature can inoculate you against ever understanding a word of it. The awful irony of my situation isn't lost on me. But then I'm hopelessly out of step."

"Me, too."

"People listen to you. I'm a crank and a crackpot."

"They seemed to be listening this morning."

"To their stomachs growling, maybe. How many of them have even read *A Farewell to Arms*?"

"Look on the sunny side, Ernest. Your department provided you with airfare to Ireland."

"And shoe-horning my way into an International Women's Congress with a paper on a hairy-chested, elephant-slaughtering, philandering sexist male pig is no mean accomplishment in and of itself." My little presentation argued that Catherine Barkley, the witty and complex heroine of *A Farewell to Arms*, spends the novel fantasizing the novel's oafish, purblind narrator to be her beloved fiancé of eight years, slaughtered on the Somme. In the words of yet another Ernest, she is "faithful in [her] fashion." It's struck me as obvious for years that Hemingway did this deliberately and for clear aesthetic reasons. Yet nowhere in the Critical Canon can I find my reading of the novel, and the occasional colleague to whom I'm foolish enough to broach it regards me with glassy-eyed disbelief. Well, what the heck! Might as well spell it out chapter and verse, present it as a paper, and ultimately—in the sublime service of Beauty and Truth—track down some obscure academic journal gullible enough to commit the thing to print.

"I thought the other man on the panel did a good job."

"Yagh! The guy was making himself out to be so damned sensitive and *feminist* I wanted to puke . . . oh, wow! Look!" We're approaching a granite wall ten feet high that extends to the sea's edge. The approach is a no-man's-land of boulders and jagged rocks. A posting on the wall says, "Gentlemen's Bathing Area."

"This is in *Ulysses*, I suppose."

"Why, right there's probably where Buck Mulligan weights down his chemise with Stephen's key to the Martello tower!" I'm pointing toward a flat rock lapped by small waves.

"I wish all this meant something to me," Laurel says wistfully. "What did James Joyce think of Ireland?"

"Stephen Dedalus calls her 'an old sow that eats her farrow.' Mulligan calls her a 'country full of rotten teeth and rotten guts.' Joyce went into self-imposed exile in 1904. Though it's the only country he ever wrote about, much to the chagrin of the locals. In 1941 when he died, *Ulysses* was still banned in Ireland. The ban was lifted only recently."

"They haven't lifted their ban against women swimming here."

"Because men here swim in the nude."

"So what?" Laurel runs ahead onto a walkway skirting the wall and takes a peek around the corner. I touch my groin. Goddamn lump. Laurel is stripping off her clothes. I snap her picture. She's waving some article of clothing at me. I snap a picture. She dons her blouse and returns to where I'm waving the camera over my head.

"You didn't by any chance take my photograph, did you?"

"And miss an opportunity for blackmail and extortion?"

"Good thing there's no one else around."

"No naked Irishmen?"

"Thank God, no."

"What's the most useless thing on a woman's body?"

"Is this a joke?"

"You'll have to tell me."

"Okay, what?"

"An Irishman."

"It's a joke."

"Better follow my orders from here on out or you'll wind up as the Miz Universe Centerfold in the family album."

"One of your former graduate students told me your teaching copy of *Ulysses*, with all its annotations and what not, resembled an album containing the entire universe."

"Same old Modern Library Edition I've been teaching out of since fall of 1964. Even before I'd actually read *Ulysses*, I was teaching it. Couple of years later an ex-student from my maiden seminar in modern lit runs into me on campus. 'Professor Lockridge!' he says. 'Triffin!' 'That was a great course you taught, Professor Lockridge, especially *Ulysses*.' 'Ah, Triffin, I have a confession. I was initiating myself into *Ulysses* along with the class, assignment by assignment.' 'Oh,' says Triffin, 'we all knew that.' 'Was I really so God-awful?' 'No, you were fine,' Triffin reassures me. 'Then how—?' 'We observed the progressive darkening down the sides of your teaching copy.'"

"You've told me the story, Ernest. A few times."

"Oh."

"You're all right?"

"Me? Oh . . . sure."

"You're not angry?"

"Huh-uh."

"I was putting on a little show for your eyes only."

"It's okay."

"I didn't even take it all off . . . or is that the problem?"

"Why do you think there's a problem?"

"Because you're looking . . . well, strange."

"It's nothing at all," I lie, thinking of how my brother's lymphoma first presented as a swollen node in his left armpit. By the time he got around to having himself examined the node had ballooned into a softball and the doctor informed him that within six weeks he would be a dead man.

"Then what are you thinking?" Laurel asks me.

"Oh, uh . . . about . . . about Fleming," I extemporize.

"Who is Fleming, Ernest?"

"Guess I haven't told you this one."

"Guess not."

"Fleming was an aging assistant professor several years ahead of yours truly on Yale's Revolving Bottom. It's from him that I inherited my modern lit seminar."

"The world-famous seminar with Triffin in it."

"Right. The seminar wherein I made my maiden voyage through *Ulysses*. Also through Yeats, Pound, Eliot, Hart Crane, and Wallace Stevens. I'd never studied these guys, not as a grad student or an undergrad. But in May of '64, as my first year of teaching was ending, Fleming takes me to lunch at a table down at Mory's and says Yale is tossing him off the merry-go-round in the fall, no brass ring, and I'm the Chosen One who's taking over his seminar. After downing a phalanx of ferocious doubles—"

"Ernest! You were drinking hard liquor at lunch?"

"Of course not. I still had afternoon classes to teach."

"Fleming was finished for the day?"

"In a manner of speaking. So, anyway, from his alcoholic perch Fleming issues me a warning: 'Listen, Lockridge, don't think for one moment that I envy you, trying to wring some semblance of meaning from this line-up of crackpots and lunatics.'"

"The poor man sounds utterly burnt out on teaching."

"Yeah?"

"Pity his poor students!"

"Uh-huh. So Fleming continues, 'A year from now while you're stumbling through the dark and weird maze of Wallace Stevens you'll discover that your brain has degenerated into a state of feeble-minded schizophrenia.' He proved to be a seer. The following spring I could scarcely follow the sidewalk to the bus stop."

"Like Fleming following your lunch at Mory's. What happened to him?"

"Dead and forgotten with the rest."

"No, seriously."

"Fleming was hired on at Swarthmore."

"Sounds like an improvement."

"Swarthmore required faculty members to teach themselves into oblivion."

"Like our own Ohio State. Didn't Swarthmore offer *you* a job?"

"And I phoned Fleming for advice, and he advised me I'd be crazy to come, that I'd never have time to write, that the faculty was on call around the clock in case some poor student needed his or her nose wiped."

"Did Fleming sound sober over the phone?"

"Now that you mention it, no."

"Is Fleming a writer, too?"

"Fleming, who departed Yale trailing clouds of glory as a poet and short story writer of promise, seems to have vanished in a malmsey-butt."

"Sad. . . . But why not assign you a seminar in Shakespeare? Why did they ask you to teach a course on authors you'd scarcely even read?"

"I'm the youngest of the English faculty. Ergo, I teach the most recent authors."

"You call those denizens of the Stone Age 'recent'?"

"As 'recent' as Yale allowed itself to go back then."

"Why did you agree to teach such difficult and unfamiliar subject matter?"

"Maybe I liked the challenge or merely figured I could handle it. If so, I was right. The students saw straight through me as a mountebank and a charlatan, and gave not a tinker's damn."

"So . . . where to now?"

I consult my ULYSSES MAP OF DUBLIN—labeled thus in bright red block letters, said brightness intensified by a sudden burst of sunlight through the overcast. The Irish sky is dramatic, bank upon bank of clouds like tens of thousands of simultaneous atom bomb blasts boiling into the stratosphere. "Let's hit Summerfield School."

"Do we catch a tram?"

"No, look here on the map. We can walk what was probably Joyce's route to work from the Martello tower . . . this way on . . . Buffooni? . . . it's Bible print and I can scarcely . . . Christ, I need stronger reading glasses! Those reams upon reams of goddamn grading have blinded me! Anyway, whatever-the-hell-street-name-it-is. . . ."

"Breffni," says Laurel, reading off the map.

"Turns into Ulverton, which runs into Dalkey Road, which is where we're heading."

"Looks like some distance."

"A mere half mile. It's a nice day and warming up. The air out here's clear and clean, no traffic, no crowds and cars and cacophony like downtown Dublin. . . ."

"The dirt, the poverty, the drunken reeling men and women, the total lack of pollution control on cars and busses, diesel and leaded exhaust, the filthy awful smells," says Laurel. "It's a wonder you're not dead of asthma. Or that we've not been throttled by the God-awful miasma of the place."

"You sound like Joyce."

"Dublin—yuck!"

"I didn't realize . . . I've been sort of floating above the ground ever since we got here, protected by a mental bubble."

"Far be it from me to prick your bubble. Off to Summerville!"

"Summerfield."

"Or whatever. I only live to see you lit by radiant halos."

A half hour later we're standing outside the shoulder-high cast iron gate in front of the building where in 1904 Joyce was teaching snot-nosed eighth-grade boys—and where the reader of *Ulysses* finds Stephen Dedalus mumbling through a history class. "SUMMERFIELD," says the iron lettering affixed to the gate. Trees and tall shrubs shield the house from the street. There's a swirling cloud of midges. The setting is bucolic, idyllic. The gate's ajar. We venture a few feet onto the gravel drive leading to one side of the former school, now a private residence. There's a white late-model sedan parked in the drive. Summerfield is an attractive, well-maintained, two-story stucco house with metal shutters painted in Prussian blue. "I don't see any halos, Ernest."

"I'm so anxious about trespassing that I'm not able to achieve epiphany."

"Should you speak to an epiphany-therapist?"

The walk has sensitized the lump, which tingles against my trousers. "Some sort of therapist," I mumble.

"So, what happened here?"

"Ah . . . let's see now . . . Stephen's in a distracted state, trying to teach a class about a king named Pyrrhus who won the battle of Asculum against the Romans in 279 BCE, but at the cost of most of his men. You've heard of 'Pyrrhic victory'?"

"Of course."

"Pyrrhus said, 'Another victory like this, and we're done for.' That's where the term comes from. We know Stephen's had a Pyrrhic victory over his mother that's left him desperate with guilt and grief. Class ends, and the headmaster, Mr. Deasy, calls Stephen into his office, ostensibly to pay him. But Mr. Deasy knows Stephen is miserable and should leave by mutual consent. Deasy's an anti-Semite, a miser, an old fool, but even he can see that Stephen is suicidally depressed. Mr. Deasy conveys this knowledge to Stephen obliquely, tactfully warning him against committing 'the one sin,' suicide. And he puts the hard truth to Stephen: 'You were not born to be a teacher, I think.' At the conclusion of chapter 2, Stephen is both homeless and jobless."

Laurel is silent. Finally she says, "Are we finished here?"

"Uh-huh."

"You don't want to see whether the owners might consider allowing a Joyce scholar. . . ?"

"I'm far too timid. And we've already been inside one Joycean educational facility." This was University College where we went on Monday. Joyce attended University College as a scholarship student, and after *Ulysses* appeared a Member of the Establishment remarked, "This is precisely the sort of highly literate filth one must come to expect when Members of the Lower Class are given a University Education." University College consists of a single building smaller than my Indiana high school, which burnt to the ground in 1966. There are long, high-ceilinged corridors with classrooms on either side. Black and white diamond-shaped tiles pave the corridors. We are there alone.

"I'd be happy to inquire," Laurel offers.

"No thanks. The one Joycean academic interior more than suffices."

Back in Dublin we walk to the Ormond Hotel on Ormond Quay beside the River Liffey, which flows through Dublin and provides the water for the Guinness Brewery. The Ormond Bar provides the setting for the "Sirens" episode of *Ulysses*. During the Great War when Joyce mailed this particular chapter to a little magazine publisher in America, Allied authorities intercepted the manuscript on suspicion that Joyce was an enemy spy writing in code. It was ultimately decided, however, that the manuscript merely represented "an oddly incoherent and incomprehensible piece of literary writing."

The Ormond Bar has been recently desecrated. The décor of a traditional Irish bar lies buried beneath a plywood Sherwood Forest all slobbered-over with Kelly green. Paint fumes nearly overpower the omnipresent tobacco smoke. We escape to Eccles Street and the dwelling occupied by Leopold and Molly Bloom for all eternity.

The entire block of dwellings on the Bloom-side of Eccles has been demolished to make room for a redbrick hospital complex that looms over us. An identical row of dwellings across the street still stands . . . vacant, the fenced-off basement-level areas awash in debris.

"No halos, huh," says Laurel, who sees my disappointment.

"How about heading out to where Leopold and Molly first got it on? And I'll declare the pilgrimage officially at an end."

"Where are you taking me, Ernest?

"Some lurid back alleyway littered with the detritus of mythological beasts," I say, trying to boost myself into a sunnier state of mind.

We catch the train to Howth Head hill, northwest of the center of Dublin. It's late afternoon as we climb the road to the summit of the huge formation, which we have to ourselves. The surrounding vegetation is lush and verdant, bending in the warm, hissing, sweet-smelling breeze. The summit affords a clear, sunlit view of Dublin, Dublin Bay, and the Irish Sea. The cloudbanks are straight out of Rubens. In the rays of the lowering sun I visualize the nacreous swirling swarms of winged putti.

"Where did you say they did it?" asks Laurel.

"Somewhere down there."

"Out in plain view?"

"Molly's this incredibly hot babe who takes it all off whenever the mood hits her. Irish father, Jewish mother, you know."

"You have in mind someone of your acquaintance?"

"I was thinking of that gully-like spot where we're not quite so exposed to the naked gaze."

"And yes I said yes I will Yes."

That evening following dinner we go for a nightcap to the Clarence Hotel's Octagon Bar, a wood-paneled eight-sided saloon where tobacco fumes gray the air. A plump befreckled young woman in a pinafore-style dress whose fraying hem gives out at midthigh wanders over from the bar. "Ma'am and Sir?"

"Ginger ale," says Laurel.

"Would a lemon soda suit you, Ma'am?"

"It'll have to."

"Double Jameson's, please," I say. The exertions on Howth have granted the lump a life of its own. "In honor of Fleming."

"I didn't marry Fleming, Ernest."

"Um . . . on second thought, Miss, ask your barman to pull me a Guinness."

"A full or a half, Sir?"

"Um . . . half a pint."

"Go ahead, Ernest, order a full one."

"No thanks."

The waitress wanders back to the bar.

"Please have one if you want one," Laurel insists. "It's been a long, strenuous day, God knows."

"The sheer artistry of it requires entirely too much time," I explain. "All that filling the glass a quarter full, allowing the foam to settle, then daring to fill it all the way up to half-full, and on and on. Pulling a full pint of Guinness in Dublin is like playing a Stradivarius in Cremona."

"Where should we head off to tomorrow, do you think?" Laurel asks.

"Well, it's either up the coast or down the coast. Or east across the Midlands."

"That's a big help."

When the waitress returns with our drinks, Laurel asks, "What is your opinion of the Midlands, Miss?"

"Sure and they're a dreary wasteland, Ma'am. You'll not be wanting to waste your precious stay in Ireland fooling around with the Midlands." She walks back to the bar.

"The Irish regard their Midlands the way the Australians regard their Outback," I observe. My Guinness leaves an aftertaste reminiscent of the Eel River where I swam as a child in Indiana.

The racket in the alley beneath our hotel room after the pubs close awakens us, a clattering of feet on cobblestones like insomniac tap dancers on parade. "Must be the custom here to have tappets fastened to the toes and heels of everybody's shoes," I murmur into my pillow.

"It's a poor country," Laurel murmurs back. "They're trying to save their soles."

In the hotel restaurant before checking out we order the full Irish breakfast, the "Fry." "This tastes really great," I say amidst shoveling down the two fried eggs, the fried potatoes, fried tomato, and fried bread.

"And so good for you."

"Righto. My doctor's encouraging me to putty-up the old arteries."

"It's no joke, Ernest. Wasn't your last cholesterol count through the roof?"

"Somewhere in the shtratosphere," I say, masticating my fried bread.

We head over to the Avis office a few doors from the Hotel Clarence and rent the red Opel we reserved through our travel agent. There are no snakes in Ireland, and no rentals with automatic transmissions. Straight shift, four-on-the-floor with the left hand! I've been dreading this moment for months.

"How are you doing, Ernest?" We're driving south along the west coast of Ireland. Thus far I've remembered to remain in the left lane. No accidents yet, not even nonfatal ones. I frequently swerve onto the berm unleashing the irate drivers that accumulate behind me. The mood of Ireland will lighten upon my departure and I alone will know why.

"Easy as pie, like falling off a log," I mumble, feeling brain-dead from the night before. Whenever I'd lapse into fitful slumber I dreamt of being strapped to the operating table whilst a grunting, perspiring team of surgeons played tug-of-war with the eighteen-foot anaconda they were dragging from my rectum. My brother experienced this nightmare all through his agonizing year of chemotherapy.

"You seem distracted."

48

"Only trying to recall Saint Patrick's technique for ridding Ireland of its snakes."

We reach Wexford late Friday afternoon and check into a bed and breakfast before taking a leisurely stroll about the compact coastal village. "Not to worry," I assure Laurel in our tiny room. "To my knowledge James Joyce never came anywhere near Wexford."

"So long as he didn't write about it."

We stroll to the end of Kilmore Quay, a long pier with iron railings. Sailboats and fishing boats lie at rest in the calm waters of Wexford Harbor. The sky is clear. The sun's starting to set. Beautiful.

We're crossing a cobblestoned open space on our way back to the B&B when Laurel notices a small bronze plaque. "I didn't know Ireland had bullfighting."

"Bull baiting. With bulldogs. What we now call pit bulls. They'd tether a bull to a wooden post in the center of the ring and sic the dogs on him. Not as thrilling as feeding Christians to the lions but great fun nonetheless." An insufferable know-it-all, I deign merely to glance at the plaque. "This is the site of their bullring, the movie house of the day, Saturday matinees, the works. It's also where in 1649 Cromwell slaughtered eighteen hundred souls of Wexford's total population of two thousand. Mere Roman Catholics, you see."

"Why not all of them?"

"Knives, swords, pikes, axes, primitive muskets—mass slaughter was pretty work-intensive back then. Say, I've managed to work up an appetite. How about you?"

The following day, Saturday, we end up at a much-touted B&B on Hook Head Peninsula jutting south into St. George's Channel in the Irish Sea. Getting here has been slow-going. We trailed a tractor-drawn peat wagon down a narrow, winding road with bogs on both sides where workers wielding long-handled turf-cutters extracted trapezoidal bricks of peat. The bricks stood stacked at intervals along the roadside.

"Speaking of work-intensive work," observed Laurel.

"I'd take early retirement in a split second."

The circular for the four-star B&B platonically offers boating, sailing, fishing, tennis, croquet, grounds for horseback riding and hiking, a wide variety of indoor entertainment, luxurious accommodations, gourmet dining. Where the road dead-ends we discover the actual B&B to be more

Aristotelian. The half-dozen rowboats are full of water. No tennis courts, no setup for croquet and, except for the patch of dirt between building and stony drive, no lawn. No horses, no grounds, no place to hike. Bare wooden cubicles with a two-foot hiatus between ceiling and walls.

"I love our privacy," Laurel says.

"Thank God we're the only guests."

At dinner Laurel orders sole, which comes to the table complete with skeleton. Will the waitress (the proprietor's wife) please request of the chef (the proprietor) that he debone the filet? The waitress returns Laurel's plate to the kitchen, whence cometh the chef's furious "NO!"

Seated at our table is the proprietor's mother. A stained surgical dressing covers her left eye. The day before yesterday surgeons removed the cancerous eyeball. She describes the operation. Postprandial entertainment consists of *The Quiet Man* on videotape. Laurel and I are ushered onto a brown couch in front of a decrepit Zenith TV in a brown-walled living room with brown ceiling, brown curtains, threadbare brown rug. "Sure and we've seen *The Quiet Man* already," the proprietor's mother says, leaving us on our own. John Wayne plays an Irish boxer who retires to a charming little Irish village and transforms it into a virtual Paradise of well-being and bonhomie. Maureen O'Hara plays the winsome Colleen.

"Ever thought of retiring, Ernest, and operating your very own B&B?"

"I think of nothing else."

Sunday finds us on a sidewalk in Cashel behind two elderly American couples. The husbands are decked out in green polo shirts and red-and-white checkered golfing slacks. Their wives are immaculately groomed, nary a blue hair out of place, as though heading for luncheon at the country club. Before a shop window displaying plush wool sweaters one of the men fiercely asserts, "We can buy that!"

"So can we!" asserts the other.

"We can buy the whole doggone store!"

"So can we!"

"I'm on our Liberry Board! Are you on your Liberry Board?"

"I'm *chairman* of my Liberry Board!"

"Well, I'm *president* of *my* Liberry Board!"

Laurel and I fall behind our "Fellow Amuricans" until they're out of earshot. "Will that be us?" I ask.

"Let's hope not."

"I think those are the first Ugly Americans I've ever actually run across."

"The marvelous thing about being an Ugly American is that even when you don't act ugly, the ugliness is there, ineradicably there in your bones," Laurel says. "You don't have to actually *do* anything, just simply *be*."

"It's almost Zen. 'Cease to strive.'"

"Are you quoting someone?"

"The ubiquitous Joyce. Leopold Bloom, who's fed up with his job in advertising, thinks about giving up before it's too late."

"As in, to heck with 'buying that'?"

"But you know, Laurel . . . sure, our 'fellow Amuricans' would rather discuss yachts than Yeats, but I think we may be missing something far more significant."

"Which is?"

"That they have a lot more money than we do and they no longer have to work."

We ascend the Rock of Cashel, Ireland's Holy of Holies. The ruins of a twelfth-century cathedral now clutter the summit, once the throne of Celtic kings. I deign to consult the guidebook. "Hey, Laurel, it was on this rock that while Saint Patrick was initiating King Angus into Christianity, he inadvertently skewered one of the royal feet with his pointed staff."

"What happened?"

"Angus grinned and bore it as part of the ritual. No pain, no gain."

Laurel stretches herself out atop an intact sarcophagus about whose limestone base foot-high saints stand in relief, palms pressed together. She shuts her eyes.

"Talk about ceasing to strive," I remark, my battery-powered camera clicking and whirring.

A vast outcropping of limestone rising two hundred feet above the surrounding plain, the Rock of Cashel affords a clear view of the country-side for miles in all directions. Those old Celts knew a good vantage point from which to spot invading hoards. Lots of good it did them, conquered as they were by a lone invader armed with a shepherd's crook. I spot a ruin about a half-mile away amidst the lush green Irish vegetation that stretches out below us to the horizon. According to the guidebook it's Hore Abbey, a Cistercian monastery founded in 1272 and dissolved in 1541. "Wake up, Laurel! I've got us another ruin!"

"I love ruins," she murmurs, opening her eyes.

We forge our way through meadow grass and heather where a herd of cattle stands placidly grazing. "Not to worry," I tell Laurel.

"About what?"

"No snakes in this grass."

"Thanks for reminding me."

Seen from the crumbling abbey Cashel's spires and escarpment resemble Camelot against a baroque cloudscape. Rampant vegetation swaddles Hore Abbey. My feet stumble against a shattered sarcophagus. "Uh-oh." I pluck a long bone from the waist-high heather. "What's this?"

"A femur?"

Bite-marks punctuate the gray staff. I raise it to my nose. No stench. I drop it into the heather where it lands beside a gray dome that resembles a XXXL yarmulke. "Are turtles any relation to snakes?"

"I don't think so, Ernest. Why?"

Picking it up I find myself in possession of a human being's cranial vault, hollow and commodious, empty but for the small black beetle that hastily releases its grip and flits away. "Alas, poor Yorick!"

"Is that what I think it is?" asks Laurel.

"Should we spirit this fellow of infinite jest back to Ohio with us?"

"And then what?"

"Well, Stalin used the top of Hitler's skull for an ashtray."

"We gave up cigarettes five years ago."

"When Lord Byron took Newstead Abbey over, he unearthed the cranium of a monk and had it fashioned into a wine goblet. Wrote some verse on it, too. 'Start not! Nor deem my spirit fled! Behold in me the only skull from which, unlike a living head, whatever flows is never dull!'"

"Have you seen it?"

"Naw. Some religious fanatic reburied the thing following Byron's death in 1824 at the ripe old age of thirty-six."

"Ernest, don't you think we should leave Yorick here where we found him?"

"Okay. . . ." Peering at the gnarled innards of this thimble that at one time held a universe I seek words to express whatever it is I'm feeling. "All the dead voices. . . ."

That night seated at table 3A in the dining room of the Cashel Palace Hotel we enjoy our best dinner by far since arriving in Ireland. I feast on kidneys, sausages, sweetbreads, lamb chops. Laurel has a veal chop. Our experience is tarnished only slightly by the presence two tables away of our quartet of "Fellow Amuricans" whose scintillating banter, inaudible to anyone more than a half mile from the Cashel Palace, calls for a second bottle of Muscadet on our part. The couples met in first class during the Aer Lingus flight over the Atlantic. Both men are retired bankers devoting their retirement to travel and to golf. They've come to Ireland with their golf clubs because Ireland boasts the world's finest links. It's their good fortune to have run into one another: now each has the other with whom to compete. They're planning a month-long orgy of betting for dollars, a different golf course every third day, wagering to begin at £500—US$750—per hole. "I can afford that!"

"I can *more* than afford that!"

"That's more money than I have in the bank," I say.

"Do you think they're twins separated at birth?" murmurs Laurel.

"The wives, too. Have you noticed how they're both mutes?"

We make a side trip the following day to Holycross Abbey with its fragment of the True Cross, a hair-thin splinter shielded by a thick rind of glass, then head over to Killarney where we arrive during the Festival Races, run on a racecourse whose green turf appears only a wee bit unsettled by two days of racing. The stands are crowded and raucous. Pints are in evidence. Bookies on stepladders work out of bulging leather valises. "Let me take this opportunity to add to my retirement nest egg," I say.

"What 'nest egg,' Ernest? What 'retirement'?"

I purchase a racing form for 50P. "What about 'Happy Eater' for the third race?"

"Why, Ernest?"

"Well, he's paying seven to one."

"Have you bet on the horses before?"

"No. Here's 'Candy Smile' at ten to one. Doesn't he pay the most?"

"Only if he or she wins, places, or shows."

"The Sport of Kings, right? Bet to win!"

I approach the bookie with the shortest line and place a bet on "Candy Smile" to win. According to the cardboard stub I receive for my five pounds my bookie is Paddy Kelly. "Now bet with the best," says the stub on both ends of which are printed three numbers: a blue two, an orange seven, a green three. I return to Laurel in the stands. "How poor old Paddy

Kelly keeps anything straight is beyond me," I tell her. "What does any of this have to do with Candy Smile?"

Ten horses take off around the track for a steeplechase of "about two miles" according to the racing form. Turf muffles the hooves. "It's like that deer park in Oxford," I say above the madding crowd. "Dozens of deer running like wild and you can't hear a sound."

"How is Candy Smile faring?"

"The track announcer's like listening to *Finnegans Wake* on Recordings for the Blind!" I shout.

Horses and riders are passing the stands to the hoots and shouts of spectators. I consider all the horses to have crossed the finish line when along comes Candy Smile, dead last. "There goes my meal ticket."

"Good," says Laurel.

"Why 'good'?"

"Now poor old Paddy Kelly won't have to worry about keeping things straight."

The following race, "an extended handicap flat race for four years old and upwards," I bet to win on "Lost Art" with "Turf Accountant" Sean Lynch. "Lost Art" loses badly. Next, "an upside down handicap flat race for four years old and upwards, mares only," I bet on "Sly Grin" to win with "Pleasure-to-Pay" P. Carty. "Sly Grin" comes in next to last.

"Here's 'Out to Pasture,' Ernest, at ten thousand to one," says Laurel, pretending to consult the racing form.

I pocket my stubs. "Let's hit the trail, Podner, while we're behind."

That night I spot something gleaming halfway up a rock retaining wall outside the pub where we've just finished dining on steak and kidney pie. Someone's shoved a pint glass into a cranny. "Lose some, win some," I say, extracting it gingerly. Holding the wide-mouthed glass feels, for a split second, like holding a World Cup.

In the morning we hire a horse-and-cart ride through the Gap of Dunloe. Seated behind the leathery, rake-thin driver we meander along the exact same Last Mile down which Saint Patrick in 447 CE hounded the writhing, hissing mass of Irish snakes into bottomless Serpent Lake, gleaming like a slab of polished basalt beneath the melodramatic Hibernian sky.

In the Opel, Laurel and I and my gutta-percha lump circumnavigate the Ring of Kerry. We explore the Dingle Peninsula, its ring forts and beehive dwellings designed, constructed, conceived in, born in, lived in, and died in by our Stone Age ancestors. We locate the exact same inlet from which on March 22, 532 CE, Saint Brendan sailed off in a canvas boat to America, beating by a millennium some Christopher-come-lately out of Italy by way of Spain. From the easternmost tip of Dingle we take a ferry piloted by an Irishman with insane searchlight eyes to Great Blasket Island, once the site of a thriving culture, uninhabited now for over a quarter century except for one mad hermit. Great Blasket is thick with vegetation, the ground wet and spongy underfoot.

"What is that you're mumbling, Ernest?"

"Place seems plenty large enough to accommodate *two* mad hermits."

"Yeats's is much bigger than Joyce's," says Laurel.

"Joyce's may be thicker."

"What is it about these Irish writers?" Laurel's sizing up Thoor Ballylee from its stony foundation to its stony breastwork.

"There's Robinson Jeffers's tower in Big Sur, and he's an American. So maybe it has something to do with writers in general."

"*Men* writers!"

"I guess women writers inhabit caves."

Thoor Ballylee's a thirteenth-century Norman tower on the Cloon River in County Galway. William Butler Yeats purchased it as a ruin in 1916 for thirty-five pounds and had it reconstructed to serve as the main residence for himself and his young wife and children. Yeats was fifty-one when he bought the tower. He lived there off and on from the summer of 1919, until 1928, eleven years before his death. Thoor Ballylee now serves as *his* shrine.

"Did Yeats retire here?" Laurel asks.

"Far from it. Yeats even had a Steinach operation—"

"A *what* operation?"

"Named for this quack German surgeon who implanted monkey gonads into old men's thighs to juice them up."

"You're making that up!"

"Thanks, but no."

"Doesn't the body simply reject them?"

"Not Yeats's. The operation seems to have given him a second wind sexually and creatively." Surreptitiously I finger the lump on my groin.

"Anyway, he married a girl in her twenties, half his age, sired two off-spring, commandeered his very own castle, churned out a raft of poems and plays, wrote a long crackpot thingamajig titled *A Vision*, became a nonstop sexual athlete conducting affairs with women all across Ireland—including the Midlands—entered politics—"

"That figures," says Laurel.

"As a Senator of the Irish Free State, no less."

"What did Yeats's wife have to say about her husband's philandering?"

Except for the woman who collects our two pounds admission fee we're alone in the tower whose setting is rural and isolated. We arrived here over winding country roads. Touring the rooms we are on our own. Each room comprises one entire floor. The furniture looks primitive. A spare and austere dwelling, this old man's castle. "His wife said nothing at all that I'm aware of," I answer Laurel. "She was happy merely to be the Great Man's vessel."

"Boy oh boy," says Laurel.

"Something the matter with that?"

"No, Ernest, of course not. Go on."

We're in the master bedroom. There's a small adjoining bathroom.

"See, Yeats was hopelessly in love from boyhood on with a woman named Maude Gonne who from the start made it perfectly clear she would not have him. Maude marries an Irish revolutionary named John McBride and bears his child, a daughter. Years pass. The Brits hang McBride and Yeats proposes to the Widder McBride, who sends him packing. Whereupon he proposes to her *daughter*! *She* turns him down. So on the rebound from both mother and daughter Yeats proposes to the girl in her twenties, who gives him the green light."

"Yeats sounds like a hopeless jerk."

"Now you sound like Fleming, Laurel. Anyway, during the honeymoon Yeats's brand-spanking-new bride, who's fully aware of her third-place finish in his affections and a distant third at that, suddenly lapses into a trance-like state and starts blathering all this spiritualistic gobbledygook. Yeats, who's a longtime devotee of spiritualism in all manner and shape—séances, Madam Blavatsky, the Order of the Golden Dawn—tells his bride to commit the words to paper and Mrs. Yeats dutifully commences a bout of 'automatic writing,' supposedly dictated through *her* by some other-worldly spirit. Based on his wife's scribbling Yeats cobbles together *A Vision,* which he says 'enables him to hold together in a single thought all of history, all of philosophy and all of time.' You should see the thing, full of illustrations—"

"Full of something."

"Gyres with their tips touching, whirling in opposite directions, representing birth and rebirth, the phases of the moon, the cycles of history. . . . Deep down maybe it had something to do with toilet-paper rolls."

"Did you teach this *Vision* thing?" Laurel asks.

"'Fraid so. Back then I was blind as a bat to the fact that my first marriage was making me insane, so its lunacy fit right in. Following Yeats's death his widow admitted it'd been a hoax. She'd played Scheherezade to prevent her wheezing ancient of a Sultan from waking up one fine morning and giving her the ax. Still, one must admit that the monkey gonads coupled with a hoax of crackpot theories—"

"As in, 'a murder of crows'?"

"Enabled old Yeats to crank out some pretty impressive poems during his final years."

"I know," sighs Laurel, who is a poet.

"What do we do now, Ernest?"

We're on the peak of Diamond Hill, 1,460 feet above sea level, in Connemara National Park.

The climb posed no problems. During a dinky "Nature Walk," an eighth-of-a-kilometer macadam loop behind the "Information Centre," I'd spotted the faint beginnings of a trail in the heath, heading in the direction of Diamond Hill. "It's unmarked," Laurel had said.

"Yeah?"

"Maybe that means we're not supposed to take it."

"Look across the heath to the mountain. Any stone walls that you can make out?"

"No."

"Then it may be our first honest-to-God hiking opportunity since leaving Dublin." Thus far our attempts to explore the countryside have been blocked by stone barricades, the most frustrating instance occurring only this morning when a road sign told of a "City of Ring Forts" a mile off the road. The first wall we came to, a mountainous eight feet in height, stopped us dead in our tracks.

"Listen to what the information center's circular says, Laurel. 'The view from a mountaintop puts the entire area into perspective. Diamond Hill is a reasonable climb—so reasonable, in fact, that there may be sheep grazing on heather waiting for you at the top.'"

"Okay, Ernest, but here's what *my* circular has to say on the subject. 'Do not go walking without proper clothing, including walking boots, and proper maps and compass and the ability to use them, and sufficient food and spare warm clothes. Do not venture into the hills alone.'"

"Who's 'alone'?"

"'It is important that intending hill walkers should call into the Information Centre, and leave details of their planned route and expected time for return.'"

"Let me see that. . . . It also says right here that 'Diamond Hill, which towers over the Park Information Centre, is worth climbing to view the Park lands and surrounding scenery.' So there."

"What are you saying, Ernest?"

"That it can't possibly be all that big a deal."

Nor was it. Until now.

"Ernest, which one of those . . . *things* is our trail down the mountain?"

"I don't know."

"You may be right."

Surveying the moss-blanketed turf of the descent I'm confronted with an insane spider's web of intersecting, crooked, meandering pathways "I just supposed we were on a human trail but those look like grazing paths made by sheep," I observe by way of assessing our situation, though we have yet to run across any sheep. "Or mountain goats," I add.

"If we see one, perhaps we can ask directions."

"Which of those things looks like the road most traveled by?"

"They all look about the same. When does it get dark?" We've brought bottled water but no food. No flashlight. No extra clothing.

"We have time," I say, glancing at my wristwatch. Not much time. "Hoo boy! How time flies when one has fun! Well, as that great Irish philosopher Heraclitus once said, 'The way up is the way down.'" I draw a deep breath. "Let us go then, you and I."

I choose one of the paths at random and down we go, each step sinking in the spongy turf. Sparrow-like birds twitter and flit in the liquid summer air. According to our circulars darkness brings out bats. The path makes a gradual descent before dead-ending abruptly at the lip of a fifty-foot sheer drop, jagged boulders beetling about its base. I teeter dizzily on the brink.

"Ernest? What is it?"

"Don't come closer!" I'm back-stepping.

"Where to now?"

"Off we go-ohh. . . ." Earth drops away at my feet. I'm falling . . . falling . . . facedown onto a foul carpet of marsh and moss. A skull-sized stone brushes my temple.

"Ernest!" Laurel is far above me, frightened and small. "Are you alive?"

"Thanks to the good Lord," I murmur, rising, brushing myself off. One inch to the left would have dashed out my brains, such as they are.

The next path I choose takes us down the mountain to the Opel in the parking lot by the information center.

We're at Yeats's grave in Drumcliffe churchyard in the shadow of Ben Bulben, more plateau than mountain and shaped like an ill-formed loaf of bread. Yeats wanted his gravestone made of limestone quarried near the spot. To me his gravestone looks like granite.

"Is his brother buried with him?" Laurel asks, pointing at a foot-square slab of slate inscribed with a single name resting atop the gravel covering the grave.

"'George' is Yeats's wife."

"Poor, poor thing," laments Laurel.

On our way here we drove around Lough Gill so I could see the Lake Isle of Innisfree of Yeats's magnificent poem, perhaps the ultimate retreat from the workaday world in all of poetry.

I will arise and go now, and go to Innisfree,
And a small cabin build there, of clay and wattles made:
Nine bean-rows will I have there, a hive for the honey-bee,
And live alone in the bee-loud glade.

And I shall have some peace there, for peace comes dropping slow,
Dropping from the veils of the morning to where the cricket sings;
There midnight's all a glimmer, and noon a purple glow,
And evening full of linnet's wings.

CHAPTER 2

I will arise and go now, for always night and day
I hear lake water lapping with low sounds by the shore;
While I stand on the roadway, or on the pavements grey,
I hear it in the deep heart's core.

From the roadway I glimpsed the Lake Isle twenty yards or so from the lakeshore. The tiny island consists of a steep hillock jutting abruptly out of the water. Thick with trees and shrubs it's the size of my back yard in Worthington, Ohio.

The evening before we're to cross over into Londonderry an I.R.A. sniper shoots a twenty-two-year-old British border guard through the skull. We cancel our plan and take a room in Rathmullan House, an "Irish Country Home" on Lough Swilly. The accommodations are sumptuous, equal in luxury to the Royal Suite in the Royal Crescent in Bath, but that's another trip, another story. The restaurant truly does deliver gourmet dining. There *is* a golf course, a wee little one. We eat and drink. We play at playing golf. We walk the beach at sunset. "Now, here's someplace where I'd consider retiring," I tell Laurel.

"Pricey accommodations even for *your* retirement, Ernest, and that's not counting breakfast, lunch, and dinner."

"Whenever the necessity arises I shall simply go out and win the Masters."

We pass two idyllic days and nights before being rousted for a pair of teenaged Brits in a Bentley. They're poorly dressed in designer clothes. A heavy encrustation of gems and chains appears to have wrecked their postures. The young man's hair—protean variations on the theme of "blond"—dusts the small of his little back. Excepting microscopic bits and pieces the young woman's anatomy stands exposed to the four winds.

"They must be awfully successful at something," observes Laurel.

"Dope dealing? Rock and roll?"

"Not fashion modeling. . . . Why are you looking at them like that?"

"Trying to determine whether they're ex-students of mine."

The morning of our departure I palpate my lump and find its bulk to have receded more than a mite. Could it actually be that I do not have cancer? We strike out boldly toward the Midlands, our destination the village of Tyrrellspass, whence once upon a time Laurel's Norman ancestors the

Tyrrells—rogues, revolutionaries, bandits, scallywags, and scoundrels—cowed and scoured the surrounding countryside, which as we head further south has become increasingly beautiful, the fields more green, the landscape more gentle and appealing, the cloud-piled sky awash in inlets of periwinkle blue.

"Laurel, have we entered the Midlands?"

"An hour ago, at least. Why?"

"Because they're simply *gorgeous*! Do you think all that bad-mouthing's merely part of a conspiracy to keep us tourists from overrunning Ireland's most valuable national treasure? It's a dead ringer for Ohio on our best day of the year! But it's this way all the time! The Midlands are *Paradise*!"

"Ernest! Pull over!"

I swerve onto the berm, where a sign proclaims,

Baile Locha Riach
LOUGHREA

"'Lockridge,' do you think?" I ask.

"What else could it possibly be?"

"If the denizens of Loughrea all toe-out like a lockridge of ducks we'll know for certain."

I pose beside the sign. Laurel shoots my picture.

Like all the Irish villages we've driven through Loughrea resembles a ghost town. "Why aren't they all outside enjoying this beautiful day?"

"You know us Lockridges. In front of the TV like hermits."

"People are no different in Ohio," laments Laurel.

In Tyrrellspass we call at Tyrrell Castle, a Norman fortress resembling Thoor Ballylee though thicker at the base. An elderly gentleman in tweeds and bow tie swings inward the oaken slab of a door.

"Hello," says Laurel, extending her hand. "I'm Laurel Tyrrell." As the Tyrrell motto proclaims, Truth Is the Way of Life.

"Well, we mustn't deny a Tyrrell admission to her castle," says the gentleman, welcoming us. He's the owner, chief architect of the castle's restoration and now the sole resident of the castle. The restoration has preserved much of the original interior. A two-hole stone privy triangulates one corner of the master bedroom.

"This castle has grown a wee bit too large for its man." The gentleman hands us a colorful brochure. "I'm a widower now."

Tyrrell Castle is going on the auction block, bidding to start at US$350,000.

"Let's buy it!"

"With what?" Laurel asks.

"Those aren't pounds, Laurel, they're *dollars*! Why, houses in Worthington are selling for far more than that."

"You'd make a tip-top property agent, Mr. Tyrrell."

Laurel is silent.

"I'm in the market for a retirement home."

"This one is nothing but work, young man."

As we're returning to the Opel, Laurel places something at the foot of the wall, against which in 1650 Cromwell's soldiers executed the castle's occupants—all of whom had surrendered.

"What's that?"

"Lucky stone from Diamond Hill."

We're over the Atlantic. It's night. Behind us in Smoking someone is coughing out his lungs. We can't sleep. "Know what you're teaching in the fall?" Laurel asks.

"I don't want to think about it."

"Yeats?"

"Never again."

"*Ulysses*?"

"No I say no I won't No."

"It'd be like falling off a log. Why not?"

"Because I've come to believe D. H. Lawrence when he said the technique of *Ulysses* may be new but its values are a wasteland of old cigarette stubs, worn erasers, dust balls, rancid chestnuts."

"For example?"

"Intercourse without conception is obscene. Birth control's an evil, especially coitus interruptus, which women particularly loathe. Man's mission is to populate the globe. Intercourse during pregnancy results in deformity and death. Daughters are of no value to a father, who must sire sons to maintain his line, his reputation, and his self-respect. A woman requires a manly man who takes charge and smells of cigars. Women are earth-mothers, whores, and nitwits. Homosexuality? Forget it. James Joyce is one of the all-time champions of 'family values.'"

"Isn't it fortunate for his reputation that he made himself nearly impossible to read?"

"It gets worse."

"How is that possible?"

"Though Joyce wasn't an anti-Semite, you have to give him that at least," I ruminate, chewing the cud of thought. "Unlike Pound, Eliot, Lawrence himself. . . ."

"You said it got worse, Ernest."

"Huh? Oh . . . I mean where I'm concerned."

"Oh?"

"Laurel, I've arrived at the grand conclusion that Literature is a false god and I stand among its legions of false priests."

"That sounds serious."

"Which is one of the reasons why I don't want to think about what I'm teaching in the fall."

The muffled roaring of the Aer Lingus 747 cradles us. After awhile Laurel asks, "Anything you do want to think about?"

"That I should've held onto that Cistercian's massive skull cap. Fashioned it into a goblet. Defiled it with sacrilegious doggerel."

"God provided you with a pint glass in its place."

"Hell, that Cistercian's capable of holding an entire quart!"

"Better a pint in the carry-on, Ernest, than a quart in the heather."

"Well. . . . Might just as well get on with what I really have to say."

"Okay."

"I'm thinking of a tower."

"Too many towers to keep them straight. Narcissistic male writers and their towers—"

"Our tower in Ohio, Laurel. I'm leaving it?"

"Our *marriage*? You're *leaving* me?"

"No, no, of course not! I'm sorry. I mean the Ivory Tower of Academe. The University. Teaching. I'm bailing out of the Ivory Tower."

"Oh."

"Bidding farewell to the academic life. And not a fond farewell."

"For a moment—"

"I'm going to retire from teaching. That's what I'm trying to say."

"When?"

"Soon as I can manage it."

"How?"

"Rob a bank, work at Wendy's, learn golf and win big-money championships, open a B&B, blow the blues on street corners with the sax case open at my feet. Whatever it takes. Pity my poor students."

"I've been hearing rumors of an upcoming early retirement program with generous buyouts for faculty who take it."

"Me too."

"Ernest, you've seemed distracted almost since we set down in Ireland. I'm happy you've finally told me why."

"Yeah? I mean, yes."

"And I understand."

"You do?"

"You want to get out of teaching before you've reached the point of no return and it's too late."

"Yes, I do. Yes."

Conversation: Ireland

March 17, 2003

Ernest: Right off the bat let me alert the reader to the fact that I did not have cancer, though the fear of it got me thinking seriously about how I might and might not want to spend the remainder of my life. That lump concentrated my attention wonderfully, though it turned out to be a benign "subcutaneous cyst."

Laurel: But the scare propelled you toward getting retired.

Ernest: And I did retire. Within four years of our trip to Ireland.

Laurel: At the ripe old age of fifty-two!

Ernest: Shakespeare's age when he died. The Buyout came to pass, whereupon I seized it with greedy claws. And, bless her soul, my Great Aunt Marie left me a small inheritance that was enough, however—

Laurel: To buy the extra years—

Ernest: Five years out of the eight I taught at Yale. Those five, plus the five the Buyout gave me, plus the twenty years I taught at Ohio State all added up to a grand total of thirty years' worth of "contributions" into the State Teacher's Retirement System. And now a monthly stipend that's almost enough to live on. The mug shot on my Emeritus ID shows some old guy grinning like he's just robbed Fort Knox and gotten away clean.

Laurel: The trip had major consequences for both of our academic lives. It pushed you into wanting to retire, whereas the International Feminist Conference experience—particularly my appalling arrogance and ethnocentrism—pushed me into postmodern and poststructural theory. You were getting ready to retire, apparently, and I was getting ready for a radical intellectual shift. So, although I write about the Dublin conference in rather negative terms, the conference had very positive consequences for my subsequent intellectual growth.

Ernest: We'd played out our current hands and were ready to move on to something else. It's interesting to me that my "something elses" didn't include fiction writing—for dollars, anyway.

Laurel: Mmm. . . .

Ernest: Bitter experience as a novelist had taught me I couldn't count on it. I'd had one major financial windfall—

Laurel: From writing novels—

Ernest: But for the rest, small advances and a trickle of royalties. I didn't want retirement and old age to be an impoverished stroll down the yellow brick road of illusions. And I'd grown weary of fiction. And of Literature as some Grand Ideal. And I'd come down with a tough case of futility, the Vanity of Human Wishes, vanity of vanities and all that. Literature in its various forms and avatars seemed to have played itself out. Reading, teaching, writing—that wasn't where the remainder of my life wanted to go. It's difficult to talk about this, even after so many years.

Laurel: I'm moved hearing about this.

Ernest: Thanks.

Laurel: I was moved by the emotions in your piece, too. In it I sensed two seemingly contradictory emotional strands. You are both totally immersed in the works of famous writers—Joyce and Yeats—and screaming to leave the English professoriate.

Ernest: I know it.

Laurel: You do a lot of teaching of the literature in your Ireland piece, too. Teaching of Yeats and Joyce. Given that the audience are not English professors—

Ernest: Back in 1987 I was still a professor, so writing about Ireland now meant pulling my dusty old teaching hat out of cold storage. When I took it off in 1991 I swore I'd never teach another class.

Laurel: Never teach another anything, you crowed.

Ernest: Well, yes. Though now when I find myself in discussion groups I can't seem to keep the—

Laurel: Lid on? Hat off? Lips closed?

Ernest: The superglue binding my lips together seems to melt and the words start pouring out, the outrageous opinions—increasingly outrageous the longer I live. If I'd written my Ireland narrative for an audience of English professors I might've softened some of my more outrageous judgments, but what the heck, here I go again. . . . Much as I love Joyce, I never want to reread *Ulysses*. I see problems with it that go beyond even the ones I've already mentioned, in spite of its powerful reputation— which in and of itself may be a root cause of some problems I have with contemporary fiction. Large portions of Joyce are by any reasonable standard virtually unreadable. But unreadability *per se* is no great virtue in writing, even fiction [*laughter*]—no automatic indicator that the writing is great, or even any good. Look at the growing chasm between some of the truly unreadable "literary" fiction, and the glut of "trash" that's rushed into the void because people can wallow through it without falling asleep or pitching the book across the room. *The Bridges of Madison County*, say, versus Thomas Pynchon's *Gravity's Rainbow*. Which is a hoax, you know, a practical joke—

Laurel: I haven't read it.

Ernest: Well, it's a long-winded prank to trap the Literary Establishment into making a monumental ass of itself by heaping laurels—

Laurel: So to speak.

Ernest: Onto a mop-bucket of tomfoolery. Nonsense. Seven hundred and sixty pages of woolgathering and cerebral nosepicking.

Laurel: Why?

Ernest: Pynchon holds the Literary Establishment in profound contempt . . . I suppose because they're always rewarding his work. Anyway, he hired this oddball comedian who called himself "Professor Corey"—

Laurel: Professor *Irwin* Corey?

Ernest: Right. The Maestro of Doublespeak. Pynchon hired Corey to impersonate him at the 1974 National Book Award ceremonies where Pynchon was scheduled to receive the prize for *Gravity's Rainbow*.

Laurel: I gather the prank succeeded.

Ernest: Oh boy, and how!

Laurel: But how could Corey pass in public for Pynchon?

Ernest: Pynchon's a recluse. No one knew what he looked like, not even his editor. So, Corey-impersonating-Pynchon got up and delivered an "acceptance speech" composed of pure gibberish. Sort of like the prize-winning novel—which literary critics still refer to as The Great American Novel. Oh Literature! Oh Fame!

Laurel: Father knew Irwin Corey.

Ernest: Father knew Lloyd George.

Laurel: No, seriously. They were friends in Chicago. With my fake I.D. in hand I saw the professor perform in a Chicago nightclub, where that same night I was also hypnotized.

Ernest: Step right up folks and be hypnotized by a fake!

Laurel: It was someone else who did the hypnotizing.

Ernest: You're sure of that?

Laurel: How many have actually gotten Pynchon's joke?

Ernest: One—that I know of. You make two.

Laurel: Speaking of "outrageous"?

Ernest: I guess. Plus a certain willingness to make a monumental ass of oneself.

Laurel: Some pundits think the popularity of the memoir is thereby explained as well.

Readers wanting to read readable stories.

Ernest: That's been my own experience

Laurel: If I knew the Tyrrell family motto when we went to Ireland—"truth is the way of life"—I had repressed it.

Ernest: Hmm.

Laurel: So maybe it's not strange that I have devoted much of my academic career to epistemological questions. How does one know what's true? Where does your authority come from? On what grounds can anyone claim to know anything? Epistemological questions have been of interest to me since childhood—probably because I was a bright child who felt defensive when some grown-up know-it-all challenged me with that impudent question, "How do you know that?"

Ernest: Your grandson, Akiva, is like you.

Laurel: Yes. When he's asked "how do you know that," he gets riled-up, too. "I just know things," is what he says. And he does.

Ernest: And you think he would make an excellent lawyer.

Laurel: Yes, he would. Like my father.

Ernest: And you thought you would have made an excellent lawyer.

Laurel: Yes, I would have.

Ernest: But your father discouraged you because you wouldn't have been able to enter the smoke-filled men's clubs where the deals were made.

Laurel: And no jury would take a woman lawyer seriously. So, "truth as a way of life" as the Tyrrell family motto is one that I did not enact in a court of law. Instead, I have been busy deconstructing it! What constitutes truth? Whose truth? Under what conditions? And, I find myself, of course, still searching in that field. Reason is no longer the ground of truth, for me. Nor logic. They're false gods; they will not lead you to Truth.

Ernest: With a capital "T."

Laurel: Yes. I've dismantled the binary in my own soul between "reason" and "feeling." They're interconnected. One is pretty useless without the other. So, Truth is a way of life for me, but it's not what the Tyrrells had in mind. It's a postmodern sense of truth with a lowercase "t."

Ernest: You know how music's been a big part of my life since I retired, and the truth of music transcends both reason and feeling. I recall getting into an argument, way back when, with someone who said music was more beautiful, profound, and universal than literature, and, further, that the universal language of music brings us closer to the Truth. . . . whatever it is. I wouldn't even join the argument now. And so . . . to bring all this down to earth—what's the "truth" we're trying to embody in this joint project of ours? What do we think of when we think of "truth"?

Laurel: All right. Let me think about this. At one level it's straightforward. When I describe our book to people, I'll say it's "he sees, she sees—he writes, she writes " and how our differences in gender, discipline, religion, ethnicity, birth order—

Ernest: Sociological categories—

Laurel: Yes—those differences and other ones affect what we see and what we write. While abstaining from "Capital T Truth claims," we create a different kind of truth—modeling the possibility of "both . . . and"—both your vision and representation, and my vision and representation. These don't collide or collude, but create a complex vision that invites other people in, invites them to enter our worlds through their own imagery. So, our book is an example of crystallizing. And, because of the book's structure, we are creating a new truth between us.

Ernest: Hmm.

Laurel: But, at another level, what we are doing is not straightforward. Two weeks ago, when Rabbi Gary Huber began the Sabbath sermon by saying, "We all die," I was taken up short. Of course, he is right. The truth of life is that we all die. In some ways I think this whole project is about that truth. We know we will die. But how do we want to be remembered? I think we've talked about this before.

Ernest: Yes.

Laurel: In this piece, I acknowledge my father's death, and write about him, as I want him to be remembered. He'd been a minor character in other pieces I've written—sometimes my hero, sometimes my nemesis—but I'd never honored his background, his family, his history as *my* background, family, history. Consequently, I have never fully honored a simple truth about my own life: I did indeed grow up in two cultures. My struggle was and still is how to be "both . . . and"—how to integrate the two cultures into my Self. I'd love to feel myself as unified, although I doubt that is possible, just like I doubt you and I can write one unified text in a single voice. So, in some ways writing this book with you in this form is replicating what goes on in my head all the time—there's this about me and that about me and Hello! What is coming into the forefront now?

Ernest: Go on.

Laurel: When I wrote about my dad singing lullabies to me, I was a child again. I could see my room, my storybook dolls, my bed. I felt cherished. I've always credited my dad with stimulating my intellectual interests. Of course, him claiming to be a Druid—well there it all is—memorization, learning, teaching. But until I wrote this piece, I didn't credit him as my spiritual teacher. My mother was Jewish, but I didn't experience her as a spiritual person.

Ernest: And she didn't want you to be Jewish.

Laurel: Apart from even that, she wasn't spiritual in her approach to life. She was practical. Probably depressed a lot. My dad's happy-go-luckiness and his attitude toward life—joyfulness, learning, kindness to people, animals, and other living things—maps right onto Reform Judaism, my spiritual home now. It comforts and grounds me to discover that my father's spiritual teachings concerning everyday life are the ones I practice today.

Ernest: That's a lot to respond to. [*Long pause.*]

Laurel: Start anywhere.

Ernest: Well . . . three things come to mind. First, I noticed small differences in the way you and I recall and write about some of the concrete details of our experience. The reader will notice them or not—no need to be specific here. But neither of us feels a need, now, to "get our stories straight." I think it's really something that sixteen years after going to Ireland we recall things so similarly, give them similar weight, select similar events to write about. Okay . . . second, we're not Thesis-Antithesis mongers—"his account," "her account," plus a dialogue posing as "synthesis." Our approach is open, fluid. And, third . . . following your lead, perhaps, I'm putting more and more of my history and feelings into what I write.

Laurel: You said to me that you like writing creative nonfiction—or what some call literary nonfiction, a name I rather like. We've both moved away from our earlier genres toward this genre. You seem to really like it. I like it. I love it.

Ernest: Deep down it's not all that different from writing fiction for me. Both draw on a vivid concrete memory, for instance, though in fiction I'd alter that memory, create a vivid, detailed "memory" of something that didn't exactly happen—though God knows we all do this sort of thing constantly when we're supposedly "telling the truth." [*Laughter.*] Or, more superficially, I'd alter details so as not to . . . get myself sued! But the essential process of imaging and looking behind the image, trying to figure out what things mean, how they hang together, how they connect, where they're heading, what the true consequences are—those remain the same, whether in fiction or "creative nonfiction." In fact it's what defines the "creative" part—not description, dialogue, so-called "fictional techniques," so much as discovering, *imagining* the underlying pattern, what Henry James calls "the figure in the carpet." The imagination roots out the underlying connections, the pattern—what we don't know about what we know—and embodies this knowledge throughout the writing.

Laurel: That's really nice, Ernest. I think there were two underlying patterns in my narrative, juxtaposed but not really integrated. One is "academics"—and the need to move on in my theorizing; and the other, which became the title of the paper, is "all in the family." The narrative begins with me trying to integrate the two by looking for "family" in the international feminist movement—to no avail. Through the narrative my father and his family's history appear. The narrative ends with the appearance of my oldest son Ben, who was the last member of our family to see my father alive. Through the writing I claim my spiritual, intellectual, and biological relationship to my father—and my son's relationship to my father. We're Vikings!

Ernest: Skoal!

Laurel: And Begorra! Today is St. Patrick's Day. My brother Barrie phoned this morning to thank me for the St. Pat's Day card. The card, he said, had brought back his feelings about our father.

Ernest: Oh?

Laurel: Yes, Barrie said he was feeling guilty. When father tried to talk to him, Barrie shut him out. I've been ruminating on that phone conversation, and wondering if one of the reasons my dad nurtured me was because I would interact, argue, engage him. To what extent did Barrie's unwillingness to be the son my father wanted clear the field for me? The youngest. A girl. Could I be heir to the intellectual world my father revered? So, everything really is "all in the family," no?

Ernest: You're still struggling, trying to figure out what these basic dynamics are and how they've shaped you. And we'll never come to the final truth regarding ourselves, let alone God and the Universe. But that's—I think these pieces of ours and these conversations are efforts to grapple with what's really going on back then, and now—

Laurel: Right now—

Ernest: With us. And how "back then" is "right now." Once I started writing about Ireland, sixteen years ago became one with the present.

Laurel: And I wrote from photos, which I had never done before—except in poetry—and it was fun. It was a different experience, creating different writing problems around tense and so on. What is past is not past.

Ernest: Yes.

Laurel: And, of course, we're struggling with all of our family right now. Our family is entirely too complex—five children between us, each with a mate, eight grandchildren, siblings. . . .

Ernest: Unresolved problems with siblings.

Laurel: With yours. Thankfully, my sister and brother and sister-in-law and brother-in-law and you and I are good friends.

Ernest: Complex, indeed. I'd say that in some ways writing these accounts has been a process of reconciliation as well as comprehension.

Laurel: I like that—reconciliation and comprehension.

Ernest: So when I have one of my narratives in a more or less completed state it's like existing in a place where things feel peaceful and whole and harmonious.

Laurel: Yes.

Ernest: The personal seems to be the deepest driving force for my writing.

Laurel: Reconciliation and comprehension. Those are beautiful words. I like them.

Ernest: Achieving of some kind of harmony and peace. That's what Yeats is writing about in the "Lake Isle" and what I am trying to grant myself now when I write. Peace.

Laurel: We can drink to that in our Irish pint, snuggled in our carry-on and not chipped to this day. Speaking of which, I looked up My Castle in Tyrrellspass on the Internet. And guess what?

Ernest: What?

Laurel: My Castle is now the "Adlib Restaurant."

Ernest: What do you make of that?

Laurel: [*Hearty laughter.*] It is soooo literary. And if we—

Ernest: That's what you were doing when you walked up to the castle and introduced yourself as "Laurel Tyrrell"—ad-libbing.

Laurel: And that's what Mary Daly was doing for her keynote at the feminist conference in Dublin.

Ernest: Well, yes. . . .

Laurel: And, that's how I teach. I ad-lib.

Ernest: Well, so did I.

Laurel: I like ad-libbing. It gives one hope.

Ernest: Life is an improvisation.

Laurel: Yes.

Ernest: Though shouldn't there be an underlying melody?

Laurel: You do jazz—but I think of improv in theater.

Ernest: Let's see, I was Stanley Grapplenewsky in my Bloomington High School Junior Class Drama—a stereotypically idiotic football player—and I didn't ad-lib a single syllable.

Laurel: I sure have.

Ernest: Doesn't there need to be some sort of basic notion—?

Laurel: Yes, a basic theme—a conflict that needs resolution. The players know the conflict and they know something about who they are in the conflict.

Ernest: Elaine May/Mike Nichols—with whom you were trained—practiced a humor of allusion that depends on the audience's sharing a common culture with the performers that they can refer to in a kind of shorthand.

Laurel: The Jewish mother—

Ernest: Yes.

Laurel: The therapist, the telephone operator.

Ernest: That's it. And at the University of Chicago you could talk about the telephone operator and Camus in the same breath.

Laurel: And Aristotle—and Thucydides, Thermopylae, Peloponnesian War, x-squared, y-squared, H^2SO^4. . . .

Ernest: Are we doing something like that? What you and I have is a shared past we're writing about—

Laurel: And we're doing a little improv number right here.

Ernest: Any conflicts needing resolution?

Laurel: Well, I do have a little question. You know Bloom—

Ernest: Harold Bloom?

Laurel: No, Leopold Bloom.

Ernest: *Leopold*! God! Somehow my mind's gotten sidetracked from the greatest character in modern fiction to the greatest living literary critic. A guilty subconscious reaction to what would surely be Harold Bloom's disdain for all the arrogant literary judgments I've been so glibly spewing out. I guess he's firmly ensconced now as my lit-crit Superego.

Laurel: [*Hearty laughter.*] Leopold Bloom is Jewish. So, why does a Gentile like Joyce create a Jewish main character living in Ireland?

Ernest: Let me answer in a roundabout way. There are two different strands in *Ulysses*. There's the autobiographical strand carried by Stephen

Dedalus. Really the first three chapters of *Ulysses* are what we'd now call creative or literary nonfiction.

Laurel: Which makes it very appropriate for Stephen to be in Our Book.

Ernest: Yes. But in chapter 4, Joyce brings to life someone who never existed so far as anyone knows. Joyce creates an Irish Jew named Leopold Bloom, who carries the novel's other, *fictional* strand.

Laurel: Is Leopold Bloom an alter ego? The exotic Other?

Ernest: Even though he's living in his own country, Ireland, Bloom's an exile there, thrashing about in a sea of anti-Semitism. He's barely tolerated—the ultimate outsider. For all his flaws he's basically the nicest person in the world and he's treated most shabbily.

Laurel: The way Stephen feels about himself.

Ernest: And the way Joyce felt about *himself*.

Laurel: And, in some ways that's how I feel about myself. That's the way I often felt about myself in academia. That I am an exile. I could be the nicest person in the world but I am in a sea of "anti's"—anti-everything I value in and about academic life.

Ernest: Yes.

Laurel: And to be a Jew is to live in exile.

Ernest: Yes.

Laurel: You never have a home.

Ernest: No.

Laurel: So Molly and Leopold Bloom become personally interesting to me as I try to be an Irish Jew. That's exactly right. I'm trying to be an Irish Jew.

Ernest: Good place to end this, Laurel.

CHAPTER 3
BEIRUT, LEBANON
August 18–22, 1999

Your hope chest will be filled by evening.
The noblest Phoenicians, the highest born,
Have courted you.

—Homer

City by the Sea

Ernest Lockridge

September 15, 1999
Dear Sister and Brethren,
　　Returned a few weeks back from the sun-drenched oven of Beirut. I'd've written sooner, but promptly got a respiratory infection which by all odds should have been some exotic Med-bred bug, but more likely derived from the steam room of my local health club where I deposited my carcass the day after arriving home to bake out the humors of foreign travel.
　　Our beautiful Helen is now married to that handsome and capable Phoenician, Jean-Paul, whom she met in Mali, West Africa, whilst she was in the Peace Corps and Jean-Paul was operating the West African wing of the family business. Jean-Paul's family, the Fayeds, and their circle of Lebanese Christians identify themselves (tongue-in-cheek, I think) as "Phoenicians" to further distinguish themselves from the bomb-happy Hezbollah and the Palestinians. My new in-laws are close friends of the family that once governed Lebanon, said friendship having, during Lebanon's civil war, drawn artillery fire down upon the Fayeds' reinforced

concrete villa and upon the Christian suburb north of Beirut where my youngest daughter's sumptuous wedding took place.

Following a cathedral ceremony hallowed by the participation of a full half-dozen Marianite priests we attend the lavish reception on the shores of the Mediterranean, vintage champagne effervescing in the hot twilight, banquet table groaning with earthly delights. Atop Grand Tetons of rice on three massive oval platters repose in crumbling languor a goat, a sheep, a shoat. We eat, we drink, we gyrate. Festivities wind down with the release of white doves and nonlethal fireworks whose reflections bedazzle even the wrinkled old face of the wine-dark sea.

In meager counterbalance to the generosity shown us in Beirut I did treat the bride and groom, my brand-new in-laws and family-members, the bride's sisters, my wife, and my ex-wife to a pretty fine lunch a couple of days later in the Druse-controlled mountains surrounding Beirut. In a castle. Or a palace. Whatever they call those elaborate Casbahs that once concealed the harem from the plebeian gaze, from desires more common to commoners than to Grand Emirs.

The Fayeds are immensely gracious and attractive, and as nice as anyone. Jean-Paul's father Pierre, a handsome fellow, radiates bonhomie and robust health, though due to countless bouts with sub-Saharan malaria his health is precarious. You'd never know it, however, from the way he acts. One of the most gracious people I've met. Jean-Paul's mother and sisters are beautiful. All the women of their acquaintance, in fact, seem beautiful, charming; the men handsome and sophisticated. The very air they breathe is redolent of dangers that we can scarcely imagine, yet they give off no sign of worry. Hemingway's famous "grace under pressure" describes them.

Beirut follows the shoreline like the endless scrolling of a Krazy Kat cartoon landscape. Reminders exist that this is a war zone—the bullet-pocked garden wall, the bomb-gutted apartment building, the disemboweled motion picture theater—but such touristic thrills are rare. Our drivers made no drive-by of the Beirut Power Plant, knocked out of commission by an Israeli airstrike a few days prior to our little visit.

Jean-Paul drives us on a freeway devoid of lane-markers amidst a pack of hyper-aggressive drivers violently jockeying bumper-to-bumper. Through this rampage Jean-Paul maneuvers his Mercedes calmly, effortlessly, perfectly attuned to the local rhythms. Men, women, and children rendered intrepid by poverty stand along this racecourse hawking the drooling carcasses—glisteningly denuded of their pelts—of goats, sheep, rabbits.

Exotic items are for sale off-road in a hubbub of squalid pleasure domes whose marquees tease the Middle-Eastern tourist in strange syllables, a foreign language redolent of the snake, the Infidel. "Dallas!" sings their Siren song. "Vegas!" "Santa Fe!" The Saudi pilgrim to Beirut parks his wives at the Beirut Hilton then hastens the few short kilometers to this Beirut Mecca and here savors the rarest and most-prized fruits of the Great Satan, forbidden the hometown boy back in good old Riyadh. Here at last his strenuous tongue is afforded unrestrained license to burst joy's grape against his palate fine. Booze! Hookers!

Our own little pilgrimage was perhaps no more "interesting" than it had to be. Even so, we are relieved to be back home in our own charming, prosperous and—as of this writing—unbombed suburb, Worthington, just north of Columbus, Ohio, where the Worthington police look out for our safety by routinely pulling over outsiders on suspicion of not being Worthington residents. In Lebanon, Syrian peacekeepers man the ubiquitous roadblocks, young men scanning Jean-Paul's Mercedes with their ruthless, watchful eyes and cradling battered AK-47s, arms and the men giving every appearance of having been thoroughly battle-tested—their presence no less reassuring, however, than our Columbus, Ohio police force, a rogue body that's been brutalizing, strip-searching, and shooting us with impunity, official misbehavior so barbaric that even the United States Department of Justice has at last been forced into taking notice.

All about Beirut loom billboards portraying old Dr. Assad, Lebanon's current peace-bringer, eyes shrouded in black sunglasses, and from the thin black line of his mouth extrudes a word-balloon explaining in Arabic that "it is not Syria's will but Allah's" that we are grinding your country beneath our boot heels.

The Syrian president appears ludicrously untutored in the debonair department, contrasting starkly with our own jolly madcap, Charming Billy, that irrepressible rake who oozes charm through every pore as he rains ordnance upon Afghans, Iraqis, Sudanese, and Serbs. Lebanese natives, Christian and Muslim, are not much given to criticizing their Syrian liberators, open mouths having dissolved in night and fog. Still, I consider my lovely daughter safer in Beirut than in, say, Washington, D.C., where she resided prior to her apotheosis.

The newlyweds will reside in Mali for six months out of each year. Like the Hutu butchers of Rwanda against whom the United Nations failed to intervene because the United States virulently opposed any such intervention, the Taureg insurgents of Mali are creatures of French foreign policy. Fortunately Jean-Paul is well armed, and the evening before we bid Beirut goodbye I issue a paternal directive. "Look, Helen, forget all the crap you may have heard regarding guns and just have Jean-Paul teach you how to shoot."

"Okay, Dad."

"Promise me!"

"I promise, Dad."

On the morning of our departure, Beirut International is so utterly clean, so given over to a Platonic Idea of Cleanliness that it is devoid of toilet paper. Here, too, are the young, hard-eyed Syrian soldiers, one cadre after another scouring our passports to shake loose the flimsiest ink-fleck of evidence that we have even once in our lives visited "that Zionist state in occupied Palestine," whereupon they'd arrest us on the spot.

The sole drama of this sort occurs on the second leg of our return from the Middle East, at London-Heathrow, where Western authorities search our luggage with a thoroughness I had hoped impossible, prying into all containers, twisting our prescriptions' adult-proof caps, unscrewing and squeezing our ointments, burrowing into zipper compartments, x-raying our bags when full and when depleted, a process so precise in its filtering and refiltering of our little cache of personal belongings that an earring from Laurel's favorite pair magically vanishes into thin air!

We are not x-rayed, nor are we probed in our persons, merely "patted down," although said "patting down" does occur twice—(1) whilst the polite and pleasant young English fellow, Colin by name, is ransacking all of our luggage, and (2) at the departure gate as a humorless brace of Continental airline thugs, Americans, further savage our meager carry-ons. So beaten down are we, however, so powerfully conditioned by decades of living beneath the iron claw of our own beloved government here in the West, that Laurel and I, docile fellow travelers, maintain a steady, purring drone of tameness for our would-be captors. All during their pillaging and pawing, we keep insisting aloud to our assailants and one another that, actually, we feel no outrage, no! we feel, well, *reassured* by these Byzantine precautions. And I must admit that our subsequent flight westward over the Atlantic does *not* explode—à la, say, TWA 800. Has the United States Navy taken the day off?

Airborne, I speculate aloud that the authorities mounted all this entertainment because my exotic, surly demeanor, plus the black scorpion tattoo upon my forehead, had succeeded in arousing their darkest suspicions. Laurel demurs, "It's that Beirut stamp in our passports, Ernest."

We agree, however, upon the wisdom of postponing those side trips to Baghdad, Belfast, and Belgrade.

Thine,

Brother Ernest

Laurel in Arabia

Laurel Richardson

TO: BFK123@aol.com
FROM: Richardson.9@osu.edu
Subject: Home Again
Date: September 15, 1999

Betty, Dear Friend—I'm home. Safe, but not sound. Something's seriously wrong with my shoulder. I can't raise my arm above my waist without excruciating pain. I've been at risk physically, religiously, militarily. The risks overlap and merge. So happy, so happy to be back home.

My shoulders were up to my ears for weeks before we left. The massage therapist worked on my neck, but without much relief. The United States prohibits direct flights to Lebanon so we had to change airlines—airports, too—in London.

I don't like flying, and there was so much of it; I get so tired, my body exhausted by time-zone changes—eight of them, each way—foreign waters, foreign foods. And the possibility of war, of course. That, too. The State Department had raised the travel-advisory level: "Don't go. The U.S. Embassy cannot protect you."

Most stressful though was knowing I would be immediately arrested in Beirut should the authorities discover I had been to Israel. I have a new passport, of course, without the Israeli stamp, but for all I know the

Lebanese government keeps computer records of tourists to Israel. Maybe their computer knows I am a Jew; a Jewish child who had trees planted in Israel in her name; a Jewish adult whose support of Israeli independence is recorded in Tel Aviv.

My mind settles on Jewish friends who live daily with feelings of vulnerability. I remind myself that my name is "Richardson" and that I look like my gentile father. If the Lebanese authorities ask me, I'll have to deny my Jewish heritage. I'll have to lie. I shudder thinking about it, preparing for denial and deceit.

No one who isn't Jewish seems to understand what I am talking about, how unsettling this is for me. It is as if I am no longer "half-Jewish," a safe category, but now "entirely Jewish," enduring the defining "Jewish experience": being at risk because one is not a Gentile. I think of my Jewish mother, whose witnessing of the pogroms led her to marry a Gentile so that her children would never have to face *the* Jewish Experience.

So why *did* I go to Beirut? You know why. I assessed Ernest's needs as greater than my fears, and I love him. Before we left I was telling everyone that Ernest's daughter, Helen, was getting married in Beirut. I liked how exotic it sounded, and how rehearsing nonchalance lulled my fears.

Jean-Paul and Helen picked us up at the Beirut airport in a Mercedes 500 SEL. I think there was about a six-mile "safe-zone"—no buildings, no trees, just the road—around the airport. Two hours after arrival—and after having our passports checked and rechecked by seven or eight guards, Lebanese and Syrian rifling through the pages, turning them on edge, looking for watermarks, erasures, anything out of the ordinary, I suppose, and me feeling more and more paranoid with each rifling—here we were in an Arabic-speaking hotel on the Mediterranean in the Christian sector of north Beirut.

Jean-Paul's parents, Marianite-Catholics, live outside Beirut in a stone fortress enfolding four sumptuous living rooms, five baths, a look-out tower, and a private well and generator, which they were using because the power had not yet been restored from the last Israeli bombing. Surrounding the house are acres of innocent-looking flowerbeds; beyond them an electrified fence. Under the full width and breadth of the house is another house, their bomb-shelter, intended to protect them from Israelis, Syrians, and Moslem Lebanese. The people who were to be my protectors were themselves at risk.

Speaking French, Jean-Paul's father explained the Lebanese wedding customs to Ernest: the bride rides to the church with her father only; he gives her to the groom at the door of the church; the wedding couple walks down the aisle together. Would that be all right with Ernest? Of course, it was.

Villagers lined the streets to see the bridal car, completely covered with flowers, and to get a glimpse of the bride, as if she were a Royal. Helen was beautiful, Jean-Paul handsome, and the cathedral wedding mass lovely and long. Six priests, three languages, flowers everywhere. The oldest priest told Jean-Paul to remain faithful to his wife and told Helen she could not get divorced. At the reception—Perrier water flowing like wine, food for the multitudes—a whole lamb, pig, goat, salmon, unnamed fish, a three foot sword brandished by Jean-Paul to cut the ten-layer wedding cake, a pair of doves set free, and fifteen minutes of fireworks over the Mediterranean. After dancing with Helen, Jean-Paul's father asked me to dance and the band to play jazz in Ernest's honor.

We all went sightseeing the next day. The temperature was over 100, the humidity close to 100 percent. Our camera records the soppy air. In four air-conditioned Mercedes, the families drove north through Lebanon's porno district, where Saudi men frequent clubs with American names and symbols—Black Paradise, Las Vegas Babes, Girls-a-Go-Go, Dallas. Here they find proof that the American way is the way of the devil. Some of the men have brought their wives. They are sitting on hotel steps in purdah, bodies and heads covered in heavy black wool garments. I catch one woman's eyes. I see pain. I no longer think the dress is simply custom; I feel its misogynist origins; its practice as abusive.

We stop at Biblos, the palimpsests of Phoenician, Roman, and crusader civilizations visible beneath the contemporary Lebanese culture. I remember my fourth grade report on the library at Biblos, and the purple dyes and sailing ships of the Phoenicians, the ancestors of the Lebanese, and feel centered through this remembrance. I loved fourth grade and I loved purple cloth.

But Syrian guards, young men with assault rifles, flanked by Russian tanks, stop us. Check us. What must it be like for Jean-Paul, a descendant of the powerful Phoenicians, to placate a Syrian soldier? Up into the mountains we go, up and up. The houses grow more grand. Syrian politicos have taken these houses as their own. More Syrian soldiers. More checking. I imagine how it would feel to be stopped by foreign soldiers in my own country; how worried I would be about my sons. Through Druse territory, past the Cedars of Lebanon, and finally to Mir Amine, once a sheik son's palace in Beit Edine and now a resort. Jean-Paul's parents seat us facing the best view of the mountains; they sit across from us. Ernest gladly picks up the bill. We learn later that it is the custom for the bride's father to treat the groom's family on the day after the wedding.

We stop at the Emir's palace to view the royal baths, swords, and footstools, and down we go southward following a back road. A Lebanese soldier carrying an American rifle sitting on an American tank recognizes Jean-Paul and waves us on. We reach beyond the southern boundary of Beirut. More Syrian guards. My tension rises. We are in Hezbollah territory. We drive through Palestinian refugee encampments. The road is narrow and rough. People are driving too fast. Men try to sell us live chickens and live rabbits, and dead foxes and dead rabbits; gaunt children watch us pass by, uninterested. I see the awful displacement of the Palestinians—how they are not wanted by the Lebanese, Christian, or Moslem, how they are pawns in others' political games. I feel Israel's complicity.

We drive into downtown Beirut, past bombed-out buildings, walls still studded with mortar shots and into the glare of Max and Erma's, McDonald's, T.G.I.F, Baskin/Robbins, Hard Rock Cafe. We could be anywhere. It was night. We were in Beirut.

I'm having nightmares, too. In them, I'm a passenger in a truck, rented car, or taxi. The vehicle breaks down in an uninhabited spot of land or, sometimes, on a highly congested road. I can't speak the language, I am in physical danger, and I can't decide whether to continue to my destination or turn around and head back. It is scary, this dream-text.

I am exhausted thinking about the contrasts—sea and mountains, rich and poor, Jewish and Gentile, Christian and Moslem, lies and truths, American guns and Russian guns, now and then.

All of my academic theorizing about breaking down oppositions, deconstructing binaries doesn't help me, now, in any practical sense. Or has it? Has it already? Do I glimpse that the oppositional pairs upon which my language/my Self is built requires seeing differences within a vision of nondifference?

You can tell I'm home again—at home, again—using my life as entry to the realm of the untheorized.

Meanwhile, Helen will make her life in Lebanon, while I am only comfortable in the Lebanon of my past—my fourth grade studies of Phoenicia.

My shoulder hurts. I can't type anymore.

Thanks for listening.

Love,

Laurel

Conversation: Beirut

September 30, 1999

Laurel: When I read your letter to your brothers and sister, I was struck by how different it was from my letter about the Beirut experience. I thought that the two letters offered a good example of how the ostensibly same experience is reconstructed differently through the process of writing.

Ernest: My letter's a bit like whistling in the dark. I'm uneasy about my daughter's new place of residence, so I'm trying to "beat the blues" by positing the notion that, hey, Beirut's really no more dangerous than America. Whether or not I believe it's true. . . .

Laurel: Your fear regarding your daughter and your daughter's life maps onto my mother's fear for my life as a Jewish child, and my desire to avoid that which might endanger me. I've come to a deepened understanding of it because I put myself at risk.

So as different as our texts are in terms of writing style, apparent language choices, cadences and so on, what's driving both of them is the same emotional issue—the safety of daughters.

Ernest: That's true. If Helen were Jewish, it would be really impossible for me to imagine that she could live either in Beirut or in Mali. Mali, of course, is a Moslem country, and I think I'd just be in constant terror for her safety, that she'd be found out, that something terrible would happen to her. It's sort of possible to think about her living there, in large part, casting it in your terms, I suppose because she is not Jewish.

Laurel: Another parallel in the letters is that each of us begins with our bodies—with the discomforts in our bodies. Being back home is being

83

back home in our bodies. Relocating ourselves in our bodies. Of course my shoulder has not stopped hurting, and you've been off and on ill with respiratory infections since returning, so in some ways we're not yet "at home."

Ernest: I think that partly what we are doing here, both of us, is trying to write ourselves into mental and physical health. Writing this, I put myself figuratively speaking on the couch and tried to think about, analyze, even just purge some of the things that are still bothering me. There are lots of very difficult emotions that went into the writing of both of these letters.

Laurel: I wrote to enlist the healing power of writing.

Ernest: And it helped.

Laurel: I've always liked the epistolary form, but as we continue our conversation, I find myself entranced with its power for poststructuralist theorizing. In a letter, you get the sense of a particular person writing to particular people; there is claim to authorship and authority—not about the "facts" but about the emotional state of the writer. Because of the letter's conventions, the reader/listener knows that you are not trying to reconstruct a travelogue or write a ethnographic report. If you're a little exaggerated, so what. You're trying to convey to specific people the emotional experience, and the epistle permits that.

Ernest: I agree.

Laurel: I truly believe that writing can be a method of discovery. I have a hard time nowadays writing about that which I already "know." I want writing to teach me something new about myself and the world. To sit at a desk and be engaged in the process requires that I not know where the writing is taking me. And I think you have the same sense.

Ernest: I had little clarity regarding Beirut 'till I wrote about it.

Laurel: I suppose it's this American individualism, or something, but I like saying I did this myself. My "truth" was not constructed through my conversation with someone else—a therapist, say—but rather through my conversation with my multiple selves, my history and so on. It's a very different sense of owning what I claim to feel and know.

Yet, it is clear that you and I have been to Beirut, together. We went to the same places and saw the same things. We agree on the contours and general facts, as we always have throughout our marriage even though you are a novelist and I'm a sociologist. We rarely disagree but our perspectives differ; we have different takes, different ways of claiming knowledge—

Ernest: Or what is important to us at a particular time, because it would never even occur to me to disagree with your feelings of vulnerability as you state them. In my letter I employ hyperbole—a mode I often employ with family and friends. In your letter, the only example of hyperbole would be when you say that "no one understands" and what I think you mean is "I feel this very strongly." Of course I was aware of your sense of peril.

Laurel: We've shared our letters back and forth, and each of us has done some rewriting. The letters were enriched, not substantially changed in terms of style, form, or sense of audience, but in the concrete details. The process was very similar to the way focus groups work, and the way Carolyn Ellis and Art Bochner co-construct narratives.

Ernest: After reading your letter I intensified the contrast between our respective "takes" and intensified, in mine, certain parallels regarding the United States and Lebanon. Paradoxically, it may even be *safer* for us in Beirut where our passports invite special consideration by the authorities, who will perhaps think twice before hauling in American citizens, strip-searching us, shooting us.

Laurel: Just as you're seeing political similarities between Lebanon and the United States, I'm seeing the similarities in the emotional costs and emotional experiences of peoples such as the woman in purdah, the Palestinians, John-Paul, John-Paul's parents. Through linking of experiences, I recognize others as not "the other." It's no surprise, then, that I end my letter with a nod to poststructuralism—the "other" as "myself." A vision of nondifference.

I think our letters are complementary. Yet, they cannot be one paper. Which brings me back to a recurrent issue of mine: There is no way for us to write together.

Ernest: Yes, but we've done it and we're doing it now.

Laurel: Only as dialogue.

Ernest: "Only" as dialogue?

Laurel: As two separate voices. There's no way to create one text in which both our voices are merged.

Ernest: But isn't that what we've been doing all along—here and elsewhere? In dialogue?

Laurel: [*Long pause.*] Anything more *you* want to say?

Ernest: Yes, this. I certainly have a deep liking and respect for my son-in-law and his family, and deep sympathy for the situation they are in.

These people bring home to me how it must feel to live in an existential world close to the bone where one makes life and death decisions, but also where one is in a world where you have more choices regarding life and death. For example, if you're dying in need of a kidney transplant in the Middle East you can buy a poor man's kidney. Okay, what would you do? If I were in a situation where my choice was to let my child die, or purchase a kidney—a choice I don't have in this country—what do you think that *I'd* do? And I did tell my daughter to learn to shoot.

Meta-Conversation: Beirut

August 15, 2000

Laurel: Our editors Carolyn Ellis and Art Bochner have sent us a letter with some questions they'd like us to think about. Should we have a conversation about our conversation? A meta-conversation?

Ernest: Let's see, first they want to know whether our "conversation was helpful, illuminating, difficult, therapeutic, or what."

Laurel: That's easy. I found our conversation both illuminating and helpful because of the interplay between the personal and the political.

Ernest: I thought it was fun. And illuminating. For instance, I was aware of whistling in the dark, of a sort of manic defense regarding my daughter's safety, but I didn't get it fully under heel until our little conversation—which I wouldn't call therapeutic, alas, since it didn't cost 125 bucks an hour.

Laurel: [*Laugh.*] Here's another question. Carolyn and Art want to know about the conversation as a "meta-ethnographic and relational strategy." Great question! Definitely there are methodological parallels to ethnographic work. The Glaser and Strauss folks "memo" each other, and qualitative mentors read their students' field notes. And, definitely, the conversation strengthened our relationship. Experiencing, writing, conversing, rewriting, conversing, writing. Although we agree on what we see, we have a different edge, a different take on the experience. The differences within the similarity make us interesting to each other.

Ernest: Different—and complementary.

Laurel: Which leads to the next question: How have our "different emotional styles or forms of writing" helped us "cope with our emotionality?"

Ernest: I'd become thoroughly distressed by our own government's activities—the bombings, the cruise-missile strikes brought on by motives that look, at best, questionable. Whatever the late Dr. Assad's considerable flaws, folks around the world slept unconcerned that he'd murder them in their beds as a distraction from some homegrown scandal. More generally, though, I wanted to convey a sense of foreboding above and beyond the current situation—a general feeling of Power Run Amok as a continuing, unshakable, central part of the Human Condition. When Word War II came to an end, I was seven years old, so I've experienced the phenomenon throughout my entire life. Now, in my sixties, I've simply had it up to here. So it's an emotion that I've attempted to control by giving it voice.

Laurel: Then, there is this question about audience—one of my favorite issues. "What did we do to write for different audiences?" For the larger audience we've revised the letters, redacting some material and adding some. We've been more "artful" in crafting, too. Taking audiences into account actually simplifies the writing task. I ask myself, "What does this particular audience need to know? How can I best communicate it? It makes the writing, symbolically at least, interaction, and therefore fun for me.

Ernest: If we'd had this kind of conversation prior to our writing of the letters, it would have made writing them more difficult and the result would've been wooden.

Laurel: That's a good point, because we each used our letter as a way of coming to terms with the experience.

Ernest: We didn't write the letters in order to have a conversation. We wrote them to friends and family.

Laurel: But when I read them I thought that they, along with a conversation about them, would make a good presentation to my sociological convention—the Society for the Study of Symbolic Interaction.

Ernest: Originally we'd thought about going out and experiencing something for the express purpose of writing about it—presumably writing differently, you through the eyes of a "sociologist," and me through the eyes of the "novelist," and then analyzing the results to see how we did it differently. Then we realized that in fact we had already done the primary research. We'd already—if we were, say, geologists—collected the rock samples. So why not use *them*, and make the project smell less of the lamp?

Laurel: I think of what we're doing as "Natural Sociology"—a term my dissertation advisor, Edward Rose, coined in 1960. He'd be happy with this work of ours, and I like that here I am both experimenting and honoring my sociological roots. That the two are not antagonists.

Ernest: In the early sixties I was in graduate school at Yale, studying for my PhD in English, immersed in "New Criticism" but all the while chomping at the bit to begin a career—not as a professor or "new critic"— but as a novelist.

Laurel: Now I think we're getting to the unspoken conversation. I see it in Carolyn and Art's question as to whether this form of writing can achieve the goal of merging voices. Ernest, you said in our earlier conversation that that's what we have been doing. Although I didn't agree, I couldn't articulate why, and so I let it go, thinking we were at an impasse. But Hurrah! Now, I've had a revelation! If I were to adopt your point-of-view—that we are writing "together"—I would have to revise my deeply held and heretofore unconscious notion of what I think of as a text. You are accustomed to "writing-in-characters"—presenting characters and characters' points of view—and narrators, partial, omniscient, or unreliable, even. So, as a novelist—I'm speaking for you now—

Ernest: Be my guest.

Laurel: You're used to having multiple voices in a text, each having different points of view, different from the narrator and possibly from you, the author. Although there might be "characters" in my texts—people I've interviewed or observed, they're always *not me*—always, *not solely my constructions*. And I would never willfully be an "unreliable narrator."

Ernest: Of course.

Laurel: You and I have different ways of knowing and of expressing what we know, different core sensibilities, so that although we can create an aesthetic, intellectual packet, our voices must remain separate, distinct.

Ernest: I couldn't have said it better.

Laurel: [*Laughter.*] This is interesting.

Ernest: I don't think a single voice is necessary. I worry that you have some sort of romantic ideal.

Laurel: It may be some romantic ideal, but—get this!—it's a romantic idea about science and the single voice of science. I may be exploring here the deepest level of my resistance to my own new ways of writing. It's the idea that we can tell "a" truth together. So it is not a romantic vision about us that we can be one unified and homogenized voice, but my romanticization of the scientific way of knowing. Wow! That's a wonderful insight for me.

Ernest: And a relief to me.

Laurel: What, you don't want to be One?

Ernest: One of the things that attracts me to writing is the independence of it. It's a place . . . here is one place where, even given the, put it this way, the Iron Maiden of Language and Culture, one can experience at least the illusion of being independent and in control. It's tough to feel yourself under intimate pressure to relinquish that illusion.

Laurel: Whew! I think we're both feeling better about the co-writing because of this conversation. Unquestionably, Carolyn and Art's questions have brought us to a new understanding of our relationship to each other and to our work. I really like this. Thanks, Carolyn. Thanks Art.

Ernest: Yes, thanks.

CHAPTER 4
COPENHAGEN, DENMARK
April 8–16, 2000

The sleep of reason breeds monsters.

—Francisco José de Goya

You will hunt it on the map, and it won't be there.

—Ross Lockridge, Jr.

Lost in the Space

Laurel Richardson

I would not be writing this if it were not for the sushi dinner I shared with a visitor from Copenhagen, a sociologist who had come to The Ohio State University for postgraduate study.

"My treat," I said, being nudged by an as yet unsurfaced memory.

"So, how did you like Copenhagen? How did you like teaching at our premier university?" she asked.

Now, my mother always told me "If you don't have anything nice to say, don't say anything at all." But, I swallowed my etiquette lessons along with my tuna roll and began talking.

"You must write about it," the visitor insisted. "We in Copenhagen need to hear it. You'll be doing us a good turn."

Now, my father always told me, "There's enough misery in the world. Don't add to it. Relieve it by doing good turns."

To appease my mother's admonitions, I'll tread lightly. But Father and Visitor win.

Influences on one's writing, like on one's life, twist and turn in unpredictable ways. The deep and distant (parental shibboleths, for example) collide with the incidental and fleeting (sushi dinners). Awareness of these collisions compels me to think about my Copenhagen experiences through autobiographical refractions. Like everyone else I come to new settings with preexisting ideas and expectations that cloud the experience. Maybe that's what happened to me in Copenhagen. Maybe it has nothing to do with Copenhagen, and everything to do with me.

An earliest "literary" memory of mine is the Dane Hans Christian Andersen's story of the little match seller. I can still see the little book with its black etchings. As I remember it, the match girl is lost, out on a snowy cold night with neither gloves nor shoes. She has not sold a single match. She lights one to warm her hand, and in the light she sees a little girl warming herself by a stove fire; when the match goes out, the vision does, too. She lights another match and sees a table laden with food, which also vanishes when the light goes out. Lighting a third, she sees a Christmas tree and a shooting star. "Someone is dying," thinks the little girl. And it is so. That night she freezes to death.

I can still feel my horror and sorrow for the fate of the little match seller. I couldn't imagine anyone so poor and how something so small as selling a match might have saved her life.

When I read the story now, I realize I never "heard" its message. But perhaps, I did, and didn't know it. At the end of the story, the little girl lights a match, and bountiful food, stove fire, and her dead grandmother appear. "Take me with you," the match girl pleads. "I know you'll go away when the match burns out." So, her grandmother takes the little match girl in her arms and flies away above the earth, "where there was neither cold nor hunger nor pain." None of the townspeople who saw her corpse the next day "imagined what beautiful things she had seen . . . on New-year's day."

As an adult reader, I am seared by the child's death and outraged at a family and community that would let her freeze. I think of our homeless. But, I also hear in the story that the little match seller takes a hand in her own fate, has agency, transforming what could be intolerably agonizing moments into images of plenty and love. She sees and knows what the complacent, those not yet faced with death, cannot imagine. In the tale, we have neither a sentimental Disney ending—the girl is saved by Santa Claus and lives happily ever after with her newfound family—or the melancholy and despair that the actual unDisneyesque ending might conjure. Rather, Andersen leads me to focus on moral and sociological questions: Given a horrible event, how can it be transformed? What's fate? Personal action? Collective responsibility?

I wonder what it would be like to grow up with 150 years of Hans Christian Andersen stories shaping my country's psyche, shaping my culture, shaping me? To grow up in Copenhagen where the main tourist attraction and national symbol is—not the Statue of Liberty—but a little four-foot bronze sculpture of another Andersen fairytale character, the little mermaid? Bare breasted and fish tailed, looking lost, she sits on a rock at the sea's edge.

The Little Mermaid is a book I've only recently read, but I have inklings of a Disney version where most likely the mermaid and the little prince live happily ever after. There's probably a feminist version, too, where the prince becomes a merman and, like the male seahorse, takes care of the babies while mermama writes books.

In my mind, though, there is a version of the story that I have made up, an intermingling of my personal and cultural narratives. In my version, the little mermaid falls in love with a beautiful mortal prince, and he in turn falls in love with her voice. She trades her lovely voice for legs. Alas, the prince can neither love nor hear a woman who has no voice. Do I think my "voice" is my winning charm? If I were voiceless, would I lose my "charm?" And, have I, now, as a grown woman-scholar, transformed the literal speaking voice into the metaphoric writing voice? And what does all of this have to do with my time in Copenhagen?

I read the original story of the little mermaid now because I wonder if understanding the narrative might shed light on my Copenhagen experiences. The "real" little mermaid falls so madly in love with a prince she saves from drowning that she trades her beautiful voice, long life, and afterlife as ocean foam, for human legs, excruciating pain, and a chance to marry the prince. Should he marry her, she will become fully human and share his immortal soul. But, should the prince marry someone else, on his wedding night morn the little mermaid will immediately be transformed into ocean foam.

When the prince does marry someone else—a princess he wrongly believes saved him from drowning—the little mermaid's distraught sisters bring her a knife and urge her to kill him. If she does so before the morning light, she will once again become a mermaid. Seeing how happy the prince is with his bride, though, the little mermaid, whose love knows no bounds, tosses herself into the ocean. But because she was so good and longed so for a human soul, her fate has been changed. She is transformed into a "daughter of the air." She will spend three hundred years doing good works, giving warm breezes to the chilled, sweet scents of flowers to the ill—and then she shall receive her own immortal soul. Every time the little mermaid passes by a good child, she smiles at it, and a year of waiting is eliminated; but every time she passes a wicked child, she sheds tears. For every tear she sheds, a year is added to her wait.

If I had grown up with this story—and seen the little mermaid, perched on a rock waiting for her immortality—would I not have felt guilty if I behaved badly? Would I have valued the prospect of transformation through personal action? And maybe, just maybe, I'd absorb the cautionary tale: Know your place in the scheme of things.

Oh my, how real the consequences of the fairytale's message!

My actual trip to Copenhagen began with an engaging e-mail from Dorrie, a graduate student in sociology at the University of Copenhagen. She had read my book, *Fields of Play: Constructing an Academic Life*; indeed from the e-mail, I thought she might have committed some of it to memory since she was quoting me to myself. She invited me to come to Copenhagen to (1) teach a three-day graduate seminar at the University of Copenhagen, and (2) give a keynote address and workshop for the annual all-Scandinavian conference on gender to be held in Roskilde. The conference was called, "Between the no longer & not yet." Could I come in April 2000?

How could I not? I was flattered and enthused, because I thought of Denmark as a socially, academically, and culturally progressive country. How wonderful to share my work with the like-minded. I was also feeling a little financially opportunistic, as Copenhagen was on the way to Russia, where I would be heading next to see my stepdaughter and her family.

Dorrie gave my seminar a "headline," "Post-Positivistic Qualitative Research: Representational Practices and Legitimacy."

"Will I grade papers?" I e-mail.

"No, we don't write papers."

This university is beginning to sound quite European to me.

"How many people in the seminar? What departments?"

"Probably between ten and twenty. It'll depend upon the advertising strategies."

Now, it sounds American.

"We have had to turn many people down. Everybody tells how wonderful and interesting the readings and the programme look." Dorrie e-mails in early March. "Thus, there's absolutely a very positive atmosphere."

Why shouldn't there be a positive atmosphere?

"Any progress on my reimbursements and housing arrangements?" I e-mail. "I'll need two rooms because my husband Ernest will be with me."

"My sociology department will not take care of your expenses. They will only give an honorarium for the course," Dorrie e-mails me back. I check the exchange rate and figure the university will be "honoring" me with a princely sum—enough to cover a few Danishes and black coffee. "They arrogantly assume that your work is not as relevant as quantitative methods seminars; they're paranoid regarding poststructuralist thinking and even more so when this thinking is done by a woman, or even worse, a feminist! Thus negotiation has been very difficult. But I suppose this is not an entirely new and surprising situation for you to hear about?"

Why did I not heed the warning in her e-mail? How did my beliefs about Copenhagen's progressiveness blind me to the words upon my screen? My mind must have been stuck on financial matters. I didn't want to be their new little match girl.

"Any progress on expenses or housing?" I e-mail about two weeks later.

"The gender conference can give you the subsistence-money-rate given to Danish researchers going abroad—fifty kroners a day."

This converts to about US$8 a day. How in the world do Danish researchers live in America and how could I live in Denmark on that amount? And why should the gender conference—where I will spend but one day—be financially responsible for my university teaching? I feel the edges of guilt moving in upon me. I am not comfortable with "gouging" other feminists. Wait a minute, I remind myself. This is not gouging. And, I am not the one making the decisions. And, I am not a little match-seller. I will not perish for want of a kroner.

"Regarding the conference," Dorrie e-mails, "there's also a lot of enthusiasm, and the questions put forward are very inspiring. Your workshop is already overbooked. And deadline is not even due yet."

"What will the weather be like? And, any progress on housing?" I e-mail about two weeks later.

"About the weather—coldish—yes and probably also rainy. It could begin snowing in a just a few minutes from now." And at last, she e-mails, "Regarding housing, we will borrow an apartment for you and your husband. We hope it'll do."

I have never written this long an introduction in my life. Why am I avoiding Copenhagen? Why won't I allow my writing to place me in that time and space again?

The Saturday morning of our arrival at Kopenhagen Lufthaven, we take a cab to Anna's apartment off Gønnergade. The entrance to the apartment building abuts the narrow sidewalk, like my cousin's loft in Soho, I think. The litter reminds me of Soho, too. We push the button for 7D. Dorrie and Anna, a new sociology graduate student, bound down the stairs, open the worn wooden doors, and greet us in near unison, "We are so glad you are here. Let us help with your luggage." I like them instantly. We spontaneously hug. They give us fresh flowers, cheese, bread, wine, a map of the city, and important phone numbers.

The apartment reminds me of the student apartments that surrounded the University of Chicago in the 1950s. High-ceilinged flats were divided into "units"; although each unit had the requisite bath, bedroom, living room, and kitchen, the layouts were peculiar, mazelike. We enter 7D through a narrow hall that leads into what was probably once a dining room, but now contains Anna's desk, books, and clothes. Off that hub-room through pocket-doors toward the street, one enters the little living room, probably once a parlor. In it there is a couch, chair, rabbit-eared television set, high-end stereo equipment, and tall windows, covered with Indian cloth. Behind the hub is the little bedroom, its floor covered nearly wall-to-wall by the bed, a mattress on the floor. By the head of the bed a narrow opening leads to a hallway where my elbows brush the walls. Turn left and go down two little steps to reach the little bathroom. Note the little washing machine/dryer combination appliance in what was once probably a linen closet. Turn right out of the bedroom and down a step to the 1940s American kitchen. Look out the back door. See the wooden steps that lead to a little spot of yard, shared by all the apartment buildings flanking it.

I have no sense of direction. None. I am someone who could get lost in a thimble. So as to not get lost in the apartment, I think in the imperative mode—"Go here, step down, see that." I always choose the same pathways through the apartment, always retrace my steps. The labyrinthine nature of the apartment stays in my psyche, probably greatly exaggerated, but I cannot remember any of the colors of the walls, furniture, linens, or any of the design motifs, despite my proclivities to remember such details. My guess is that my expectation of Danish design in primary colors was not met—that everything was muted.

Anna explains how to turn on the hot water heater, reminding me of the Seattle apartment I lived in, depressed, forty years ago. "Please don't wash the sheets or towels, and please turn off the hot water heater when not in use," she tells us. She shows us how to use the telephone, television, and stereo.

"I'll come for you on Monday at 8:30 and walk you to the university." Anna says, putting on her backpack. Dorrie hoists the suitcases. "It's not far."

Monday morning opens cold, dark, and bleak. Anna arrives on a bicycle. "Ernest and I did some exploring over the weekend," I say, pulling my scarf close around my neck, grateful for my full-length fleece coat. "Pay attention," I tell myself, "so you can retrace your steps back to the apartment."

"We got wonderful Danishes at a bakery—ah—I think in the opposite direction," I say, feeling hopelessly lost already. Backpacked Anna walking her bike, and me with Mephistos on my feet and my trusty purple Danish schoolboy's bag over my shoulder, we begin our trek.

"We ate twice in the restaurant next to the apartment. The dolma and aubergine were good," I venture, "and the people were very friendly."

"Mm. Yes."

"Hafez restaurant. Of course, we had trouble reading the menu."

Our apartment is located on the central-city side edge of the Norrebro quarter. Almost 200,000 Moslem immigrants mostly from Turkey, Somalia, Pakistan, and Iraq live in the quarter. Whiffs of coriander and cumin and cinnamon and cloves emerge from the fifteen

Turkish restaurants near us; kiosks sell sesame candies, spices, and oils. Graffiti, in Arabic, are painted on the churches. Women's heads and bodies are covered, and from the play parks no Danish is heard. Young men look restive. I am not certain if I would be safe walking alone into the quarter at night. Or day.

"Turks were brought to Copenhagen to do the hard physical labor required by industrialized countries everywhere," Anna explains. "Other peoples from the Middle-East came, too. Last year they rioted because certain social benefits were retracted. It's still not resolved."

"I didn't know you had ethnic conflicts here?" I say, surprised, and saddened, that my vision of an egalitarian Denmark has been marred. But why would I be surprised?

"It's not ethnic so much as racial," she answers. "Some Danes think of Turks as"—she hesitates, trying, I think, to find the right American synonym—"as not-white." She does not bring up the religious difference issues, nor do they occur to me at the time.

I pull my scarf over my head and transfer my bookbag to the other shoulder. Up one street for a few blocks, across another, down some steps, through a brown patch, to a pedestrian path beside a river, across a bridge, circling a construction site—"where some of the rioting occurred"—and then through a maze of streets jutting here and there into the center of Copenhagen, until, at last we reach the university, the "City Campus," consisting as best as I can tell of one large restored stepped-gable building. We walk up stairs to the third floor, where Anna shows me my office. It is 9:45. My seminar will start at 10:00. My shoulders ache.

Twelve students—six men and six women—sit around a wooden table. Everyone is drinking coffee. If it weren't for the notebooks, book jackets, and conversation all in Danish, I feel I could be in any American university. Other than the large number of men—and maybe my sense that the students were older and the women quieter than I expected—there is nothing distinctively different. All of this is blissfully familiar.

"So we welcome Professor Laurel Richardson. . . ."

Dorrie introduces me, and the students give a little round of applause. That's how I like to remember it, anyway.

"Please call me 'Laurel' if you are comfortable doing so," I say.

My plan is to compress my stateside ten-week graduate seminar into three days. I begin, as I always do, by asking the students about themselves. They are all sociology majors, with "sociological" interests who are "interested" in the seminar. That morning, I lecture on postmodernism and answer questions. I go to lunch with the women students at a nearby café, shocked at the high prices and the menu's listing of fifty different kinds of beer. The women order their favorite beers. I refrain. That afternoon, I engage the students in discourse analysis of an interview segment. All is going well.

"See you here tomorrow," Anna says, as we leave the building. I button up my full-length fleece coat.

"Uh . . . uh. . . ." I stammer. "I don't know how to get back to the apartment." I don't have the slightest idea. The crisscross of walkways, breaking spaces into irregular triangles, and the sameness of the rows of period six-story buildings confuses me. "Stop gloating," I say under my breath to a gargoyle under an eave.

"Oh?" Anna says, clearly surprised by my ineptitude. "Then let's get started." She walks her bike and I put on fleece mittens.

"This bridge looks different," I say. "Where is the construction site? The river walk?" The wind cuts through my fleece coat. It is getting dark.

"I am taking you a different way," Anna says, smiling. "You'll see more of Copenhagen this way." Great, I am thinking, now I'll never find my way back to "campus" tomorrow.

"I'm so glad you're home," I say to Ernest as I collapse on the bed. It is 6:00. "Ernest, please call a cab to pick me up tomorrow morning."

"Sure." He looks dubious.

"Did you have a good day, Ernest?" I ask, but fall asleep before I hear his answer.

"Are you sure this is the university?" I ask the Turkish cab driver. Nothing looks familiar.

"Yes," he says.

"Are you sure?

"Yes, yes."

"Yes?"

"*Yes!*" He turns and scowls.

Does he think I don't trust him because he's Turkish?

"It looks different," I say, trying to explain my hesitation.

"It's the *back* entrance!" Under his breath he says something in Turkish.

99

"Keep the change," I say, handing him a lot of kroners. I feel bad that he feels bad. He scowls again. I give him some more kroners.

"Go in that door," he says, and peels away from the curb like a cab driver in America.

"Good morning, Professor Richardson—uh, Laurel," Karin says, as she steers us toward the seminar room.

My lecture on the second morning is about voice—the researcher's and the researched. "Break into groups of two," I tell them. "Interview each other and then write up your interview in either a traditional or creative way. But be sure to honor the voice of the person you are interviewing."

The students nod.

"Any ideas for the general topic of the interviews?" I ask.

Silence.

"Well, you know I am a feminist, so I would be interested in learning more about gender relations in Denmark at the millennium. Let's reconvene at 1:30."

Feeling proud of my pedagogy, welcoming some "down-time," and looking forward to learning more about the feminist successes in Denmark—and feeling confident that I will not get lost if I don't stray too far from the campus—I set off on my own to explore the environ that my trusty *Lonely Planet* guidebook calls without any explanation, "The Latin Quarter." I pay strict attention to where I have walked, doubling back and retracing my steps every few minutes. I am least likely to get lost when I am alone for then I am not distracted by conversation or the expectation that someone else will lead me back. That's why, I boast to myself, I am a writer.

The "kultorvet," a pedestrian plaza that *Lonely Planet* says might have street musicians, flower stalls, beer gardens, has only dour looking people, refusing to make eye contact with me, or anyone else. Everyone seems lost in their own world, oblivious to what's around them. Blank faced people on ten-speed bicycles whiz by each other. The bright red and blue single-speed bikes *Lonely Planet* says are free for anyone to use fill a rack, unused. A bookstore in a building well is closed. A massive neoclassical cathedral is open. I enter. I see a familiar-looking sculpture of an open-armed Jesus, and around him twelve disciples. I am alone in that space.

"Why don't people greet each other?" I ask Dorrie as we simultaneously enter the university building.

"Oh, they do—they will—when the sun comes out," she says. Sunshine apparently transforms the winter-weary Danes into Danes with spring in their soles. Spring souls.

Now, it is time to write about that which I have been resisting.

Five pairs of interview reports go smoothly: the rave scene; music; art; social benefits. Anna and Soren are last. Anna gives a sociologically traditional report. Then Soren reads his report, the psychological/emotional gist of which I paraphrase here:

I like doing this kind of research, feeling the power of getting into Anna's mind and feelings. I ask her questions—any questions I want—and she answers. I have power over her. I can do anything to her I want to. I can enter her body like I enter her mind. She answers me. She comes to me. She wants me. I am going to follow her home, watch her undress. And then watch her again and, when she is not home, I am going through her underwear drawer. She wants me to. I know she does. See? She answers my questions.

Anna is shaking. I am shaking. In my thirty years of teaching, I have never had an experience even remotely like this one—humiliating, mortifying, violating, threatening verbal violence from one student to another. If a man had done anything remotely like this in one of my classes back in the States, the feminist women would have been up in arms and would have shouted him down before he finished his last horrid words. But here no one speaks.

"Any comments?" I ask, waiting. Incredulous.

Silence. Like little mermaids, the women have lost their voices.

"Soren, in my country," I say—aware of my jingoism, but unable to stop myself—"you would be called a stalker."

More silence.

"In my country, it's against the law to stalk."

Another long silence.

A male voice. "What's a stalker?"

I dismiss class early. Four women follow me into my office. "We want to walk you toward your apartment. So we can talk," Dorrie says.

"Gender relationships in Denmark are in backlash," Karin begins. "When you raised the gender-relations issue, you raised a red flag."

"I did?"

"Few women choose to get married, now. Most choose single motherhood because the state will provide for their children. They don't need husbands," Dorrie explains.

"What about the fathers?"

"They have no rights to their children if they're not married to the mothers. Many of the men are angry about this. They have meetings about this."

My sympathies are with the men, as I think of my son Josh's struggle to gain joint custody of his son.

"The backlash is everywhere," Anna says.

"I was a women's studies major before I came to the sociology department, but I don't want it known because I won't be taken seriously, if it is known," another student says. "It is too dangerous for me."

"What?"

"Feminists are not welcome," she says.

Then they tell me about Soren. He had made uninvited passes at a sociology graduate student. When she told him to stop, he didn't. Then he spread nasty rumors about her and undermined her credibility by calling her a feminist. Many of the male students supported him. Soren's advisor was a powerful man in the department. The woman was forced to leave.

"Soren was empowered to do the same thing to another woman. She's gone, too," Karin adds.

"So Soren is a real threat to my body, mind, and academic future," Anna says.

"And we can't talk about any of this—feminism, anger, sexual imposition —in the department," Karin concludes. "We're afraid."

The University of Copenhagen is the largest, oldest, and best research university in Denmark. According to the social science department's website, the university's location contributes "to the inspirational atmosphere that characterizes the study environment of the faculty"; and there is a "long tradition" and "great demand" for the social science graduates to fill "leading positions" in "the public and the private sector."

"Can you get to your apartment from here?" Anna asks. My confused look is not just about getting back to the apartment; it is about admiring the courage of these women who had invited me and who have taken the seminar, women who endure the chilly environment—and, then, I find myself back in time to another place. My own state university. It is my experience, there, that has come to dominate my sense of Copenhagen, and why I have resisted writing about it.

"Do you know where to go from here?" Dorrie asks. We've just crossed a bridge.

"Draw me a map," I say.

Seven years earlier my body and soul had rebelled. I was exhausted from defending the right of my specialties—gender, qualitative research, feminist theory—to exist in my sociology department. I was tired of being marginalized, undermined, and dissed; troubled by the treatment of feminist graduate students interested in qualitative research. Adopting the university's new "business model," the sociology department devalued commitments to diversity in research methods, theories, and pedagogies. I was lost in the emergent space. Worse, I had lost what had deeply mattered to me all of my professional life—a sociological community committed to understanding and improving the world.

"I'm thinking of taking the 'early retirement buyout,'" I told my department chair. Before I had finished the rest of my prepared speech, the chair was on the phone giving the dean the good news. Each of them, I think, got bonuses that day.

"I'll still be doing research and working with my graduate students," I said, "So, I'm interested in my Emeritus privileges—like supplies, secretarial help, office space."

"Retirees? They just fade into the woodwork," the chair blithely said.

Like cockroaches? I thought.

"Ernest, there's something rotten in the state of Denmark. And it's the sociology department," I say, telling him the grim tales.

"I guess, sociology departments seem to be Sociology Departments the world over," he says.

"How can I possibly teach tomorrow?"

"You can. You've been doing it for years."

I arrive by cab the next day at 9:55. The weather is brighter. The students and I act as if nothing happened yesterday. This is the first time in my teaching career that I avoid debriefing a class. I cannot put Anna through the experience again; I cannot trust Soren; and clearly, the women have lost their tongues.

For the next days, Ernest and I do touristy things, and I try to forget the seminar. We take the train to Hamlet's castle in Elsinore and the boat to Sweden. Then we explore Copenhagen: Stroget, the longest pedestrian mall; the grounds of the Royal Danish family's home; the fence enclosing Tivoli, which is not yet open for the season; the Round Tower, from which we can see red tile roofs, church spires, and patches of brown. We greet rambunctious tow-headed children running down the tower's spiral walkway; stroll along the canal, liking the row houses and boats; stare at the sixty-foot building wall painting of a big, bare-busted blond woman holding two blue-eyed snow-white babies, happily pointing to her breasts—"Maelk" the lettering says. We wonder about the humungous scary monsters of the night painted on a building abutting a play yard. There are sculptures everywhere—a gigantic sculpture of Hans Christian Andersen looking like the mad-hatter; bronzed little people; and gargoyles, in small, medium, and extra-large sizes, freestanding and as scuppers. On four Palladian windows of a restored gothic building are blood-red renditions of the Woman's Liberation Movement symbol—the clenched fist inside Venus's mirror. It is one of the largest buildings in Copenhagen: it is the battered women's shelter.

A few days later we check into Hotel Prindsen in Roskilde, a short train ride from Copenhagen. From the train station, we walk up a hill, cross a small graveyard behind an imposing stone cathedral, and enter our hotel. "On this site," I read from the brochure, "there has been a Hotel Prindsen since 1695 . . . Hans Christian Andersen stayed here in 1842."

"Maybe we're in his room?" Ernest says, getting that dreamy look he always gets when he's in the actual space where another writer wrote.

"No such luck," I say. "This reincarnation of the hotel dates only to 1876." I had already noted the French Renaissance architecture and the "Best Western" sign.

"Shall we go to the Viking museum? The Cathedral? Eat Danish Ribs?" Ernest asks.

"Thrice yes, Milord," I say, getting into the spirit of this Medieval trade city.

The next morning Dorrie picks me up from the hotel. "Everyone is happy you are here," she says. She hands me the conference flyer: on the cover, a quartet of photos of life-sized eyeballs; above the eyeballs, the bold banner reads "Between the no longer & not yet"; and beneath that banner in small Danish letters, "refleksioner over aartusindskiftets konsforskning"—reflections on sex/gender research at the millennium.

Women from all over Scandinavia fill the Danish modern auditorium at Roskilde University, an expansive, elegant campus. Everything feels open and fresh here; expectant. Hugs, greetings, laughter. I breathe a sigh of relief and begin my speech, "Writing for Your Life: A Feminist Practice."

Thank you for honoring me with your invitation. . . . When I began writing this speech a month ago I asked myself, "What do I most want to say?" Here is the short answer: I would like academic women everywhere to understand that, although their lives are in part controlled by larger forces, they have agency: they can make choices, they can transgress.

As I reread my speech and write about it now, I realize how deeply my keynote maps onto the lessons of Andersen stories: Whatever the dire circumstances, if you are true to your own spirit and take action on your behalf, you can transform your plight.

After my speech, women stand in line to shake my hand, hug me, and thank me—"for giving me resolve," "for understanding what we women face," "for encouraging me," "for modeling creativity and courage," "for talking about women who have been abused . . . I am one." I feel overwhelmed by their generosity.

"Are you sorry we didn't go see *The Little Mermaid*?" Ernest asks, as we settle into our airplane seats, flying way above the earth to Russia. I am feeling comfortable in this space.

"No, not at all," I say. "I really didn't want to see her." And, now I think I know why. Too many little mermaids have traded their lovely voices because they fell in love with Prince Universitates, who can do no wrong, who neither knows nor cares about their pains, losses, lives. He doesn't even know that the little mermaids saved him from drowning in alphanumerical soup. He allows—even encourages—outlandish abuse of them to take place in his kingdom for they have violated his sacred dictum: Know your place. But when all the little mermaids come together in a different kingdom—"the no longer and not yet . . . ," lithe and happy, they regain their voices. But must they wait three hundred years to gain immortality—not for their bodies, but for their words?

I settle into my airline magazine. "A Journey Away from the Cold" captures my attention. This is no retelling of the little match-seller story. It's about a Danish woman who has finally received her "license to kill." "Long overdue," she says, "because I'm a woman." Now, having realized "her ambition to become a big-game hunter in a male-dominated world," she's leading buffalo hunting groups in Tanzania. "It's dangerous as hell," she says. "But tracking a cunning old bull, bringing him down—that's the greatest pleasure on earth."

Stranger in a Stranger Land

Ernest Lockridge

"That makes Darryl Hannah look like Mrs. Tom Thumb," I remark, pointing at the head and stark-naked torso of a mural that consumes one side of a six-story building. Each snow-white breast is ten feet wide, with a big black bull's-eye.

"Who's he?" asks Laurel.

"Tom Thumb?"

"Darryl Hannah," says Laurel.

"*She's* a movie star."

"A man's first name, a woman's . . . ? I'm jet-lagged, Ernest. . . . Wait . . . isn't she the mermaid in *Splash?*"

"It's *Attack of the Fifty Foot Woman* I was thinking of," I say.

On the apartment building wall the Queen of Brobdingnag—red-lipped, smiling, blue-eyed and blonde—holds a naked snow-white blond male twin crooked in each arm, mother and infants aglow with religious ecstasy. Under the troika, bold capital letters spell out, "MAELK." And further down, in script: "det er lejligt," or "dej er deiligt," or "led en lellijtj"—?

"Some sort of hidden e. e. cummings message?" I ask.

"Such as?"

"Suckled by Wolves?" I suggest.

"Wrong city and species. What about, Dunk your Danish?"

"Or, Sure Beats Crack?" I say. "Have you ever seen such delirious happiness?"

"Maybe it's The Little Mermaid," Laurel says.

"What's 'Maelk'?" I ask.

"Her name?"

"She doesn't' have one," I say. "Not in grim old Hans Christian."

"You're certain?" Laurel asks.

"Grandma Lockridge read me *The Little Mermaid* when I was eight and I've not so much as glanced at the thing since, but I'm certain, all right."

"You didn't read it to your daughters?" asks Laurel.

"Slicing her fishtail up the middle to give her a pair of legs and the pain's always there and dancing's like treading on knives? She gives up her royal oceanic family, has her tongue cut out by the Sea Witch, plays voyeur while her dreamboat spends a blissful wedding night with some Princess who got the credit for saving his life after the Little Mermaid really saved him? And in the end she turns to sea foam and evaporates into thin air? This is a role model for daughters?"

"You can recall all that?"

"It made an impression.

It's late afternoon of our first day in Copenhagen. The sky is cobalt blue. We're making a little foray into our neighborhood, the Arab Quarter, where walls and fences swarm with Arabic graffiti. Arabic explodes over the brick wall surrounding the Roman Catholic cathedral, past which we're strolling. Loops and whorls, crescents, scimitars adorn a splintery fence behind which there's a playground. It's over this playground that the Goddess of Breast Milk presides.

"Let us be thankful that Arabic is Greek to us," I remark.

"Why?"

"The ostrich in me. We'll sleep easier tonight if we don't know what they're trying to tell us."

"Maybe I want to know. I'm a sociologist."

"The writing on the wall looks more than a little menacing to me."

"Ernest, I'm so jet-lagged I could sleep on that rock with *The Little Mermaid.*"

CHAPTER 4

Returning to our second-floor graduate-student apartment I feel forty years falling away . . . and I'm in my dingy 1960 digs across from the YMCA in New Haven, fish out of water, awaiting the exam that will expose my weakling grasp of French, German, and Latin, said torment to be inflicted in the Castle Keep of a Gothic skyscraper, a medieval fortress called the Hall of Graduate Studies. Mere days ago I was in bucolic Bloomington. Now I'm imprisoned in an Urban Waste Land. To consummate my matriculation into the Yale Graduate School I must pass two languages prior to the start of classes. *Mein Gott! Tempus fugit! L'heure a sonne!* I hit the street and walk the last mile to where some tweedy Torquemada awaits with his Iron Maiden, his Turn of the Screw. I screw my courage to the sticking place and. . . .

Lo! It's 1962 and I'm cramming for my PhD generals, stuffing my piddling lump of blood-pudding with Beowulf, Chaucer, Spenser, Shakespeare, Milton, Dryden, Pope, Wordsworth. . . . How am I squandering my one and only life, longing for Retirement before my "Career" has even begun. . . ?

The New Haven apartment and this apartment in Copenhagen both open onto squalid cityscapes. The air is fetid. Horns blare. Street lamps are glimmering. Rats with wings flutter to rest on windowsills and eaves. Pigeons.

Laurel's readying herself for bed. "Any plans for the next few days?"

"Thought I'd drop in on the set of one of those porno movies Denmark's famous for and see whether they're taking applications. Maybe hit the top bookstores and sign any rare unautographed copies of my books. . . . Or maybe I'll just hang out."

"Just hanging out sounds like Heaven."

In the morning Anna, whose apartment we've co-opted, rings the bell, and I buzz her in. Anna's in her early thirties. She's tall and slender like Laurel. They wear identical glasses—oblong ovals, wire-rimmed. Anna shares the space with Gerd, who is away somewhere researching one of the articles he writes for left-wing publications in several languages. Anna, who's staying with friends while we're here, is taking Laurel's seminar. Laurel's looking forward to teaching the seminar because Denmark is reputed to be far more advanced than the United States.

"How do you find everything?" Anna asks.

"Terrific," I tell her. "It's really generous of you to let us stay here."

"You had your breakfast in the apartment?"

"An omelet," says Laurel.

"Oh my! A world-famous scholar, and a cook!"

"Ernest does the cooking. And the grocery shopping."

"No Danish man would perform such tasks."

"Just call me the new womanly man."

"I have him well-trained."

"I fetch, but I don't roll over," I quip.

"Oh, ha ha. Ernest, would you like to accompany your wife and myself to the university?"

"No, that's okay."

"May I at least provide directions?" offers Anna.

"Won't be necessary, I have a map. But thanks."

Anna's eyes are intelligent, bright, but I glimpse something in her mien that looks a little cowed . . . fearful. I ask, "Hey, Anna, from here to the university—it's safe? You don't run a gauntlet getting there?"

"Copenhagen is quite safe," Anna says.

"Copen*hayg*en?" Laurel asks.

"That is how we Danes pronounce our city. The 'ah' is German . . . as when the Nazis were occupying our country. We are now perhaps still a bit sensitive."

Laurel says, "Ah. . . . Well, Ernest, you're on your own."

"The little match boy," I quip.

"Don't get lost," Laurel says. "Or you're liable to freeze to death."

"We must bear our going hence, even as our coming hither," I say. "The readiness is all."

"Oh, ha ha," Anna laughs. "Laurel, is your husband always such a card?"

"The joker," I quip. There's something I want to ask Anna, but I can't recall it. A new concern has short-circuited my memory: that whilst showing off I've scrambled my Shakespeare, whisking some Lear into my Hamlet.

Following their departure I lounge at the kitchen table and skim *The Lonely Planet*, a travel guide. Tivoli would be the natural starting point but I see that it's closed for the duration of our visit. So I decide to explore "Copenhagen's main shopping street, Stroget," where "you can find numerous speciality [sic] shops selling everything from clothing to Danish porcelain and electronics." I want a few Cuban cigars as a birthday gift for my son-in-law Joe. Joe and Susan, my eldest daughter, are missionaries to the Russians. We'll be visiting them in a little over a week, in Petrozavodsk. I leave the apartment armed with Kroners, Credit Cards, Passport, and a City Map.

Out on the street I can't find Stroget on my map. Two miles of World-Famous International Shopping and it might as well be located in Timbuktu or the Twilight Zone. Something from my father's novel comes to mind: "You will hunt it on the map, and it won't be there."

I set off down H. C. Andersen's Boulevard in the direction of central Copenhagen.

On a bridge over a river I see on the map that the "river" is, in reality, an outsized pond snaking through the city. Segmented by bridges the pond has three different names: Skt. Jorgens So, Peblinge So, Sortedams So. In Ohio I run, swim, lift weights, but after only a couple of miles in Denmark my legs are beginning to ache. Thrombosis due to circumscribed movement across the Atlantic? Death in Copen*hay*gen . . . my anonymous corpse sprawled on the embankment of a mud-hole called a "So."

I make my way through a throng of pedestrians scanning the pavement with gloomy eyes.

My soles are smarting. The sky is gray. A wind blows across a vast cobblestone-paved courtyard. I spot a street name. "Stroget." And below it, in English: "Foot Traffic Only." Stroget's a pedestrian mall, and my map is solely for motorists.

Stroget throngs with shoppers. Ah, a tobacconist! I limp up a flight of ornate cast-iron steps and enter Rappaccini's Garden. The fragrance! Delicious!

"Speak English?" I ask a pink-cheeked young man wearing a double-breasted suit.

"But my dear Sir, naturally!"

"Well, I'd like to buy some Cuban cigars. Not for myself, of course."

"But my dear Sir, of course not! And let me assure you that we have a more fabulous selection of the very finest in Havanas than does Master Fidel, himself. And now, Sir, may we get down to business? May I suggest that you follow me into the Humidor in order that you may appreciate the full array of selection, and I may better direct you in your choice?"

The Humidor's about the size of our master bedroom in Ohio. But here in Denmark I'm a Sultan in a Seraglio of Cigars. Bolivar, El Rey del Mundo, San Cristobal, Romeo y Julieta, Vegas Robaina, Cohiba. . . . I select four Cohiba Robustos sealed in screw-top torpedo tubes. "Boy will Joe go for these!"

"And for yourself, Sir?"

Oh God! I've not smoked for eighteen years. Nothing. Yet I can taste the ambrosial Montecristos my brother-in-law smuggled down out of Canada. One puff brushing the surface of my tongue and my scalp would brush the ceiling plaster. The Humidor is an Occasion of Sin, the temptation overwhelming.

But to start smoking again. . . . Mornings squandered in hawking phlegm. . . . And my wife with whom I quit cold turkey on tax day, 1982, partners in the mortal struggle, buddies supporting one another through the craving, the hideous withdrawal. . . . I envision *her* enslaved again.

> Some it do chew, and some it smoke,
> Whilst some it up their nose do poke.

Thus wrote my great-great grandfather, Methodist circuit rider and physician in nineteenth-century Indiana. On the spot I take him for my role model.

Vile weed begone!

"Thanks all the same, but no thanks."

"If I may be permitted to inquire, Sir, 'Why not?'"

"I gave up smoking for my wife."

"One cannot but admire such selflessness."

"Thank you."

"If I may be permitted, Sir—"

"But of course."

"Well, then—" He draws a breath. "Even for those of us in robust health and in our prime, life does not linger forever. And one has the right, indeed the duty, to reserve certain pleasures to oneself alone. If, however, you are committed to your decision—"

"Ah. . . . I'm afraid so."

"Then, Sir, I must respect your decision, mustn't I?"

"Alas."

"However, Sir, we are always here for you, in the event that you were ever to change your mind."

Safely out on Stroget, Caribbean swag in a gold-embossed bag, I feel that I actually belong among this throng of shoppers. *Ich bin ein Copenhaygener!*

MUSEUM OF SEX. A poster behind glass shows a woman with black rectangles blocking out her breasts and crotch. She's holding some spiked device that drips with chains. The entrance features crimson wallpaper, Persian carpeting, a mannequin whose plaster flesh peeks out between her veils, plaster fingers beckoning. No Danish Modern in sight.

During our maiden year of cohabitation, I motored with Laurel to Bloomington for the Lockridge Family Reunion. We took a room at the Big Red Motel across from the Monroe County Courthouse. Beside the Big Red stands a single-story family home transformed into a porno shack.

ADULT BOOK STORE
OPEN 24 HOURS
LADIES COME INSIDE!

We're returning after dinner at Mom's. It's around midnight, and Laurel's been introduced to my mother, stepfather, siblings, in-laws, nephew, niece, aunts, uncles, cousins, Powder Puff the cat. My stepfather grudgingly permitted the tiny cadre of hardcore degenerates among us to consume the wine provided by my New York City brother and my sister's German spouse.

"Been inside an adult bookstore before?" I ask Laurel.

"What about you, Ernest?"

"Why, of course not!" I reply. "What about it? Are you game?"

"If you are."

We enter into what was once upon a time a family's front room. It's brightly lit with shelves displaying shrink-wrapped magazines, books, and an array of amorphous-looking objects. "Hi there, folks," says the young man behind the cash register. "Out-of-towners?"

"We're from next door," Laurel says. "The motel."

"Actually, I'm a native Bloomingtonian," I tell him. "Born and raised."

"Checking out your old haunts, hey buddy?"

"Let's hope not," Laurel says.

"Folks want something in particular or just looking?"

"I'm a sociologist," Laurel says. "It's research."

"Research away to your heart's content." The clerk points to a green door. "There's a back room there in back if you're interested in more research."

"What's *she* for?" Laurel asks me, pointing to a fish-mouthed face.

"One of those blow-up dolls," I inform her.

"And—?"

I explain.

"Yuck!" Laurel says. "How do you know *that*?"

"Want to find out what's behind the Green Door?"

We enter into a twilight space with booths on both sides of an aisle. Sounds are emanating from the booths. The air's thick with aromas reminiscent of a dog pound. At the room's far end stands a plastic wastebasket full to the brim. There's a roll of toilet paper mounted on the wall.

"Oh, Ernest."

From adjacent booths emerge a giant and a dwarf. Making a pincer movement, their eyes on no one, they both bump against Laurel at the same time. I grab her arm. "Let's get the hell out of here!"

The Green Door slams behind us.

"How's the research going?" asks the clerk.

I give the MUSEUM OF SEX a pass. I can reach the apartment before dinnertime if I don't get lost.

On impulse I enter a small bookstore. A silver bell tinkles above the door. Bookcases stand to the ceiling in the cramped space. There's a stepladder on rollers. There's a skinny clerk, whose eyes take me in. "May we be of assistance?"

"I'm, ah, looking for *The Little Mermaid*. In English."

"Our merchandise is in Danish."

"Then . . . do you have a copy of *Den Store Dagen*?"

My pronunciation elicits a flicker of thin-lipped contempt. "And what, precisely, is that?"

"Danish translation of an American novel. Best-seller in the late forties."

"Oh, a best-*seller*."

"In America."

"Alas, we carry nothing in translation."

"Okay." The bell tinkles upon my departure.

My map. I'm on Vester Voldgade. I'll take this to Glydenlovesgade which leads back into the Arab Quarter.

I've drawn abreast of an enormous Romanesque fortress whose iron fence bristles with spikes. The four arched second-story windows display the Mirror of Venus in arterial red, with a clenched fist.

When at last I stumble into the apartment, Laurel and Anna are in the living room. "Hi, Ernest," says Anna.

"How was your day?" Laurel asks me.

"Really interesting," I say.

"What did you do?"

"Nothing much."

"What's there in your bag?"

"Havana cigars for Joe. Hey, Anna, I passed this big brick building with crimson female symbols—"

"That is our Shelter for Battered Women. Well, I must be on my way."

"Anna, everybody out there has this dour look, as though Denmark's some sort of prison—?" I say.

"Oh, we're like that for two more weeks," Anna says. "Then spring arrives and we all perk up. In two weeks you won't recognize us. Laurel, I am so looking forward to tomorrow! Please, both of you enjoy the apartment!"

Listening to Anna descending the staircase, I say, "There's something I want to ask her, but I can't remember what it is."

"You'll think of it."

"Tell me about your seminar, Laurel. How many students?"

"Twelve. Six men, which I didn't expect. They did most of the talking. The women seem restrained. So . . . you found a tobacconist."

"And almost smoked one of Castro's finest myself, but didn't. Then I didn't go to this sex museum. Thus conscience made a coward out of me. Can't say the two temptations were equal in strength. As Kipling so eloquently puts it, 'A woman is only a woman, but a good cigar is a smoke.'"

Tuesday afternoon following Laurel's seminar we take a cab to Copenhagen's Staten Museum for Kunst, which features a Goya exhibition. "Goya's my guy!" I say as we climb the museum's grand staircase. All during the taxi ride Laurel remained uncharacteristically silent.

Goya's *The Disasters of War*, a series of palm-sized etchings, occupies a vast crepuscular gallery. I place my nose mere inches from *Great Deeds*—

Against the Dead, its emasculated corpse tied head-down to a tree trunk. There's a second torso, beheaded, legs crooked over a tree limb, head impaled, severed arms dangling by the fingers. "So . . . Laurel?"

"Uh-huh . . . ?"

"How'd it go?"

Yesterday, Laurel divided the students into pairs and had them interview each other, then write from the other's point of view. Today the students read their assignments aloud. "Terrifying!" Laurel shudders. "Disgusting!"

"Uh-oh." I've moved on to *What More Can One Do?* which depicts two of Napoleon's finest stabilizing a Spanish peasant upside down so a saber-wielding soldier can more easily emasculate him.

Laurel says, "Anna paired up with one of the men, who chose in the paper he read today to imagine himself being a fly on the wall of her bedroom as she's getting ready for bed."

"You mean, *our* bedroom?"

"Hadn't thought about *that*." Laurel shudders again. "Ugh!"

A peasant with an ax beheads a dismounted cavalry officer. "Apparently the guy didn't understand the assignment," I remark.

"Oh, he understood all right. Listen to this." Laurel summarizes what the man wrote.

"Godawful!" I say. "What'd you do?"

"Informed him that 'in my country, you'd be called a stalker.' 'What means stalker?' he asks. So I'm forced to go through some sort of explanation."

"Like reinventing the wheel."

"Precisely, only worse. So when I'm finished, he says, 'Like your Benjamin in *The Graduate*. But is it not Benjamin who wins the girl?'"

"The unmitigated gall of the guy," I say. "And it's not over."

Two soldiers hold a woman down. A third soldier is flinging himself onto her.

"What about Anna?" I ask. "How was she taking it?"

"Just trying hard not to cry," says Laurel.

A handful of women battle Napoleon's army. "Ah! That's better," I remark. A woman spears a Frenchman in the gut. Another wields a rock. A woman wearing a ball gown scales a pile of corpses to light the fuse of a cannon. "The women in the class must've leapt to Anna's defense," I say.

"Not a peep from a one of them. Anna and three other woman from the seminar walked with me after class. They needed to talk. They're terrified of being labeled 'feminists.' Becoming known as a 'feminist' kills off any hope of an academic career."

"Something smells rotten in the state of Denmark."

On Wednesday Laurel bids her seminar farewell, and Thursday morning we take the train to Helsingor. We leave the Helsingor terminal beneath a row of leafless black trees whose branches terminate in clenched black fists. The day's chilly with a steady drizzle. Elsinore stands in mist across the bay. The castle's spires resemble minarets. On the way there Laurel shoots my snapshot in front of the Hotel Hamlet. I have on Levis and a baseball cap that says, "Sedona." My hands are in the pockets of my winter coat.

On a gangway of gray planks we cross Elsinore's wide moat. The castle's made of brick, with stone trim.

"Remember in Dublin when we visited that squat little castle where Joyce lived?" Laurel asks.

"The Martello tower. God, getting to climb up on top of it like Stephen Dedalus! Looking out over the snotgreen sea!"

"I'm not sure I've seen you so excited," Laurel says.

"I was excited all right."

"So—what does Elsinore feel like?" she asks me.

"Doesn't feel like anything," I say.

"I'm sorry to hear it."

"Keep your eyes out for the ghost of Hamlet's father. He sure got Hamlet excited."

"Too bad that bookstore the other day didn't have a copy of your father's novel," Laurel says.

"I need another translation of *Raintree County* like I need my own death mask. Hell, I once had crates of the damn thick, fat, heavy things."

"Had?"

"Put the whole lot out with the trash," I tell her. "All those damn foreign-language editions. Dead weight."

"I didn't know," says Laurel.

"Well, you do now."

A half-dozen workmen are pounding their hammers against Elsinore's steep copper-sheeted roof. "No ramparts," I complain. "No place for a ghost to get his footing. If Shakespeare'd actually visited Denmark he'd never have written *Hamlet*."

We purchase admission tickets and tour the place on our own. "Why, lookey here, Laurel, the royal bed of Denmark, that couch for luxury and damned incest. Nay, but to live in the rank sweat of an enseamed bed, stewed in corruption, honeying and making love over the nasty sty."

"They had to occupy themselves somehow during those long, cold winter nights without television," Laurel says.

"Suddenly I'm hysterical with nostalgia, recalling how I felt the night my mother remarried after sixteen years of celibate widowhood," I say.

"You men," says Laurel.

"She's dead now. Dead and gone. Leave her to heaven."

We enter the Great Hall. No furniture. No other visitors. Vast checkered floor, black and white. Vast fireplace at the far wall, putti flanking the mantel. Footsteps echo. "Toward the end Dad went around claiming *Raintree County* was greater than *Hamlet*," I say.

"He sounds manic," Laurel says.

It's while exploring the dungeon, a dank tunnel snaking under Elsinore, that I really get going. "I have of late lost all my mirth . . . something something . . . goes so heavily that this goodly frame, the earth, seems to be a sterile promontory . . . something . . . this majestical roof fretted with golden fire, why it appeareth no other . . . something . . . to me than a foul and pestilent congregation of vapors. . . . It is said, Laurel, that depressives build dungeons in the air. There was this Yale trivia contest? At the end of which the winner parades down a runway, Miss America style, whilst the MC serenades him 'There he goes, think of all the crap he knows!' So here I am, obscure sometime novelist, retired English professor with loads of learned lumber in his head, and what does it all add up to? Please tell me."

"I'm telling you that we are out of here!"

Consulting the *Lonely Planet* we learn there's a ferry between Helsingor and Helsingborg, Sweden, that departs on the hour. "What do you think, Ernest?"

"Well, I've never been to Sweden, but I've been to Copenhagen."

"And—?"

"What'd the Swede say when the Ivy League came calling?"

"I beg your pardon, Ernest?"

"Never mind. Soon you can ask him yourself."

In Sweden, where we must persuade the immigration official to stamp our passports, everything's closed including the Lutheran church in front of which stands a life-size bronze of a woman wearing a beatific smile. Two more arms and she'd pass as a Hindu Goddess.

Friday we travel by train from Copenhagen to Roskilde whence the fearsome Spear-Danes sailed off in longboats to sack, pillage, rape, slaughter, and incinerate their neighbors.

> Many a carcass they left to be carrion,
> Many a livid one, many a sallow-skin—
> Left for the white-tailed eagle to tear it, and
> Left for the horny-nibbed raven to rend it, and
> Gave to the garbaging war-hawk to gorge it, and
> That gray beast, the wolf of the weald.

In Roskilde Domkirke are arrayed the Royal Burial Vaults of the Danes. Meandering among the ornate sarcophagi I imagine within two of the finest the bones of Hamlet, Hamlet's father. . . . Beowulf would require thrice the volume of any vault in sight to accommodate his skeleton's epic proportions. Ophelia's a-moldering outside somewhere in an unmarked, unhallowed ditch. Now get you to my lady's chamber and tell her, let her paint an inch thick, to this favor she must come.

We devour a dinner of delectable Danish ribs, two full racks, and spend the night in Roskilde's Hotel Prindsen before returning to Copenhagen to ready ourselves for our Sunday flight to St. Petersburg, Russia.

"Ernest?" It's Saturday night. We're stuffing our suitcases with dirty laundry.

"Yup."

"Remember what you wanted to ask Anna?"

"Yup."

"And—?"

"To translate the writing on the wall," I answer. "You know, what's written below Our Lady of Twins and Tits."

"I'll make a point of asking her by e-mail."

"Forget it. I prefer just making it up. What was it that the Writing on the Wall actually said? 'Mene mene tekel uhharsin'? Bring me your tired, your meek, your thirsting masses longing to chug-a-lug irradiated milk? Your days are numbered, oh Babylon? Eat at Joe's?"

"Ernest? What do people think of when they think of Copenhagen?"

"*The Little Mermaid!*"

"And have we seen her?"

"Absolutely not!"

"So we've spent all this time in Copenhagen—"

"And done nothing!"

Conversation: Copenhagen

February 26, 2003

Ernest: We didn't write about Tivoli, we didn't see *The Little Mermaid*, we didn't see the bohemian district, we didn't write about our visit to the art museum at Louisiana. So, this raises an issue for me about the nature and aim of this book, and I'm wondering if you can help me out.

Laurel: [*Laughter.*] Good question, Ernest. [*Long pause.*] Aren't we using our travels as objects for our gaze?

Ernest: As gazing objects.

Laurel: And like the gazing ball in our backyard, what we see when we look into it is not the "ball," but ourselves and all the desiderata behind us.

Ernest: Gazing objects, indeed.

Laurel: What strikes me about our pieces is the power that Place has on our psyches. Anna's apartment and the area around it reminded both of us of other places where we lived in the fifties and sixties—New York, Chicago, Seattle, New Haven. You know it just occurred to me—this is off the cuff—that when I got so depressed living in Seattle, I was living amongst Scandinavians. And Seattle has a Denmarkian heaviness—fog, rain, chill, gloom. I think being in Copenhagen brought back memories of that terrible depressing time in my life.

Ernest: Yes. In the beginning of your narrative you say that what you're writing may not be about Copenhagen at all, which is an overstatement, but the point is, that wherever you go, there you are. It was Emerson who wrote that we travel bearing our Giants—what we've done, where we've lived, what we've read, our experiences and memories—on our backs. So, I'm lugging *Hamlet* over the moat into Elsinore, and all my grad school baggage into Anna's apartment, through whose windows Copenhagen's a dead ringer for New Haven, Connecticut, in 1960. And what does one write about when "nothing happened?" Well, we didn't see *The Little Mermaid*, that fragile bronze shell freezing on a rock in the harbor, but we've got her in our hearts and minds, deep in our bones. And when the Giant speaks there's everything to write about.

Laurel: For me the writing problem was not that "nothing happened" but that too much happened—raising an ethical problem. How could I write about things that reflected badly on my host community in Copenhagen without being offensive and rude? I tried to solve that problem in several ways. I used the conversation I had over sushi in which the Visitor urged me to tell the tale. Next, I declared that the piece was about me, not about "them."

Ernest: I understand.

Laurel: And then, I tried to understand my experience in terms of cultural issues as represented in the narratives of Hans Christian Andersen.

Ernest: Look, the visitor wanted you to expose abuses within the dysfunctional family of Denmark, to help rid her country of them. I could extemporize on a universally known dysfunctional literary family from Denmark.

Laurel: [*Laughter.*]

Ernest: There's something rotten in the state of Denmark between the men and women there. Even mentioning such matters raises another ethical issue, though—the specter of political correctness. For anyone, especially an American, to criticize another culture is politically incorrect in the current academic climate. In my opinion this academic parody of Miss Manners is pure hubris, a fascistic, grotesque pressure to curtail freedom of speech and even thought—and for what reason? To what end? But it does pose a problem for the writer.

Laurel: Of course, as a feminist, I am always critiquing cultures, but I was trying to balance telling the tale with protecting the identities of the women involved.

Ernest: It's a reflection of how really awful things must be over there—this fear of the Witch Hunt.

Laurel: Yes—

Ernest: Directed at specific individuals, who are virtually helpless—

Laurel: Right—

Ernest: What a *terrible* reflection on what's going on, that one might be even slightly concerned about such a thing!

Laurel: So, it's worrying about protecting identities of the Copenhagen women on the one hand, and making it clear through the writing that my own department is dysfunctional. Writing this piece I felt as if I was back in the pleats of time, back in the sixties and then back ten years ago when I chose early retirement and discovered the people in charge were happy to see me go.

Ernest: Yes.

Laurel: It's a painful thing to see where you have placed your life and to wonder whether what you have done has lasting consequences or not.

Ernest: You see me struggling with that, too.

Laurel: I know.

Ernest: It also reminds me of my take on Beirut versus the United States—yes, it's dangerous in Beirut but, heck, look at us! And you're saying, well, gee, here's Denmark, and it's like being back in the United States forty years ago—and yet you, yourself, up to the present moment have been struggling with similar issues at home. It's precisely your similar experiences in the United States that make your Copenhagen experience so dismaying.

Laurel: How long have we been together all the time now?

Ernest: Twenty . . . four years?

Laurel: I think it's been years—years—maybe fifteen, since I have written anything so feisty and feminist. Right-smack-in-your-face-feminism! My conclusion, where the Danish woman is bringing down the old bulls—

Ernest: Like Goya's women skewering Napoleon's thugs.

Laurel: Is something I might have slyly written fifteen years ago.

Ernest: Or longer.

Laurel: Yes, even longer ago. Twenty years, or thirty, or more.

Ernest: In fact, I remember some of your early work that had some of that tone.

Laurel: I know my early poetry did. Especially the poems about academia.

Ernest: Nothing since then, though.

Laurel: No. And it surprises me that I am not only psychologically brought back to a period of time when I was an angry feminist, but the tone of my writing reflects that time, too.

Ernest: Yes.

Laurel: And it's, Whoops? Who's writing this now? Who is this person?

Ernest: [*Laughter.*] I picked up a similar mood from you. I was experiencing your ordeal secondhand. "Stranger in a Stranger Land" is all shot through with it.

Laurel: I know.

Ernest: But we wouldn't want to give the impression that our narratives are only about unpleasantness and conflict. They aren't. It wouldn't be true to our total experience of Copenhagen, of Denmark.

Laurel: I agree completely.

Ernest: For me, Denmark was a complex and valuable experience at all levels. I was surprised at its impact, the detail with which I bring it all back, the feelings, the sensations. It's as though my entire life converged upon me there in an almost symphonic flood of memory and desire.

Laurel: So what you write about when "nothing happens" is everything that's happening inside you.

Ernest: That's how it feels. I could write a book about being in Denmark.

Laurel: I spent a long time trying to choose a title. I like the one I finally chose, "Lost in the Space" because I did feel lost in every space. The apartment, the city, the classroom. And as I talk about it now, I still feel lost in the space—as if I'm back in a time that I'm not in anymore. Lost in time and space. It's bewildering and distressing. As you know it took me a very long time to write this. It was a very painful piece to write. One of the most painful I've written because it meant going back to reexperiencing leaving my sociology department.

Ernest: Right.

Laurel: I summarized that experience in less than a half page, an experience that is still niggling at me. . . . Well, maybe more resolved now. . . . But. . . .

Ernest: I've never seen you struggle so much with writing. And it was you who suggested we should write about Copenhagen.

Laurel: Yes.

Ernest: And I had misgivings when you brought it up because, gee, what was I doing but playing hanger-on, kicking footloose around Copenhagen for a week? Yet once I started writing it came out in a flood.

Laurel: I was so envious!

Ernest: Well, I wish writing were always like that. But know what? It isn't.

Laurel: We were also working on what epigraph might start this section. And, I thought the line from your father's novel—

Ernest: "You will hunt it on the map, and it won't be there."

Laurel: The map, yes.

Ernest: I, too, felt lost in the space. And you see me using memory as a crystal ball to find my moorings, telling me what to do and where to go—or, in the case of the Museum of Sex, not to go.

Laurel: Hmm. Mmm.

Ernest: Recalling my father's novel helped me moor myself, in a confounding situation. Also, his words suddenly became concretely clear to me—connecting me with my father, my past, and with myself in ways I won't even try to explain here in the interests of ecology, of preserving entire forests that'd have to be slain for any book this might appear in.

Laurel: You know, in our pieces on Death Valley both of us intertwine getting lost and dying, and here we've done it again. You are lost, with so many death images in your paper. Me lost, and death underpinning mine as well, even when not written explicitly—such as my cousin's death and the 9/11 destruction of her Chambers Street loft. So this is part of our shared emergent mythology, yes?

Ernest: Well, yes. But also the fun I was having with Goya's morbid etchings in the context of our conversation about the gender-relations. We were indeed having that conversation when we were looking at the Goyas. There it is. Life's a veritable smorgasbord of symbols.

Laurel: And I have not a single memory of a single Goya etching. I was so burdened by my experience, my memory is defective.

Ernest: I don't know whether it was for *The Disasters of War* or another series of his etchings, but Goya wrote the epigram, "The sleep of reason breeds monsters," which may underlie our experience—especially yours.

Laurel: That's good.

Ernest: Nice and dark.

Laurel: Let's use two epigraphs for this section.

Ernest: Two for one! And regarding "the sleep of reason," you must have felt in that seminar that you'd been challenged, under conditions of dire threat, to reinvent the wheel, and then justify its very existence.

Laurel: Right.

Ernest: Or, to switch frames, you must've felt like Sisyphus. You've been pushing that boulder up one side of the mountain for your entire professional life and there you are in some seminar room in Copenhagen, and Lo! The boulder's tumbling down the other side.

Laurel: That was one of my favorite myths in college. I was drawn to it because I didn't want a life that begat that kind of hell.

Ernest: The first thing I ever published was an essay on Camus's *Myth of Sisyphus.*

Laurel: I didn't know that.

Ernest: Connections keep turning up.

Laurel: And maybe we're bound to the women of Copenhagen as well, as they try to push back that boulder.

Ernest: Sure. . . . You know, I think the entire experience of Denmark was an epiphany of sorts. I can't recall another place or time where so many strands of my life converged at once. And literature. Shakespeare, Hans Christian Andersen, Beowulf—

Laurel: Don't forget Kipling, Ernest.

Ernest: "A fool there was, and he made his prayer, even as you and I, to a rag and a bone and a hank of hair—we called her 'the woman who could not care,' but the *fool,* he called her his 'Lady Fair,' even as you and I." No, by all means let us not forget the Gospel according to Kipling!

Laurel: I don't know how you do that.

Ernest: What?

Laurel: Just spout out those quotes.

Ernest: Including Tennyson's invigorating translation of *The Battle of Brunanburh*, with which I embellish my narrative?

Laurel: I was wondering where those lines came from. . . .

Ernest: So . . . I feel a powerful spiritual, even a religious quality about our time in Denmark that I'm finding hard to express here, but I wanted to embody it in my piece. For instance, it's in that sculpture in Sweden, outside the church.

Laurel: But what does it mean to you for literary quotes just to pop into your head? For myself, I suppose, it's sociology concepts. . . .

Ernest: Okay, Laurel . . . consider me a Literary Fundamentalist. Your Christian Fundamentalist spouts the Bible—

Laurel: [*Laughter.*]

Ernest: And this particular Literary Fundamentalist spouts English and American Literature.

Laurel: Do you then see the world through those words? Or do those words describe the world to you?

Ernest: I don't know . . . I'm not sure. . . .

Laurel: Do the words enlarge the world? Settle it in a different place?

Ernest: Perhaps in the same way a myth deepens and clarifies raw experience. *The Myth of Sisyphus. Hamlet. The Little Mermaid.* Myth and literature help order and direct your life, so you're not just traveling fecklessly about. They're like a map. We're able to map ourselves onto literature and onto myth.

Laurel: Yes, a map.

Ernest: You will hunt yourself on that map—

Laurel: And here we are.

CHAPTER 5

PETROZAVODSK, RUSSIA

April 16–26, 2000

There's a divinity that shapes our ends,
Rough-hew them how we will—

—William Shakespeare

Out of Russia

Laurel Richardson

So many stories. My mother's, my stepdaughter's, mine. Like travelers, the stories sometimes collide; sometimes pass each other in the night; sometimes glimpse each other in a reflecting pool.

In 1908, my Russian Jewish grandmother brought my mother to America when she was eight. They escaped the pogroms. If they had not, some thirty years later, they would have died at Babi Yar, and I would not be writing this. When I look at pictures of Ellis Island refugees, I scrutinize the black eyes and hair, the tattered brown shoes of little girls. Any one of these girls might have been my mother. She has now been dead some thirty-three years. She would not like me writing about Russia. But the need to do so grows more urgent, for I am now the age my mother was when she died.

An astrologer once told me that in my most recent previous life I was trampled to death by a brace of horses in St. Petersburg. She said I had been a radical Jewish woman, disobeying my well-to-do father, fighting for women's rights. I always liked this past-life metaphor; I had thought of it as commentary on my present life, and probably the only life of which I would be conscious of, anyway.

127

But, when I am in St. Petersburg, I feel as if I am visiting a past life. It's a feeling unlike any I've ever had. I recognize St. Petersburg square, the buildings, the horse sculptures. One golden building declares: You lived here once. When I peek in the doorway, I feel a rush of remembrance, and displacement—the crown molding seems unchanged, but the hallways have been painted a different color. At one street corner, I feel overwhelming sadness.

My step-grandfather, "Jampa," was the only grandfather I ever knew, as my mother's biological father had himself been trampled to death by a horse in Milwaukee before my mother arrived in America. Jampa had been a jewelsmith and watchmaker in St. Petersburg. He escaped from Russia, on foot, carrying his most prized possession, his brass samovar in a black felt bag, on his back. Gramma kept it in her dining room, using it to make pungent tea. When I was five, I asked that the samovar be given to me someday, which it was when Gramma died. It is in my dining room, now. My son, Josh, has asked that it be given to him, someday; and his five-year-old son, Akiva, having heard the story, says, "And someday, it will be mine and then my son's and my son's son's."

I see a similar samovar in a restaurant window in St. Petersburg. Earliest memories return, memories of the first three years of my life, when my grandparents lived with us in a South Side Chicago mansion. My grandfather, then nearly blind, was the only warm hand in that castle. I remember the nightly ritual of sitting on my grandfather's lap. He told me no stories; there were no plots, no characters. But in spectacularly rich detail and always in the present tense, he described what he must have been seeing in his mind's eye, in his memory: the lively horses, carriages, massive gates, brick streets, and golden buildings of St. Petersburg.

Perhaps, when I am in St. Petersburg, I feel Jampa's youth, Jampa's life, asserting itself. Or, perhaps, I am reliving my own "past life" as a little child living amongst Russian-speaking Jews. Jews who took their children out of Russia.

"You don't marry a man," my mother used to say, "you marry the life." Ernest's daughter—my stepdaughter, Susan—married a man, Joe, who wanted the life of an evangelical Christian missionary. She wanted that, too. Eight years married, still childless, they were preparing for a missionary life in Russia, when Susan's fertility surgery succeeded. We rejoiced.

Surely, Susan and Joe would not go to Russia now. But off they went, Susan seven months pregnant.

Three years later, they are raising our two granddaughters, Nadia and Vallia, in Petrozavodsk, a town eight hours north of St. Petersburg by overnight train—or, as Ernest and I traveled this last trip, ten tiring hours by car on a two-lane, pot-holed, bermless, rest stop-less road, the major and only highway going north.

Joe's Russian "right-hand" man, Ivan, a jack-of-all-trades and former professional trucker, tied our luggage on the roof of a small borrowed car, and then climbed into the driver's seat. After four years in Russia, Joe is still not willing to drive outside Petrozavodsk without Ivan: too many unknowns—language barriers, mechanical failures, infrastructural assaults, Vodka-enhanced drivers, and renegade police.

Armed guards stopped and checked us only twice. I wondered if the guards knew we were Americans, and if that was a good or bad thing. Joe thought on average "good." Police did ticket us for going seventy kilometers an hour in a thirty-kilometer zone. The paperwork took close to an hour; Joe paid the police the one thousand rubles—about thirty-five cents. No points were put on Ivan's driving license. "Nyet! Nyet!" he said, laughing, finding the idea absurd.

We arrive in Petrozavodsk. We will stay in the kids' seventh floor, four-room "suburban" apartment, "Stalin Arms." This is 2000. We cannot stay in the town's one hotel because the mafia does not run it, and therefore it is not safe.

We enter a refrigerator-box-sized elevator, inhaling its recent military overstock camouflage green paint job. I'm coughing, and Ernest is almost having an asthma attack. Smiling, Joe comments, "If OSHA were to come to Russia, they would close down the whole country." A few days later, the brake breaks in that elevator, and we zoom toward ground zero. There is no emergency exit, no custodian on duty, no English-speaking 911. Two hours later we are extricated. From then on, Ernest and I climb up and down the seven flights, and three-year-old Nadia happily climbs up and down with us.

The apartment is guarded by a heavy iron gate and multiple steel key locks installed by Ivan. We enter and take off our shoes. Cupboards that Ivan built rise from floor to ceiling down the hallway. They hold a medical arsenal—routine shots, antibiotics, prescription painkillers, allergy medications, syringes, needles, ointments, Band-Aids; off-season stuff; books; secret safes; a shoe rack.

The kitchen, although much smaller, reminds me of the separate kosher kitchen my grandmother kept in our Chicago mansion: crazed porcelain sink, zinc faucets, high cupboards, limited counter space, small refrigerator, old green stove, smooth porcelain-topped table. Boxes of cereals, breads, and grains sit on the counter, the table, and the refrigerator; five-gallon water bottles on the floor. Vallia's highchair blocks the doorway.

Throughout the apartment, the wooden floors shine, windows sparkle, and walls gleam with flowery Wall-Tex. Matruskas, Russian hand-painted boxes and artworks decorate shelves. The air smells of freshly baked apple pies. For thirty-five dollars a month, Susan has a full-time housekeeper/cook/nanny/gofer. Thirty-five dollars is more than the housekeeper earned as an accountant, a job that she lost when the Iron Curtain fell.

Eagerly, Susan turns to the packages containing the things she has asked us to bring her: oregano, cumin, tarragon; Pot-X medium-hot curry sauce; three jars of Jiffy creamy peanut butter; balsamic vinegar; Ponds pore cleanser; Rembrandt toothpaste; Estée Lauder moisturizer; four large tubes of Desitin; shoes, in ascending sizes, for baby Vallia; Carter's size 2 big-girl training pants; size 4 Gymboree turtlenecks, tights, and socks for Nadia in black, forest green, dark blue, light blue, red, pretty pink, white, and cream.

Susan opens the socks, looks at them and sighs. "No. No," she says. "They're too small."

She sighs again.

"Nadia won't have any socks, now!"

"Check them against her old socks," Ernest suggests.

I go with Susan to Nadia and Vallia's bedroom. There is a built-in cupboard holding fancy dresses, underwear, corduroys, turtlenecks, sweaters, tights. Susan takes out a pair of Nadia's old socks and measures them against the new ones. The new ones are much bigger. She sighs and says, "Well, that's a relief."

In Russia, how could one be the kind of loving, caring mother Susan is and not be overcome with anxiety? Just focus on the socks; just focus on the socks. Did my grandmother focus on her children's socks? Did she ever question her choice to leave Russia? Did she question her choice when my mother married my Gentile father?

Joe turns on the television to his favorite station, international CNN. Bombings, tortures, starvations, earthquakes, fires, and plagues enter the living room.

"How can you stand to watch this horror," I ask.

Nadia and Vallia are playing with the Furby we brought them.

"Whenever I feel put upon," he says, "I look at the screen and see how much worse it is for others."

I don't think we even get this station at home.

I look out the picture window to the south. I see the bus stop, kiosks, outdoor market, groves of birch, forests of pines, and, to the north, the apartment complex's backyard dovecote, play equipment, clotheslines, and beyond those, rows upon rows of similar apartment complexes, and then, the Prussian blue of Lake Onega. How pretty! From up here, I cannot see the grime, debris, and animal filth on the pavement and earth or the pigeon dung on the play equipment. Our grandchildren cannot play outdoors.

"I'll just put my shoes on," Nadia says, "and you can take me to America."

My mind turns to our visit two years earlier. The family lived then in a three-room basement flat in central Petrozavodsk. Their toilet could be safely flushed only once a day. Water was never safe for drinking; filtering it three times, though, made it safe enough for laundering the baby's clothes. Vodka-soaked neighbors and passersby, at any time of day or night, used the flat's entranceway as a urinal.

Russian doctors advise parents to take children outside for at least two hours a day, regardless of the weather. Daily, Susan and Joe would take then-baby Nadia out for a carriage ride through the nicest part of their neighborhood, the Petrozavodsk cemetery. We walked with them, admiring plantings and statues, the smooth path and tended lawns, ignoring the grim faces of passersby. No eye contact; no smiles or "oohs and ahs" over the baby carriage; no "hi's" or "*prebyet*'s."

Seeing a wrought-iron fence with what looks to me like a wrought-iron menorah, I ask Joe, "What's that?"

"It's the Jewish cemetery," Joe answers.

The first and last stanzas of a poem I wrote some thirty years ago about a Ku Klux Klan rally in Skokie comes into my head:

> From Moscow to Dachau
> There are cemeteries
> For Jews . . .
> "We are everywhere."

I walk under a blue Star of David suspended between two arches. The cemetery gate is gone; the gravestones broken, markers smashed, Hebrew words defiled. Weeds grow between and on the graves. I suppress my tears. I place a small stone upon a desecrated gravestone. I am thinking that Russian Jews fortunate enough to have been buried and not gassed—as my mother would have been had her mother not taken her to America—do not rest in peace.

I take some photos; Ernest takes some photos. I wish I were alone in the cemetery.

Missionaries Phil and Alice invite some dozen people for dinner, including Ivan and his family. His daughter, Sonia, shows me a picture of her best friend, "a brilliant scholar" of Jewish ancestry, denied admission to the University of St. Petersburg because the quota for Jews, Sonia said, had already been filled. In defiance, this friend named her out-of-wedlock daughter, Rivka, a traditional Jewish name.

"My friend and her daughter will have to leave Russia," she says. "They will not be able to have a life here because of the naming."

The child, a sacrificial lamb? I wonder. The Jewish mother's strategy for getting out of Russia?

I want to tell Sonia about the story I wrote for my synagogue's literary magazine, when I was ten or so, about medical school quotas, but I don't. I let myself pass in Russia, as my mother wanted to in America, and could not in Russia. Now, I let the Russians believe that my mother was a Russian just like them.

Grushenka, the Russian tutor, commands my attention. "We were taught to fear and hate Americans people and you feared and hated Russians people during cold war," she says in broken English.

"Actually," I say, "we were not taught to fear and hate the Russian people, only the government."

Grushenka repeats her statement verbatim twice more.

I say, "Here is a joke I learned in graduate school. What's the difference between Russia and America?"

Shrugs.

"In Russia, man oppresses man, and in America, it's vice versa."

She does not laugh.

"I went to America," Grushenka volunteers. "In Minnesota by Visconsun. To a Christian teaching house. No one shot me. I got back from America without being shot."

I retreat to the one comfortable chair in the apartment, and read a magazine. Ernest snaps my picture.

When it is finally time to leave, I disentangle myself from the kisses, hugs, and petting of Phil and Alice's newly adopted Russian son, Yuri.

"The people at the orphanage liked us so well, because we helped out so much," Phil is telling the assembled group, "that they gave us the choice of three children to adopt: an eight-year-old girl, who was blind; a bedridden two-year-old boy; and six-year-old Yuri!"

Yuri is tinier than three-year-old Nadia. Abandoned by his parents, he has lived his entire life in the orphanage. He has a severe cleft palate, a clubfoot, and genital abnormalities. He will fly Aeroflot to America for surgeries. He is not toilet-trained, yet, and he shows signs of attachment disorder. Attachment disorder children appear to be very loving and warm. They are so needy, though, that their adoptive parents cannot make up the losses they have experienced. Unless treated, when the children grow up their clinginess turns to anger, hostility, and eventually violence toward their parents and others near to them. I am concerned for Nadia and Vallia.

Later, I discuss my concerns about Yuri with Susan.

"Yuri's fine!" she says, emphatically.

She has to believe that, I know. Like immigrants everywhere, these missionaries depend upon each other for friendship, help, community, support—and, for something more—a sense of belonging, meaning, and purpose. The team distributes food to 2,000 families each month; they provide medical supplies to the local clinics; they are setting up a computer center with medical information and online physicians. Because their church is not a registered church in Russia, they cannot promulgate their faith, only model it through their actions.

Two little girls rattle the apartment's iron gate. Susan tells us that their mother is always drunk and doesn't feed them. She gives them each a bag of food and tells them they're always to tell her the truth about their lives. She tries to be a good surrogate mother to them. Nadia looks on.

We get our shoes on; we're going shopping. We buy a dozen hand-painted boxes, about a dollar a box. Three-year-old Nadia translates. We buy her a porcelain doll with little white leather shoes, and laces that won't stay tied. The doll costs about US$10.00—about as much as two hundred loaves of bread or about what Nadia's pediatrician earns in a fortnight. Susan looks for new shoes for herself, but there are none.

"Even old worn-out shoes are snapped up in the outdoor market," she tells us.

Without warning, I am back in the Holocaust Museum in Washington, D.C., and once again overcome by the stench generated by the roomful of gassed people's shoes. There would be a market for those shoes, even now, here in Russia.

We take Joe and Susan by public bus to a Korean karaoke bar and restaurant, the only place in town with good food and genuine imported bottled water, pure and spring-fed. We are the only group in the restaurant. Scattered at tables and standing at doorways are men, alone. Occasionally, one man joins another man. They don't eat or drink or leave together. They barely talk. The restaurant is the place where Russian Mafia hitmen, bagmen, and drug dealers meet and exchange rubles, dollars, goods, and contracts.

Susan and Ernest sing a duet on the karaoke.

My mother had married a criminal lawyer, a Mafia lawyer, my father. Did she think that would protect her from the lawless? Does Susan think she is safe in a mafia-owned bar? Is she? Was my mother?

On our last full day, we take an outing in Ivan's thirty-year-old van, "the loaf." Ivan says he drives the safest vehicle in Russia because, over the years, he has himself replaced all its working parts. The last time I was in the loaf, it hit a bump and I slipped off the hard metal bench-seat, landing sprawl-eagle on the hard metal floor. No bones broken; only bruises.

I enter the loaf with caution. There are seven of us. None of us have seatbelts. Ivan is driving. Joe sits next to him. Nadia is on my lap and Vallia is in her stroller. Ernest is riding backward. The heater is on because the weather is in the forties. We are going two hours north, almost to the Arctic Circle, to see their dacha. It is situated in a little community, on a little hill above a clear little lake, surrounded by big birch and bigger pines. The setting is idyllic.

Wearing a bra and cotton underpants, a heavyset woman in her forties nods to us, and goes about stoking her sauna. Wearing only underpants and work boots without laces or socks, a toothless man in his sixties works his potato field. He engages Joe in conversation. "He wants me to find him an American bride," Joe says, chuckling. "A young, pretty one."

Nadia and Vallia love being at their dacha. Here, they can be outside, touch things, smell flowers, pick up stones, throw sticks in the lake. Susan looks ecstatic. I like it here, too. The air feels fresher; the land sweeter; the people happier; my grandchildren freer.

I wonder if my grandfather's family had a dacha. Do Jews have them now?

After less than an hour of country life, we take our places in the loaf and drive away. A speeding Mercedes throws a rock from its wheel, shattering our windshield into thousands of glass slivers. Ivan, the truck-driver, knows what to do. He slowly—ever so slowly—slows down the car. He slowly, slowly pulls off the road and slowly, slowly stops the loaf. We are in slow motion, but this is not a movie. If he had stopped suddenly, the shards would have flown, like so many daggers, into our faces.

"Joe!" we yell.

Joe doesn't answer.

"Joe! Joe!" We don't know if a shard has fatally wounded him

"I'm okay," he finally says.

He is as white as a Russian winter, as white as my grandmother's porcelain sink, as white as my mother wanted to be. Reliving the terror, to soften it, I have reverted to metaphors. Joe picks broken glass off his jacket, hat, and boot-tops. Ivan and Joe stretch a blanket across the inside of the shattered windshield, and in tandem push the shards out onto the loaf's hood and the roadway. Ivan turns on the windshield wipers, and hands Joe a pair of sunglasses. We laugh. Two hours of driving ahead of

135

us. Police stop us at two checkpoints, but they don't notice or don't care that we are driving without a windshield.

"Has this ever happened to you before?" I ask Ivan.

"Only four or five times," he says.

Nadia and I sing-song the ABC's, "To Market, to Market," and "Yankee Doodle."

Nadia asks if she can come back with us to America.

"I'll just keep my shoes on and we can go," she says.

To Russia with Love

Ernest Lockridge

Four of us, full-grown adults, are crammed into a box only a tad larger than one of those vacant-lot freezers where, too late, they find your missing child. Our oubliette sports a foul coat of Railroad-Salvage-vintage rust-and-barnacle-proof molasses-thick khaki goo, through which peers a substrate of Cyrillic graffiti run amok. It's Friday evening in April 2000. Out for a night on the town, we had stepped into the elevator, my wife and I, my daughter and her husband, heading for the best little restaurant in Carelia, a Korean karaoke owned and operated by the Russian mob. Creaking steel doors a half-foot thick clamped us in. A bulb extrudes ten watts worth of corpse-green light as the elevator heads into free-fall and lurches to a grinding screeching halt somewhere between the seventh and first floors of the Stalin Arms in Petrozavodsk, Russia, on scenic Lake Onega, where for the past three years my daughter and son-in-law have served as missionaries.

In kicks my claustrophobia. My wife touches the shuddering small of my back. "Look, Ernest, we'll be fine."

"This sort of thing happens all the time," my daughter reassures me.

Son-in-law Joe slams a big fist against the elevator's gluey wall and Lo! From some invisible intercom floats a disembodied female voice, abrupt, annoyed, speaking Russian. Joe translates sporadically.

"Why is it you are disturbing me?"

"Look, there are four of us stuck here in the elevator."

"And what this has to do with me?"

"We urgently require help in breaking out of here."

"Is Friday. Everyone gone. Expect Russian people to place lives on hold for your convenience?"

"Nyet! Here we are on the verge of suffocation."

"Must extricate own selves. Otherwise you are trapped there 'till Monday, perhaps Tuesday."

"Okay, Ernest, let's give 'er the old college try." My son-in-law, an ex-wrestler, pries at one door with both hands, fingertips abutting the crack, while I apply myself to the opposing door. In spite of our grunting effort the doors fail to budge, and I suppress a cheap crack regarding the Power of Prayer, respecting their mission, and seeing advantages in their current life when they're not trapped in elevators. Ohio found them trapped in low-paying, work-intensive jobs. There, Joe was hawking industrial-strength valves over the telephone. Here, during the long winter now drawing to a close, he and his Petrozavodsk buddies ice-fished on Onega, a frozen expanse the size of Lake Erie. With machine pistols they pursued moose over the tundra. Once an overworked social worker, my daughter can now devote herself to full-time mothering. She even has a full-time helper, Veruska, a KGB accountant whose job expired with the Soviet Union. Worn-looking at thirty-seven, Veruska worries endlessly that her draft-age son will be dropped into the Chechnyan meat grinder.

Joe slams the elevator's side for a second time.

"Have succeeded, no?" proclaims the ectoplasm.

"Nyet! Doors will not budge by even a hair."

"Weaklings!"

"Nyet! Is being deprived of breath!"

"Don't worry, Dad, Joe's exaggerating to make a point."

"Four Westerners in one elevator! All own doing!"

"Nyet! Help required, not bickering!"

"There must be a little air coming from the elevator shaft, Dad. Otherwise we'd all be passed out."

Making a feeble effort to appear suave, even graceful under pressure, I manage to gasp, "I could be bounded in a nutshell and count myself king of infinite space," plagiarizing this witticism of sorts from the Bard. Only a couple of days prior to our arrival in Russia my wife and I, during a stay in Denmark, had taken the train to Helsingor, where we made our timorous way through the crepuscular dungeons of Elsinore, ancestral palace and sarcophagus of Hamlet, Prince of Denmark. The dungeon-master had called in sick. The tour was a do-it-yourself affair. Fading arrows on the dank, oozing walls had directed us over the slippery cobblestones of the maze and, at last, out into a dismal Danish drizzle.

"Westerners!" says the Phantom of the Elevator. "Fat!"

Joe shouts, "NYET! Do you imagine for one instant that when we expire horribly, suffocating and starving, that our two governments will be at all pleased with your grudging reluctance to send even one of your countrymen to our aid?"

Long silence, then sullenly, "Have contacted workman. Maybe there in hour, two hour, three hour. Must await *with patience*."

"Ernest and I would really enjoy hearing the story of how you two got together," says my wife.

While my daughter is recounting the blithe familiar romance, my mind, bounded in its nutshell, is busy assailing me with other aspects of our predicament. Shortly before boarding the flight from Copenhagen to St. Petersburg we learned that a phantom Swedish SAS agent, one "Beata," had summarily canceled our return, reassigning our seats to strangers. Return flights are now full, and we have been transferred onto a waiting list. Everything is up in the air 'till we get back to St. Petersburg International, a hard day's drive from Petrozavodsk, and Joe's Lada SUV, fresh from the factory, has broken down, transmission a clamorous chaos of sheared bearings and stripped gears. Not knowing when Moscow will send a replacement. Then there are our visas. Upon entering the city limits, we non-Petrozavodskians must present our papers to the Local Authorities, who inform us that our visas, cut to order by the Russian Embassy in Washington, D.C., emit the distinct aroma of rot. Local Authorities confiscated them on the spot. They confiscated our passports. Without papers we are trapped.

Our 1997 visit to Russia three years ago taught us the supreme importance that Authorities here attach to a sound visa. Cooling our heels at Petrozavodsk International (closed the following month to nonmilitary aircraft), awaiting the puddle-jumper back to Helsinki, we watched Visa Control unceremoniously pack a tuxedo-clad dignitary back onto the aircraft in which he had just arrived. Even the welcoming throng with their musical instruments and bouquets could not save him. We watched helplessly as an infant was stripped of his reentry visa after the parents,

Petrozavodsk residents, had bundled him past the point of no return. The two officials in the cramped booth, grinning crocodiles clothed in shabby Stalin-era uniforms, a man and a woman, emerged to pronounce these cruel verdicts from their marathon bout of mutual flirtation. The bewildered parents remained free to reenter the Motherland at any time simply by walking back the way they came—having first, of course, abandoned their infant son on the tarmac.

The Korean karaoke club is to be our first restaurant dinner since arriving in Petrozavodsk. 'Till now we've been dining out with missionaries and local friends in their apartments. Last night at the apartment of missionaries Phil and Alice, a half-dozen Petrozavodskians were in attendance, including an English-language instructor and her husband, an unemployed former bank manager. He wears the bewildered, stunned look of any well-groomed and educated, law-abiding, dignified professional man when he's told: "Sir, it is my unpleasant duty to, so to speak, kick your ass out!" Fired three years ago, he utters scarcely a syllable all evening. "Actually, we, ourselves, have visited your United States," says his wife. "You have heard of someplace called Minnesota?"

"Minnesota is one of the United States," I reply.

"Well, then, Sir, many years ago as part of an exchange of educators between our two nations, United States and Soviet Union, I and this husband, who was allowed to accompany me, were sent to a village in Minnesota named"—some rural Shang-ri-la floating in an ocean of grain. "And here is most amazing thing!" Her eyes widen with wonder. "Neither I nor husband are shot at. Since three entire days in Minnesota we are not even robbed."

Is she joking? "What a strange coincidence," I venture. "I've lived in the United States for six decades, and that hasn't happened to me either."

Constructing a thin-lipped smile, the English instructor replies with utter scorn, "You are no longer under any necessity to present your slaughterhouse of a nation in an insincere or overly flattering light. This evening you are among friends. You may tell exact truth. I guarantee, upon my word, that nothing you say will ever leave these premises." She indicates the cramped dining room. Like other Russian apartments we've seen, Phil and Alice's would fit tidily into the kitchen and dining room of our modest Ohio Cape Cod. Stalin decreed that no one required square footage greater than his own miserable boyhood hovel's.

Several days ago while flying over the Atlantic I happened to read a *New Yorker* exposé of the Russian Mafia, brutes with doctorates in physics and math, and a bottomless cynicism toward all legal authority thanks to their years under Communism. These thugs, with their genius IQs, now dominate organized crime worldwide. By all odds Russian mobsters should have already mugged me back in Ohio. Here in Petrozavodsk, according to Joe, mafia thugs burglarize the old women, pensioners, whom we see begging kopeks for bread and rent. The burglars cut their elderly victims' throats to tidy up. The one hotel in Petrozavodsk is not safe for tourists because it does not belong to the mob. In the Stalin Arms my daughter and son-in-law's apartment has an iron gate, triple-locked. They could be in Minnesota, of course, where the living is dangerous. "Well," I say, "uh, what about your uh Russian Mafia?"

"If I may be so bold as to ask this of you, Sir," the English instructor coldly replies, "what precisely is this putative 'Russian Mafia'? Personally, I have never heard even the slightest mention of a 'Russian Mafia.'"

As I fumble out a kopek's worth of my *New Yorker*ish knowledge, cynicism infuses her pale face with color, with fiendish glee. Witheringly she cuts in, "Surely you are not meaning to leave me with the totally ludicrous impression that the people of your nation believe everything they read!"

Phil and Alice have just adopted six-year-old Yuri from an impoverished Russian orphanage. Yuri was born with a cleft palate. His appearance is heart-rending. We have been told that his genitals are deformed. A series of corrective surgeries in Ohio is in the works. Smaller at six than my granddaughter Nadia at three, Yuri greets adults with yelps and embraces, his eyes gleaming with a wild joy that announces, "At last! Mamma! Papa!" Poor little guy. No need to worry, yet, when Nadia appears now in the dining room to announce that she and Yuri plan to get married.

Retreating from the English instructor, I join the discussion Joe is having with Alexander, an artist whose exquisite icon of the Virgin Mary we've purchased for pocket change. Alexander worries that democracy is merely a euphemism for "kleptocracy." Russia, he says, has ousted the Tyrants from their den only to replace them with Thieves. His beloved country is not merely "For Sale," it is "On Sale." To us, this is old news. Yesterday in downtown Petrozavodsk's "Official Outlet for the Sale of Antiquities" we shelled out a mere thirty bucks for a nineteenth-century enameled box and a couple of eighteenth-century icons. "Isn't there a problem smuggling uh getting national treasures such as these things across your border?" I asked the clerk, an impeccably dressed Andrei Gromyko look-alike.

"Oh, not to worry, my good friend, all is quite legal and above board. Here we are already drawing up official papers attesting that these national treasures are of no further cultural value and may therefore be permitted out of the country." The papers, with their florid John Hancocks and ornate seals, are fit for framing. Spiriting our swag from the shop, I'd remarked to my wife, "When we get back to St. Petersburg let's find out the asking price for St. Isaac's Cathedral."

Joe is saying, "Yeah, Alexander, in lots of ways capitalism really does suck. Unfortunately, everything else seems to result in these really terrible tyrannies." The long drive north from St. Petersburg International to Petrozavodsk had taken us through countryside of unparalleled openness, and through hamlets within whose constricted boundaries the citizens had once been trapped by law. I think that Shostakovich's twisted melodies, his rancid anthems and lullabies deformed in nightmares, give voice to the tyranny of Stalin writhing within the human spirit. Back in 1997, Joe's driver Ivan had taken us to "oh, Ernest! the most beautiful spot in all of Russia." This turned out to be a picturesque little waterfall, a stone's throw from Petrozavodsk. Bright cloth streamers festooned the scrub birch along the riverbank overlooking the waterfall. "Hey, Ivan. These things left over from some sort of festival?" I'd asked.

"Oh no, Ernest. We tear cloth from clothing and leave it as pledge that one day we shall return."

"Wow, Ivan. You must've been coming here since you were a kid."

"Oh no, Ernest. Petrozavodsk was prison. Three years ago Ludmilla and I are permitted here for first time."

Ivan and Ludmilla, married thirty-five years, are here at Phil and Alice's, along with their daughter Sonya and her year-old daughter. This is no country for young men. The few jobs pay next to nothing. Young men spend their days chain-smoking the toxic Russian cigarettes, two cents a pack, and swilling the cheap Russian vodka. Sonya, attractive, lively, and in her thirties, selected the best among the unmarriageable young men of her acquaintance with whom to become pregnant. She carries a snapshot of a bewildered-looking fellow holding her child in his lap. Ivan and Ludmilla are happy with their granddaughter, and with Sonya, their only child.

Ivan, built like a boxer, has the eyes of a Cossack. A local trucker for most of his working life, he now works full-time for Joe at two hundred dollars each month, a salary placed solidly in context for us by the glamorous-looking couple here at Phil and Alice's, physicians—he's a pathologist, she's a pediatrician and an Olympic silver medalist—who receive a combined monthly salary of thirty bucks. They and their nine-year-old son live with her mother, a pensioner, in the mother's rent-controlled cubicle, and are saving a few rubles per month toward their own apartment. There are no mortgages in Russia. Ivan is overseeing construction of a dacha and sauna on a sylvan lake for my son-in-law and daughter. The existing dacha is being demolished and carted away. Labor and materials are dirt-cheap. The purchase deed names Ivan the owner. Russian law forbids selling off the Motherland to foreigners.

As we were returning from the dacha site a pebble slung by a Mercedes with blackened windows shattered the windshield of Ivan's weather-beaten Lada van, called a *bohonka*, or "loaf," for its resemblance to the coarse cheap staple of the Russian diet. Ivan calmly steers his loaf onto the berm. From inside he spreads an old Army blanket over the spidery chaos of glass and, in tandem with Joe, gently nurses it out. A precious Cohiba smoldering ambrosially in the ashtray must be discarded: a dusting of glass has rendered the cigar lethal. On the road again, Ivan dons sunglasses, hands a pair to Joe and switches on the windshield wipers, which dance a slapstick pas de deux in the empty space. . . .

We've been boxed inside the elevator for nearly two hours when there occurs a violent clanking below us in the shaft. The feeble elevator light goes dead, suspending four fragile souls in silent, endless night. Then Lo! Our straitjacket begins a nearly imperceptible upward movement followed by rapid acceleration, levitating us to the ultimate story, the eighth, where the portals creak apart and out we stagger onto the grimy concrete apron of the Penthouse of Liberty.

A half hour later my daughter and I are belting out a duet. "Country roads take me home!" Her voice is a Salvation Army angel's, mine the croak of a bullfrog that gargles with Rustoleum. The karaoke's local clientele appear exhausted from their ferocious daylong Slaughter of the Innocents. The following day brings the restoration of our passports and visas. "I bet you offered a bribe to those bastards, Joe." "Aw, Ernest, come on." "Well, would you at least let me reimburse you?" "Aw, Ernest, why don't we just chalk it up to the grace of You-Know-Who."

And that's the news from Lake Onega—except for a trail of scraps, a kite string's-worth of leftovers. Furby, for instance, the gift we brought from Copenhagen, resembling a koala bear crossed with an owl. "Oh tolu!" it cries to the grandchildren. "Me koko! Yooom, Da Da, frightened!" Joe wonders aloud how much longer he can expect Furby's batteries to hold out. Eerily from the garbage shaft of the Stalin Arms there floats a haunting ultraviolet glow, Stalin's ghost condemned for his foul crimes to fast in fires and doomed to walk the night. Ten years after the fall of Communism pedestrians still cringe reflexively whenever an officer in the Russian Army wearing full uniform, pistol strapped to his waist, strolls casually into their midst. Three years ago the golden girls of Petrozavodsk, heron-legged, were flocking the sidewalks. They've vanished now into the chicken coop of White Slavery. Spring thaw reveals a city defaced with trash. Within a single day, the citizens of Petrozavodsk have raked this into smoldering piles. In the Jewish cemetery we wade through weeds and scrub, stepping over the shattered markers, shards, granite splinters scored with letters of the Hebrew alphabet. Begging food and clothing, hoydens with sticks clang the apartment's iron gate like chimes. A month later, while my daughter, son-in-law, granddaughters are away in London, burglars steal everything. They steal the iron gate.

A fresh transmission arrives from Moscow for the SUV. At St. Petersburg International Airport no official even asks to see the fancy documents absolving us of the theft of national treasures. And soon, our lost seats having been restored unto us, flights of icons wing us to the West.

Conversation: Russia

January 23, 2001

Ernest: What I want to write about now are my own experiences. Experiences I'm trying to understand. Whether I communicate them to someone else is secondary. And I'm not much interested in making things up. I'd rather weave real experiences into a pattern for the sake of understanding them, or find the pattern that underlies the experience. Connecting the dots. Or discovering a pattern that expresses what I'm feeling. Russia disturbs me. Are my children and grandchildren safe there? Or, just how unsafe are they? How much should I worry?

Laurel: I'm intrigued that you are more interested in making meaning of actual experiences in your life than in writing from your imagination. Do you think hanging out with ethnographers has affected you?

Ernest: Yes, it seems that I'm in good company. I'm especially impressed to observe that ethnographers never, but never, make anything up.

Laurel: [*Laughter.*] Of course not! But I also hear you say you're not interested in necessarily tying your experiences to some Grand Truth.

Ernest: Right. Capturing the concrete experience is more than enough, thank you.

Laurel: Are you mind reading my list of Top Ten Writing Thoughts? That's number four. . . .

Ernest: Hmm.

Laurel: Writing is always done in a specific, local, historical context.

Ernest: Maybe we're trading dreams again, but daydreams.

Laurel: Lucid ones, I hope. My own writing's become more focused on concrete experiences, too, letting a detail communicate my deeply felt, internalized experience. I've come to view writing more and more as a sacred activity.

Ernest: And reading can be sacred. You're taking life into yourself; you're giving life to someone else's soul or spirit when you're reading . . . Longfellow, Dickinson, Shakespeare. . . .

Laurel: But first there's writing, mine, yours, somebody's. What I'm thinking about, here, is that often when I'm writing a first draft time passes unnoticed, space unnoticed, and, then, Whammo! I know something I didn't know about the world or myself. And then sometimes during the revision process, I feel deeply connected to others. I shape my text with others in mind. Then, too, I experience time and space as a single dimension. I think our Russia papers try to recreate or represent time and space as inseparable.

Ernest: Right.

Laurel: And, yes, when you're reading, time and space become one. You are connected to others historically—those in your space and not in your space, those alive and those who have never lived off the page. I find this one of the most fascinating things about written language.

Ernest: The past can seem to stand still, unlike the present as we live it. Then, when we write about the past we set it back in motion, but in whatever order we may choose, connecting the dots to reveal hidden similarities, camouflaged patterns of cause and effect—

Laurel: Discovering or creating thematic connections.

Ernest: You observe this array of the past as standing still and say to yourself, "oh, that and that and that all seem to match." So, you rearrange them together on a shelf.

Laurel: That process of putting things on a shelf offers to others a strategy for reshelving, if you will, the boxes and jars that have constituted *their* lives.

Ernest: We appear to be spawning a whole new intellectual discipline. The Mid-Ohio School of Cultural Study and Interior Decoration.

Laurel: Why not? Relevant here, I think, is that in the past I worked to make my writing's structure invisible, seamless, like hiding the decorator's touch. But now, I want the reader to see my writing choices, the structure of my texts. I like having a visible structure, a "bookcase" that holds the shelves that hold the boxes that hold my memories that hold my experiences. I think seeing structure helps readers make connections to and in their own lives, too. I may be wrong about this.

Ernest: When we write, there are things we're conscious of and things we aren't—cultural and biological modalities, for instance, that inevitably shape our perceptions and how we transform these into language. The reader may be more aware than the writer of these influences.

Laurel: That's right. Multiple interpretations. Different decorators. Other people's boxes on my shelf; my boxes on their shelves. One way to accomplish this may be buried in a writing technique we both used— the dislocation of ourselves/readers in space and time. My thematic material just took over—as though I had no choice. But, how come you did that? Was it the shock of being stuck in an elevator? Was it a literary decision?

Ernest: My most intense experience over there was being trapped in the elevator, and this seemed to embody so many other experiences that it became a sort of synecdoche, if I may be permitted a lapse into overt pretension. My experience seems almost to have dictated my technique. On the other hand, there's always my surname, Lockridge, ready-cocked to deliver perhaps yet another unconscious aftershock.

Laurel: What? Now, you're mind reading my reading! The last thing I underlined in Cixous last night was about the unconscious effects of our proper names. I fell asleep thinking how my name is at odds with itself. The anagram of my given name is "Allure," and I write to fulfill its promise. But my surname, "Richard's son," is something I'm not—something my writing resists.

Ernest: There are more things in heaven or earth than are dreamed of in our philosophy, looks like. Trapped in the wrong surnames!

Laurel: And in the elevator where you begin your narrative. But I had a terrible time getting into mine. Other stories kept intruding. Other boxes kept falling off the shelves and hitting me on the head. But when I finally let myself write about those boxes, I discovered that my topic was not our trip to Russia: it was *allure*—the allure of emigrating from Russia, the allure of moving to Russia, and the consequences thereof for children. And, then, the literary device of shoes as metaphor for coming and going, moving and changing, walked all over my text, moving the text through three centuries and three continents—from my grandfather's history to my grandson's future.

Space/time felt like one. In Hebrew, there is a single word, *olam*, which means unending space or unending time, the universe or eternity. Perhaps I'll construe *olam* to mean both simultaneously. Why not? It's my life. My paper. I'm not making sense—

Ernest: I think you are. Go on.

Laurel: The process of writing was not only making meaning of our difficult trip to Russia, but it was making meaning of my grandparents' life and my life as a young child. I obviously had spent the first three years of my life with Russian-speaking people. I must have known rudimentary Russian. I don't remember it.

Ernest: Whatever we're experiencing involves our entire past—the causal skein that brought us here, what we recall and what we don't, what's in our body-memory like typing or playing piano—and this holds true whenever and whatever we happen to be writing.

Laurel: And, then when we are writing about local, concrete experiences, the interiorized cultural critic can arise, also, in a site-specific, time-specific way. For example, although I am deeply concerned with anti-Semitism in Russia, historically and contemporaneously, I consider it in particular sites, not as generalized anti-Semitism. Readers can perhaps see where the critique applies to their heritage and future.

Ernest: How does it feel to be trapped at the mercy of some mechanical, inhuman tyranny even now? What must it have felt like under Stalin? And lest we feel complacent, here's our Russian visitor simply terrified of being at any moment mugged and shot in the Minnesota outback. And the United States is a place where people do get mugged and shot. Including, I imagine, the occasional Minnesotan.

Laurel: If one writes to make meaning of one's experience in one's life and does so with a certain ruthlessness, suffering through the writing anxieties, I would submit, one cannot help but simultaneously connect to others and do cultural critique.

Ernest: Hamlet—probably the archetype of someone trying to understand his life—is also trying to understand his country and his culture. There's something rotten in the state of Denmark, and by golly he not only researches the problem, he attacks it sword in hand.

Laurel: Shakespeare lives!

Ernest: *Hamlet*'s not just about some mythical ancient Denmark, of course. It's about—well, just about everything, isn't it?

Laurel: Ah, yes!

Ernest: And as part of our quest to understand ourselves, we must have some understanding of the culture in which we are enmeshed—

Laurel: Or the cultures we've inherited. Speaking of which, I can't be in Russia without bringing in my Russian family history. So, I wonder about you and Russia, and where your hometown, Bloomington, Indiana, fits in.

Ernest: "Four of us are crammed in a box no larger than one of those vacant lot freezers where you find your missing child too late"—that's Bloomington. "Rustoleum" is Bloomington, too. And Otis Elevator built a plant there in the 1950s.

Laurel: And Russia today—it's Bloomington, Indiana, in the 1940s and 1950s, your growing-up years.

Ernest: In fact, Petrozavodsk is very much as I remember Boston, where I lived as a child during World War II.

Laurel: And the trip to the Russian countryside reminded me of my family's going, every summer of my childhood, from Chicago to our "dacha" on Lake Geneva in Wisconsin.

Ernest: We're a couple of kites trailing the tails of our pasts behind us. Something rotten in the state of Russia—just something, though, not everything. Mostly, not, mostly not rotten. Something rotten in Minnesota. But Lake Woebegone's in Minnesota.

Laurel: And Lake Onega is in Russia, and it's beautiful.

Ernest: Beautiful.

CHAPTER 6
ST. PETERSBURG BEACH, FLORIDA
March 2–9, 2002

The little waves, with their soft, white hands
Efface the footprints in the sands,
And the tide rises, the tide falls.

—Henry Wadsworth Longfellow

On the Beach

Laurel Richardson

"It feels so good," I say to Ernest as the first rush of humidity hits my skin. "It is so beautiful here." The plane has landed safely, my first flight since 9/11. I breathe deeply, breathing in, I imagine, millions and millions of zaps of the happiness potions that live in the sea; some call them "negative ions."

We've come for the ninth time to St. Petersburg Beach's Gulfgate Condos, a truncated pyramid five stories high, less than a hundred yards from the sea. This time we're in condo #504, facing the gulf to the west, the Intercoastal Waterway to the east. All condos are identically furnished and color-coordinated, swirls of turquoise, shrimp, and shell on the Wall-Tex, chair covers, upholstery, pictures, dishes, towels, sheets. I sink into the comfort of the cliché.

St. Pete Beach satisfies me the way no other beach has. Five miles of white sand, neither too fine nor too shelly; just right for bare feet. To the south of our condo, low rise condos, Floridian houses, sand dunes, grasses, the confectionary pinkness of the Don CeSar Hotel, and at the tip, the dinky Pass-A-Grille fishing pier. To the north, the Holiday Inn, round and perched like a spaceship readying for take off, and past it the hotels, beach volleyball, sand castles, discos. Young couples, mid-age couples, and leathered octogenarians in skimpy suits walk the beach. Families gather in cabanas. Nobody has boom boxes. Nobody says, "Have a nice day."

But what satisfies me the most is the crescent shape of the beach, like a new moon. Anywhere on the beach I can see the whole beach, its ending and its beginning. Which is which depends on the direction I walk. Whichever direction I walk I feel cradled and safe, surrounded by beauty. "It is so beautiful here," I say over and over again as Ernest and I take our first beach walk. Nothing else occurs to me to say. Nothing else need be said.

We leave the sliding glass door open so the sound of the waves can lull us to sleep. We wake early, unusual for us. I think there must be something the matter with me because I feel so good.

Standing on our balcony, I call out, "Ernest, come look at the water! I've never seen it look this way."

"The wrinkled sea beneath him crawls."

"That's exactly right! The sea is wrinkled and it is crawling toward us."

"He watches from his mountain walls,"

"Or condo—"

"And like a thunderbolt he falls."

"Did you just make that up?"

"I'm flattered," he says, "but no, it's Tennyson's. It's about an eagle. Do you want to hear the first stanza?"

I nod my head "yes," feeling that pleasurable rush of anticipation that I always feel when Ernest recites a poem. How many poems does he know by heart? When was the last time he recited this one? Probably forty years ago. I turn toward him to hear *The Eagle*:

"He clasps the crag with crooked hands; close to the sun in lonely lands, ringed with the azure world he stands."

"The second stanza, again, *please!*"

"The wrinkled sea beneath him crawls; he watches from his mountain walls, and like a thunderbolt he falls."

Am I like that eagle, grasping my life with aging hands, high up, now, near the sun, away from home, enveloped by azure sky and sea? Will I recognize whatever it is I've come for and go for it? *Like a thunderbolt?*

We beach-walk southward, to Pass-A-Grille, the little spit from which you can see the sunrise and the sunset. The brown pelicans are back. We recognize, we are sure, the Old One commanding the "T" of the fishing pier, like a security guard, checking passports. He lets us pass. A gray heron arrives, stares unmercifully at a juvenile pelican, until the babe leaves its prime post atop the highest outcropping. Like the conquering fellow he is, the heron assumes his rightful place in this sea world's pecking order. A rotund woman catches a flat fish, the Japanese visitors do not. "No sushi," one comments as they depart.

We depart, too, and walk to Ninth Avenue, Pass-A-Grille's business district—three stores, a post office, a biker bar, and a psychotherapist's office.

"Did you bring your earring?" Ernest asks me as we ring the bell for entry into Evander Preston's store, a mélange of gold jewelry and objects for sale, and artifacts not for sale. Visiting the store is one of our St. Pete Beach rituals.

"No, I decided not to."

Six years earlier Ernest had bought me a pair of gold earrings, flat and smooth with wrinkled edges like the sea, hand crafted by Evander. The next October, I lost one earring on Doe Mountain in Sedona. We searched for it with eyes and hands, sifting through red earth, moving small red stones, and then surrendered it as a gift to the mountain. Each year when we return to Sedona, we climb Doe Mountain, wonder if the earring will show itself, and when it doesn't, we reaffirm the gift of gold.

"Would you like a replacement earring for Christmas?" Ernest had asked me.

"It was the only pair of its kind," Tiffany, Evander's assistant, told Ernest on the phone. "But Evander can make a match if you send back the one you have. It might take awhile." Two Christmases later the earrings arrived in a leather drawstring bag, "Evander Preston" embossed on it in gold script. Just like him, I thought, to have "signature" packaging.

I wear the earrings often, pushing them against my lobes so I can feel that I have not lost them. The week before we are to come this time to St. Pete Beach, I am nearly asleep when I feel the earrings pressing against my skin. I take them off and put them on my bed stand, probably near the edge, and forget about them.

"I've sucked one of your earrings into my vacuum cleaner," Dee says. "I heard it go 'thump.'" She's a conscientious and careful cleaner, and she's very upset.

"It's okay," I tell her. "Don't worry about it."

"I've looked through that vacuum cleaner bag twice," Ernest tells me coming in coughing and sooty from the garage. "I can't find the earring."

Evander has a cultivated leonine persona, a long yellowish-gray mane and beard, light downy skin; he paces and lumbers with his chin raised, and growls. He is not a pussycat. He is an epicurean, an adventurer, an artist-craftsman, and, if I can believe his "signature" T-shirt—"It is better to be a known drunk than an anonymous alcoholic"—a tippler.

A calligraphic sign on the window says, "Sometimes open from 10–3."

"I decided not to bring the unlost earring," I repeat, as Tiffany lets us in. We recognize her, but she does not recognize us. The last time we were here she seemed buzzed.

"Anything special?" she asks.

"We're just looking," we say, almost in unison.

"Enjoy!"

Tiffany disappears into the studio. We browse the cases: hand-crafted gold earrings, rings, necklaces; African masks, Indonesian jars, Japanese netsukes; a miniature gem-encrusted gold train going round on its gold track; a set of miniature working tools, gold pliers, hammer, measurers, screwdrivers, scissors, paper clips; little gold acrobats; full-scale whips, cowboy pistols, spears. Two motorcycles are on the floor—a small one with a sidecar and another, a sculpture, welded from mangled cycle pieces. The back hall holds memorabilia of Evander with notables; a framed letter signed "Bill Clinton" thanks Evander for his gift and says Clinton "will further the American dream in new ways." I wonder if Evander gave him one of the "known drunk" T-shirts stashed in the painted armoire along with a more exotic gift, like the acrobats not having sex. Beyond the back hall, I can see the studio and the kitchen. Evander's not in today.

"I miss the Harley," Ernest says. "Everything seems scaled back here from our last visit. Less imaginative and playful. Less flamboyant."

As I nod my head in agreement, I feel a presence behind me.

"That's Asia," Tiffany says, breathlessly. "She's eight months old and a perfect love."

"She's getting to know me," I say, encouraging the Great Dane to put her nose somewhere else.

"Thanks," we say, as we leave the store.

There's nothing here I want. Nothing here for me.

We beach-walk back to our condo, rest, eat, read, watch TV. Bill Clinton gives up his law practice. The historian Doris Kearns Goodwin gives up her seat on the Pulitzer Prize committee. On "West Wing," the First Lady gives up her medical license. In *The Patchwork Planet*, the novel I am reading, the narrator gives up his family fortune.

We awake to a wild sky and thirty-eight degrees. I feel wonderful, and I don't know why.

"Let's drive to Naples today," I say. "I want to look at condos." Six years ago, we had visited old Naples, and I'd found it charming. Several people I know have recently bought condos in Naples—the fastest growing community in America—and I have had it in my mind of late that I'd like one, too. Not that I can afford one, but if I depleted my stocks and made Naples my winter home, well, then, yes, maybe.

On our drive back, I spot a high-riding panel truck: Wild Animal Patrol.

A lifelong habit of mine is to imagine myself in a specific job and then recoil from the idea in horror. "That's a job I'd like," I announce, surprising myself. "I'd like to capture wild animals that have strayed from their homes and bring them back safely."

"Are you thinking about Naples?" Ernest asks.

"It was horrible, wasn't it? Malls and strip malls. Untimed lights. Gridlock. All those angry people in cars stuck in traffic."

I have trouble falling asleep that night, perhaps because the car exhaust triggered my allergies, but more likely because my friend Carolyn is coming from Tampa in the afternoon to beach-walk with me and I want to be awake and fresh. This is another one of my lifelong habits: if I have to be up for something special, I can't fall asleep because my anxiety over not getting enough sleep keeps me from getting to sleep. So, I get up and take a sleeping pill.

Ten years ago I met Carolyn and discovered St. Pete Beach. She organized a sociology conference that featured poetry, memoir, and theater—the kind of emotionally present writing that we were both doing. We see in each other kindred spirits on parallel journeys, and we choose to have our paths cross, literally and figuratively.

"A perfect day for a beach walk!" Carolyn says in her soothing Virginia accent. We begin walking northward, chit-chatting.

"I've agreed to do a workshop for a social science college, but I really don't want to do it," I tell her. "The organizer is disorganized and demanding. Now, she wants me to mediate their curriculum issues, analyze their position statements, and teach them research methods—all in two days. Plus, the flight is five hours—on a commuter jet. Plus they've not settled my lodging!" With the case I've built against the hapless college, I know I can count on Carolyn for support.

"Sounds like you don't want to go," she says. "Going won't just be treading water, it will be pulling you back to another time, like an undertow. Bail out!"

Then she smiles at me and asks, "So, what are you working on?"

I can answer her honestly. "I've been working on 'letting go'—letting go of being a professor, and letting go of writing for sociological audiences. I'm trying to 'retire.'" (*There*, I say to myself, *I've uttered that horrid, frightening "r" word*.) "I'm letting go of the familiar place where I have stood. My predictable world. I am being a *writer*."

Carolyn listens intently. She is ten years younger than I, and she sees this twist in my journey as one she might well have in hers. We reach the northern tip of the beach and turn back southward.

I say, "I'm trying to enter another world—trying to find places for my writing—but the universe does not seem to be cooperating."

I tell her the sad tale of writing venues. Literary magazines are dying out. My university library subscribes to less than fifteen literary journals, most of which do not accept nonfiction; the public library subscribes to none; Borders bookstore carries two; Barnes and Noble, none. Commercial magazines publish articles about celebrities, international politics, and how-to's, or excerpts from books published by the magazine's parent publishing house. The two thousand-magazine database of *Writer's Market Online* offers only three places that accept unsolicited nonfiction work about women.

I can whine to Carolyn. And I do.

"The *Michigan Quarterly Review* had a call on the Net for articles on 'Jewish in America.' Send papers, it said, between February 1 and April 30. Perfect, I thought, for my new piece 'Looking Jewish,' which I sent on Valentine's Day. Within the week, it was returned with a note: they've received boxes of memoirs—mine was "interesting"—but the quota had been met before the first deadline. First deadline? What first deadline? Probably that was the deadline for the invited papers from their friends," I conclude on a righteous note.

"How frustrating," Carolyn says. "Why didn't they just say 'no memoirs' in their call?"

"Well, what if Saul Bellow submitted one?"

We chuckle, and I am feeling lighter.

"I'm moving from where I was and I don't know where I'm going," I say. "I don't know who my audiences are—"

"I'm beginning to have trouble with that, too," she offers.

"Or, if I even want an audience! Maybe, I'm just too tired to deal with it all."

"Keep writing whatever you want," Carolyn says. "You know, you can always publish a book with us," referring to her ethnographic series with AltaMira Press. "We're ready for you."

That night, I have two dreams about the workshop I'm supposed to give. In the first one, the five who have shown up are in the pool wearing 1940s-style bathing caps, bobbing up and down; I have to find my own overnight accommodations. In the second, I'm given the president's master suite in the White House when I realize that I'm a *fraud*. I'm neither who they think I am nor who I pretended to be. I take a walk, then realize I need to get my stuff out of the suite. For all I know I'll be arrested for fraud! Imprisoned! But, I can't retrace my steps; I can't find my room.

"Looks like it's going to be another cold day," I say to Ernest in the morning, relieved to be awake. Then, as if my nightmares have lingered into the daylight, I say "Let's go to St. Petersburg to the Florida Holocaust Museum."

"There's none of that bad stuff here," the eighty- or ninety-year-old volunteer whispers as she struggles to enter our senior tickets—$7.00—on her computer. "Enjoy," she says. "There's none of that bad stuff here," she repeats. "We're teaching tolerance. School classes come here."

"Tolerance teaching" consumes the third floor. Rows of chairs face a display—enlarged photographs and text—of the resistance of Jehovah Witnesses, and their plight. On the sidewalls is a replica of a concentration camp chart detailing the meaning of the stars and triangles on the prisoners. Behind the chairs, there is a display of charcoal drawings of some "ordinary people who executed Hitler's ghoulish plans." Off to the side of the elevators is the "Furniture Hall of Tolerance." Entering, I read that when Hitler invaded Poland, he asked, "Who remembers the Armenians?" This exhibit does. It commemorates the "first genocide of the twentieth century," the 1915 massacre of 1.5 million Armenians by Turks. Faces look mysterious behind lace; one captioned, "Ashes—Ashes, We All Fall Down."

Rust-red triangular-shaped stairs lead to the mezzanine, protected by a rust-red double fence, like the walls of an extermination camp. There's a scale-model of Birkenau: arches, "*Arbeit macht Frei*," and a poem about dead people's shoes. A special exhibit of photographs, "Reflection without a Voice," chronicles the holocaust narrative—ghetto, camps, ovens, ashes—and concludes with a little sign of hope, a little girl, alive, running across a field. The back of the brochure advertises the museum's annual "TO LIFE" dinner.

In the central atrium, the actual fifteen-ton Auschwitz boxcar #1130695-5 rests on actual tracks from the Treblinka Killing Center. Children can read how hundreds crammed into the thirty-by-eight-foot boxcar—lacking food, water, and sanitation—suffocated. In the gift store, a replica of the boxcar, fashioned into a *Tzedakah* (charity) box is for sale ($39.95). The saleswoman puts on a CD of 1940s jazz. "Music of the era," she chirps.

"Time to go?" Ernest asks.

"Oh, yes," I say, trying to sort through my emotions. We leave the museum through the massive triangle-shaped doorway through which we entered. We look at the eternally burning gas lamps mounted on triangle bases embellishing the museum's walls, grateful to be alive.

That night I dream that I want to take my son Ben to Jewish Sunday School, but because Ben—who is eight years old in the dream—doesn't want to go, I let him off the hook. Then, he says, "Just because I say 'No,' it doesn't mean I know what's good for me." When I wake up, I feel great love and concern for Ben. Did I give him too much freedom to reject what might have been good for him? Am I having "survivor's guilt?" By not passing on my Jewish heritage, have I dishonored those who were given no chance to do so?

It is our last full day here at St. Pete Beach, and the temperature is in the eighties. We put sunblock on our faces and beach-walk to the "Pink

Palace," the Don CeSar Hotel, a Moorish fantasy of balconies, terraces, and fountains. Built in 1925 by Thomas Rowe and named for the chivalrous Don CeSar in Wallace's opera, *Maritana*, it recreated the far-off in time and space trysting place of Rowe and his lost love Lucinda. It was 1890, and her parents had refused the American's overtures to their daughter. Rowe returned to America, faithful and forlorn. "Time is infinite—I wait for you by our fountain—to share our timeless love, our destiny is time," Lucinda wrote to him on her deathbed. A ghost couple, it is said, are often sighted in the hotel, walking hand-in-hand, and then vanishing. "The Don" has had a distinguished career as host to embodied dignitaries, too—movie stars, the New York Yankees, sick soldiers, F. Scott Fitzgerald, and Zelda.

We've come "to beat around the Bush," to eyeball the preparations for President George W. Bush's appearance at Governor Jeb Bush's fundraising lunch. A helicopter flies overhead; a Coast Guard cruiser follows us. Police vehicles and police dogs guard the beach entrance to the Don CeSar, but we enter unchallenged. A dozen Secret Service men and women in black suits and white shirts, wired and armed, congregate by the elevator that will bring the president to the upper reaches; another dozen patrol the designated entry corridor festooned with black drapes solidly attached to the ceiling, cutting off vision and access from side nooks and galleys. The president won't see anything either.

"We're getting some ice cream," Ernest says to the woman agent, who lets us through to Uncle Andy's Old Tyme Ice Cream Parlor facing Gulf Drive, the president's route. We can see the covered canopy going to the street, allowing the president to step from his limo to shelter without a breath of fresh air, the routine since an assassin's attempt on President Reagan.

Ernest gets a Coke and I get a chocolate yogurt—only seven calories, says the sign. Per serving? Per ounce? We go out and up on the crossover, where we can see everything. No ghosts here.

"How'd we get so lucky?" Ernest muses.

"Sorry. You can't stay here. Go over there," a polite, gun-toting agent says, pointing catty-corner to a modest-sized crowd, standing behind a yellow ribbon. Another of my "habits" is fear of crowds. This one, though, lacks exuberance or anger, so my fear dissipates as we join them.

"Bush is late for lunch," one of the crowd says. "My son's up the road by Eckerd College. He'll phone me when the cavalcade passes," another says. "Twenty-five Thousand Dollars a Plate!" says a third. "Tax deductible, of course," a fourth declares. She's wrong, of course. "Do you think they'll have lobster?" says yet another. "There are protesters by Eckerd," says the cell-phoner. "What are they protesting?" asks an older man. A tanned, dour-faced woman in a red, white, and blue outfit arrives carrying a hand-stenciled sign: "St. Pete Beach." A stenciled dolphin swims above the "Pete." Holding the sign to her chest, the dour woman is a billboard for a dolphin-sighting cruise.

An hour passes. I'm becoming a "burnt bush." A team of bicyclists crosses over the bridge on the pedestrian walkway. Secret Service agents, I imagine, scouring the bridge's undergirth. Finally, the police stop all traffic. Cell phones ring. "He's on his way," is heard throughout the crowd. People climb up on the benches.

"You'll have to get down from those benches," says a hefty, well-armed, Secret Service agent in a deep green suit. I wonder if green signals a higher status.

"Why?" whines one of the bench-standers.

"Well, for one thing, because I asked you to. . . ." "And," I say to myself, "for two, because I have this loaded Uzi under my arm."

A full ninety seconds pass with no traffic. I see a panel truck over toward the beach, and I wish the Secret Service agents would make it go away. Maybe it's a Secret Service truck? And, there's a garbage truck. A damn garbage truck! Why are they letting it pick up garbage?

"Here's another job I'd like," I say to Ernest.

"What? Garbage collector?"

"No. Being a Secret Service agent in charge of logistics. I wouldn't want my body out there, but I'd love to figure out what has to be done to protect—"

Sirens override my soliloquy and herald the state police on motorcycles and in cars. After them a decoy limo, then a second limo carrying President Bush smiling, waving "thumbs up" to the crowd, another decoy limo, and then six white "courtesy" vans. They stop in front of us and Florida's gentrified Republican lawmakers amble out and glad-hand the crowd.

We return to the Don CeSar for our own $25.00 per plate Floridian lunch, tropical fruits and spicy seafood, in the Sea Porch Café. The room is color-coordinated, but not in the déclassé turquoises and shrimps of the lesser Florida. Here, daffodil yellows and deep greens contrast with crisp white rattan furniture, and glass tabletops reflect white fans, revolving slowly above the frond-filled room. Secret Service agents watch the door; ignore us. I pretend we're in a spy movie set in Cuba.

"I understand now why people like to come to where the action is," I say. I've been an inveterate public-action-avoider most of my life. "We're part of history, now. We are here and we don't know what might happen— there's always that chance."

"You were There!" Ernest says in his Edward R. Murrow voice.

"Oh, God," I say. "Let's hope History is not made here!"

The threat of terrorism is real, but so is my gratitude for the continuing gift of my life. The second balances the first. Ernest excuses himself, and I lounge back on my chair, cupping my head in my hand. I'm a wet noodle.

"Relaxed enough?" asks the hostess.

"I haven't been this relaxed for months," I say. "Maybe years."

We go back through the corridor, still draped in black. No ghostly couple here, just us. "Back again?" asks the woman agent. She recognizes us; she's not buzzed.

"Just getting ice cream," we say. From Uncle Andy's we can see the limos depart. The president leaves his captivity in this castle, only to be confined elsewhere. Supreme ambition imprisons.

We walk slowly back to our condo.

"I've not felt this relaxed in years. Maybe never in my life. I'm jelly, and I don't know why," I say to Ernest.

"Seems you don't want to be 'president' of the writing world," Ernest comments.

"And isn't that a relief!"

The next morning we board our flight. The pilot talks to the embarking passengers. "We'll have weather, for sure," he tells us. An hour out of Columbus, the "fasten seatbelt" sign goes on. "It's going to be rough," the pilot tells us. Winds are gusting up to forty-five miles an hour."

The plane swoops up and down like a kite on a lose string. My book falls out of my hands. As we descend, a crosswind catches us and we come in sideways, do a little tipply dance, and screech down the runway. The passengers break into spontaneous applause. Many of them are white-faced. But, I am at ease. I am not an eagle, but I am who I am and, apparently, it's okay.

Ernest Goes to Yale

Ernest Lockridge

Bright blue morning finds us perambulating along a graded cushion of sand that crunches audibly beneath our bare soles, our goal the flamingo-pink mirage shimmering up ahead in the Florida heat, gigantic yet fragile-looking, a Hansel-and-Gretel castle that might at any moment dissolve like sherbet into the Gulf of Mexico. It's the Don CeSar Hotel where once upon a time Zelda Fitzgerald, squired by her Scott, sought respite from an asylum for the mentally ill, and where a fund-raising luncheon, at twenty-five grand per plate, will take place today at noon with the forty-third president of the United States scheduled to speak. I transfer my Tevas to my right hand and pat the billfold resting in the left hip pocket of my khaki camp shorts. "You know, Honey, I'm afraid I may have left the correct change back at the condo."

"We don't have to actually attend the luncheon do we?" my wife Laurel asks. "I'm not sure I can stand to hear him speak."

"George'll wonder where I am."

"I'm sure the hotel restaurant can serve us lunch for only $12,500 a plate," Laurel says. "That way, two can eat for the price of one."

"You know, you do have a point."

"We don't have to decide right now," Laurel says. "We have a whole hour, almost."

"What do you think?" I give the water's edge a clandestine nod. Out on the calm blue surface of the Gulf, a football field's length from the little waves with their soft white hands caressing the beach, the sleek black trawler has been shadowing our southward progress down the snow-white crescent ever since we left our condo a few minutes ago. The trawler bristles with black domes, black antennae. Black radar grids whirl and pirouette.

"Better watch our p's and q's," whispers Laurel.

"Think so?"

"Otherwise, they'll get the impression we're speaking in code."

"Dot," I say. "Dash."

"You don't remember whether he was actually a student of yours, do you."

"Nope." For when I retired from university teaching in 1991 (Free at last, free at last, thank the Lord I'm free at last!) one of my impulsive gestures of liberation in the wake of twenty-eight endless years in full academic drag was to pitch my course records—grade books, lists of all my students' names, including those from my salad days, 1963 to 1971, whilst I was a neophyte assistant professor of English on Yale's Revolving Bottom of untenured faculty—into the circular file and down the Burn-hole of History a la Orwell's *1984*. Now bemoaning the reckless loss, I release a cry of regret into the beauty of St. Pete Beach embracing us like a halo of gentle reverie. "Alas!" I say. "Alack!"

"One would think that you of all people would remember." Laurel has an inflated estimation of my powers of memory. I attempt to disabuse her from time to time, half-heartedly.

Now I tell her, "Year after year back then I was facing classrooms full of smallish good-looking kids who'd rather discuss yachts than Yeats. Most of them looking like . . . oh, clones of the Kingston Trio. Hell, who'd have known one of them might grow up to be president of the United States?"

Well, for one, I should have. "At bottom, you must regard your mission as member of the Yale Faculty as that of training the Leaders of America and the World—in politics, business, medicine, the sciences"—this from a pep-talk designed to forearm neophyte Yale faculty to our task, delivered by some dean, deanling, deanlet, I forget, not my department chair, or "chairman" as he was known back when we were not as advanced as we are now. I can't recall whether my mentor-for-an-hour mentioned leaders in the arts, in literature. One could do worse, I suppose, than inspire a student to join the visionary company of distinguished Yale alumni novelists like Sinclair Lewis and John Hersey. One could do better, too. I do recall most of my foreign students—crème de la crème of Colombia, Nigeria, South Africa. Mr. Fesah-Hanana, for instance, tribal scarring on his face, three-inch commas carved in the flesh, a matched pair punctuating each cheek. Way back then I allowed myself to daydream of a distant future occasion whereupon King Fesah-Hanana, Ruler of Nigeria, invites his beloved English teacher, his Mr. Chips, to visit his luxurious palace, his deer park, his Henderson-the-Rain-King harem. . . . The current *Yale Alumni Directory* lists a Dr. Fesah-Hanana as a Park Avenue physician in gynecological practice.

Now I tell Laurel, "Guess it didn't occur to me that one of those Kingston Trio clones could become president. I lacked the foresight, I guess. Or the imagination."

"Wasn't Clinton at Yale about the same time you were?"

"Yeah, in Law School. Those characters wouldn't come within sniping distance of any course involving the English language. Besides, I'd remember Clinton."

"You're sure?"

"I gather that he never set foot or any other anatomical part on campus."

And, therefore, who or whatever may have inspired Clinton to be a Great Leader could not have been Yale, let alone some fledgling apostle of the New Criticism such as yours truly. It strikes me now as risible almost beyond belief that the New Criticism, the dogma that the Yale English faculty was pumping into its students back when Dubbya was an undergraduate, could in any way be imagined as intellectual leadership fodder to oh, I don't know, a Cub Scout! So please allow me to say a word or two here about the New Criticism, on the remote possibility that no one remembers it. Yale—its faculty rated numero uno in English during my time there (in the entire world!) despite my lowly presence hacked into the totem pole an inch or so above the dirt—was a Monastery of New Criticism, which actually was a novelty of sorts right after World War II, when GI's were flooding into colleges and universities without much background in anything intellectual, such was the scuttlebutt anyway. So N. C. was a handy tool for teaching literature when your students were ignorant of, say, history, culture, the Lives of the Poets, anything and everything else, because in order to understand, say, a poem, you could be ignorant of everything except the ability to read English. The World was excluded—thus, "Monastery," said nomenclature further buttressed by Yale's dominant architecture: Hollywood Gothic. Indeed, the more knowledge one brought to literature the worse, since external knowledge—according to N. C. dogma—merely gets in the way of the work's "true meaning," which is self-contained within the work itself. No Reader was permitted onto the premises to sully the N. C.'s conceit of the inviolable Work of Art's pristine isolation from the squalid Universe of the Creation. No Author, either! And no, I am not kidding.

My true ambition then was not to teach N. C., it was to write novels. And how anyone could imagine doing such a thing without knowing a whole lot about culture, history, current events, and just about everything else you could possibly get your mind around, was and is completely beyond me, but that's another story for another time. So, anyway, there I was teaching this stuff to students of the George W. Bush generation at Yale. N. C. spoke a lot about concreteness, tension, structure, construction. A poem became for us a fetish constructed of poured concrete and rebar, and what we did in lit class was sledgehammer the thing to pieces to find out what it was made of. Class was sometimes fun: there are distinct thrills in pounding things to smithereens. Plus, there was a religious dimension to the enterprise. The New Criticism, which had sprouted from the soil of pragmatism and expediency, soon erected its beanstalk into the intense inane of the Metaphysical and the Occult. The Yale English Department's most formidable professor, a giant, seven feet high, and brilliant, cranial cavity like the trunk of a Buick Eight, a Cardinal of the New Haven Apostolic Church of the New Criticism, spoke ex cathedra of literature as a "Verbal Icon," the incarnation of Ultimate Reality in the "concrete" art object. Gaze long enough at, say, "Ode on a Grecian Urn," you could end up spotting Baby Jesus, the way certain rural folk report seeing the Virgin on a grain silo.

And there was another crucial bit of new critical dogma (grounded in an almost unbelievably naïve, literal-minded, decontextualized interpretation of a patch of dialogue that occurs near the tail end of Joyce's *Portrait of the Artist as a Young Man*) that dictated that whereas second-rate literature was kinetic—that is, made you want to actually do something, such as, say, change your life—first-rate literature was static and left you wanting to do nothing. All of this somehow fed and was fed by the Yale Establishment's belief, solidly rooted in Robert Lowell's "tranquilized fifties," that things are fine and dandy, thank you, and don't rock the boat!

Now with the black trawler still shadowing our snail's pace down St. Pete Beach, I say, "You know what, Laurel? I hope to hell I did not teach George W. Bush anything as a young man. Not one single solitary thing!"

"Whence this burst of false modesty?"

"Altruism! In its purest form. Bear with me. You remember the New Criticism, don't you? All that rant and piffle about verbal icons, concrete universals—?"

"Watch it." She glances at the trawler. "Now you *are* speaking in code."

"Each poem hermetically sealed off from the world like a can of tennis balls? And, worse, the notion that truly great writing leaves you in a state of utter inanition, like Janis Joplin following a needleful of heroin, or Coleridge after a couple of snorts of laudanum—"

"Ernest, are we going somewhere with this?"

"Maybe. So here's a guy with the weight of the free world on his shoulders, following a vicious attack by a gaggle of delusional ghouls who actually do believe they're cutting and hacking a path into a harem of perpetual virgins, and who slash passengers' and flight attendants' and pilots' throats, then proceed to slaughter human beings by the thousands, said lunatics spurred on by the most vicious anti-Semitic fascistic propagandistic brainwashing since Goebbels, Goering, and that raving madman of a Führer plunged the whole world into war. Not to mention the Japanese militarists, whose own little *Mein Kampf* consisted of the ranting of some babbling baboon of a cocaine addict—"

"Ranting indeed. The Japanese weren't especially anti-Semitic, were they?"

"Not my point."

"Oh?"

"Look, I'm nearly there."

"So are we."

"Laurel, it's all this delusional thinking that's destroying the world. Which is why I, myself, would absolutely not want to have been one of our president's formative influences."

"Oh. I see where you're heading. I think."

"Because in these menacing, ominous, odious, malignant, and lunatic times we're living through, that frankly fill me with a sense of utter dread, the poor guy doesn't need a headful of delusions compliments of me!"

"Yes," says Laurel. "And I agree."

"You do?"

"Of course. Laura Bush is a librarian, right? She might know something concerning books?"

"Uh-huh?"

"So the president of the United States might misconstrue a Rod McKuen poem, thanks to some leftover influence from one of your literature classes, and get into an argument over it with his wife. Here's the Don CeSar."

A single-engine aircraft drones lazily out over the Gulf, flight path parallel to the shore, drawing a banner touting the virtues of Bud Lite. The trawler floats stationary now, having drifted to rest opposite the Don CeSar. An innocuous blue and white helicopter rests on the immaculate beach, the sand laundered, combed, blow-dried, puffy and white as new-fallen snow. I can make out no footprints there. Besides Laurel and myself, people on the beach consist of two wiry, athletic-looking men lounging alongside the helicopter. They are wearing crisp summer suits of khaki twill, white shirts, pale green ties. Each has a wire emerging from his suit jacket and plugging into his left ear. Their left shoulders look weighted. They have on wire-rimmed sunglasses. They wave to us like friends, and we wave back.

"Where the hell are the *black* helicopters?" I ask.

"Shh," says Laurel. "Let's go in."

"Are you kidding?"

"Isn't that why we're here? Follow me!" She angles left across the immaculate sand and strides confidently toward the Don CeSar.

Lagging behind, I give the men alongside the helicopter a submissive shrug, an apologetic grin. I display—arms at my sides—a pair of innocent palms. They smile and wave us onward toward the rear entrance to the Don CeSar. "Wow," I say. "Was that easy, or was that easy?"

"Easy for you to say," says Laurel.

We've reached the rear patio of the Don CeSar, wood slats stained gray and rough to the touch. There's a faucet to wash the sand from our feet. We don our Tevas. A score of hotel guests lounge about the patio, lazily sunning themselves. Others frolic in the pool. The outside bar is serving up drinks. "Looks perfectly normal, does it not?" I observe.

"What did you expect? Other than black helicopters?"

"Heck, I suppose those two beach boys probably each carry a huge wad of family snapshots whenever they have to be away from home," I say. "That's what makes their gun-rig shoulders look like they've got about twenty pounds of lead hanging off them."

"The Uzi family," says Laurel. "Do you think he'll recognize you?"

"Who?"

"You know. George Dubbya."

"Oh, come on."

"But wouldn't you be excited if he did?"

"I didn't have my beard back then. I was thirty-five years younger, Dante's entire age in the *Divine Comedy*. And I was nobody. And he wasn't even my student—at least, I'm pretty doggone sure—"

"Do you think he'll invite you to stay at the White House?"

"Yeah, he'll dispatch Air Force One to Columbus, Ohio on a special mission to pick me up."

"May I tag along? It'd be a wonderful opportunity to do some sociological research."

"Oh, sure. If you, I mean, I insist. And you can be sure I won't take no for an answer. I'll simply put my foot down, and you know how incredibly thankful these former students always are. Why, George'll do anything for his beloved Ernest, his mentor and guide, Virgil to his Dante, I'll bet the farm on it. We'll cavort in the Lincoln Bedroom. You and I, I mean. We'll putt on the Presidential Green, using a brand new, squeaky-clean pair of Presidential Balls! 'Mr. Chips goes to Washington.' Hell's bells, 'Ernest Goes to Washington'! Sure beats 'Ernest Goes to Jail' or 'Ernest Scared Stupid.' Where's that damned Jim Varney? Now that I really need him, he's suddenly dead as a post! They'll convene a special session of Congress, they'll write me up in the Washington Post and Call. I can see the headline: THE IMPORTANCE OF BEING ERNEST—"

"'Ernest,' without that pesky 'a'?" Laurel interjects.

"Right! Not the wretched minor virtue, but 'Ernest,' pure and unadulterated!"

"My ideal has always been to love someone of the name of Ernest," says Laurel, who was on stage with Compass Players in Chicago, precursor to Second City. "I pity any poor married woman whose husband is not called Ernest."

"Hell's bells, Laurel, once upon a time you actually married a guy called Herb!"

"That was prior to my conversion."

"Conversion to what?"

"To the importance of having my very own Ernest."

"What a God-awful name!" I exclaim. "Yaagh!"

"The only really safe name is Ernest," Laurel corrects me gently.

"Anyway, Dubbya'll fly us down to the ranch, serve up his scrumptious rattlesnake and armadillo bar-b-cue—"

"Oh, look," says Laurel. "They've changed the name of our restaurant."

"Used to be 'Zelda's,' didn't it," I say.

"What a shame!" says Laurel. "Now they're even writing poor mad Zelda out of the Florida history."

"Maybe now they'll only charge ten-thousand per plate. Still an insane price, but. . . ."

"Let's plan on having our lunch here. Okay?"

"Why not wait and see what Dubbya has to offer?" I suggest.

We enter into the lower level of the Don CeSar. A large man wearing a crisp seersucker suit stands in the hallway between the restaurant formerly known as Zelda's and the men's restroom. A wire runs from his left ear. Smiling broadly, he waves us on in. "It's uh . . . okay?" I ask. Suddenly I recall our pint-sized Olympus bulging in my right hip pocket.

"Of course," he responds in a kindly voice. "Please feel free."

"What about the ice cream parlor?" Laurel asks him.

"Not a problem," he says. "Do you know where it is?"

"Oh yes," I say. "We're practically denizens of the place."

"You're guests of the hotel?"

"Not . . . exactly," I say.

"We're staying in a condominium about a mile up the beach," explains Laurel and adds, with a nod in my direction, "He came to see the president."

"If I get lucky."

"In which case, Sir, I wish you all the luck in the world," smiles the man.

We turn right down the wide hallway. We pass the store featuring reproductions of clown paintings by Red Skelton. We pass the jewelry store, Rolex watches behind heavy, wired glass. The stores are open. When we turn left to reach the ice cream parlor we find ourselves facing an attractive pair, man and woman, flanking what appears to be a tunnel draped with opaque black fabric. "Well hi, you two!" smiles the woman. "May we be of assistance?"

"Well, we wanted some ice cream," I explain.

"Of course," she smiles, gesturing into the dark tunnel. "You'll have no trouble finding an opening that takes you right where you want to go."

We enter the tunnel and Lo! After only a few paces there is light and the tunnel opens onto our Destination. "I wouldn't have expected them to be so nice," Laurel remarks. Her reason for coming along this morning is not to see Dubbya but to study how the people around him handle things.

"Me neither. My sole experience of the Secret Service until now, you know, was those thugs surrounding what's his name? Reagan's Secretary of Defense at the time? George Schultz! Barreling out of the Smithsonian and shoving us off the steps, and Schultz himself an arrogant, snorting, crimson-faced goon. The living embodiment of your man corrupted by power." Mere taxpayers, we had that morning been sneaking into the Smithsonian in order to crash a dining hall for government employees.

"But wasn't that a lovely brunch?" says Laurel, smiling reminiscently.

We are the ice cream parlor's sole customers. Laurel orders low-fat yogurt and I forego my "usual"—marshmallow sundae with vanilla ice cream—for a Diet Coke.

After being served, we seat ourselves at a table with a circular marble top on a base of filigreed iron. "Did I ever tell you about my marching orders when it came to grading?" I say. "During the time George was a Yale undergrad?"

"Probably, but go ahead."

"Well—this was by mandate of the Undergraduate Course Director back in 1963, during the Peloponnesian War—"

"Ernest, that particular joke of yours has grown just a little stale over the years. I've been meaning to tell you."

"During the start of the Vietnam War, then—we graded on a scale of one to a hundred, and us neophyte instructors were given a clear and unmistakable directive that the vast bulk of our grades should fall between seventy and seventy-five. That anything above seventy-five should be considered a good grade. That an eighty was the equivalent of an 'A.' And that if we ever found ourselves giving out a grade of ninety and above, we must be prepared to justify it in writing to our colleagues. This was a few years before grade inflation set in."

"And?"

"Well, when I heard Bush graduated in 1968 with a grade average in the high seventies, and all these geniuses of our acquaintance were making fun of his mediocre record, I was thinking, 'No, in the context of the times that's actually kind of impressive.' Yalies were getting into Phi Beta Kappa with a grade average in the low eighties."

"We didn't have a chapter of Phi Beta Kappa at the University of Chicago," says Laurel, an Early Entrant, like Leopold and Loeb, when she was two or three years old, I forget her precise age. "Everyone would have gotten in."

"You told me. A couple of times."

"Too bad you can't talk about Bush with the people we know," she says.

"Yeah, the 'just-between-you-and-I' crowd mocking the guy for mangling the mother tongue. At least he seems to have a feel for basic English grammar . . . Hey! By golly! The Yale influence, maybe it ain't all bad! Say it good like a president should!"

"But you never really feel free to talk about him, do you."

"With you, maybe."

"Uh . . . huh."

"My fellow faux bass at our last choir party who said Bush only managed to graduate because of who his father was? You know the culprit—the one who won't stop calling me 'Ernie'?"

"I know the one."

"He believes Al Qaeda to be Allah's gift to the masses. And, since the enemy of my Enemy is my friend, and George W. Bush is the Enemy, Q. E. D. Osama Bin Laden must be . . . well, you get the picture."

"Not a pretty one."

"Anyway, I informed him that no one got preferential treatment at Yale. No one! Hell, they booted Henry Ford II out after he handed in his senior thesis with the bill still stuck inside it from the guy who wrote the damn thing for him. Ford, who was on the cusp of being Yale's wealthiest alumni ever, never did graduate. Then—it must've been all the Bud Lite—I just had to natter on about how I, a lowly and obscure untenured assistant professor on the Revolving Bottom, had flunked the son of Governor Scranton when he was a leading presidential contender

and a member the Yale Board of Trustees. And I suffered no consequences I'm aware of. And, besides, back then Dubbya, himself, was nobody either. And neither was his damn father. Jesus Christ Almighty,
Laurel! Doesn't it seem sometimes as though nobody knows a god-
damned thing?"

"So how did our Unitarian Al Qaeda sympathizer respond?"

"He said, 'High point of your life, huh Ernie?' Then he slugged me on
the shoulder like we were in high school or something. And it hurt! I
mean, it was excruciating! He's one of these mental giants who consider
all violence to be evil, except of course when some lunatic anti-Semite
launches an attack on America: then it's not merely justified, it's a fore-
gone necessity! Boy! High point of my life, huh. . . . Well, who knows,
maybe it was. I mean, what's the use of it all anyway? What is the point?"

"Let's go outside. Get some fresh air. Maybe watch Bush arrive."

"I never had one single student at Yale I thought was stupid. Far
from it."

"Ernest—"

But I keep on grousing, can't seem to help myself. "Hell, Scott
Fitzgerald's Princeton grades were so lousy they kicked him out. And he
may be the greatest American writer of all time. Goddamn arrogant Ivy
League."

"I never realized before how much you must hate Yale."

"Hate Yale? What do you mean, 'hate it'? Yale put me through graduate school, picked up the tab. Where else on earth could I have gone
from a lowly, piffling Indiana University bachelor's degree to an exalted
doctorate in three short years? Nowhere else, that's where! And my Yale
professors were brilliant. Every single one of them. And kind. Including
the Giant, poor guy, he retires and dies within the year, his body'd completely outstripped the capacity of his heart . . . as a kid he wanted to be a
Major League pitcher. . . . Then they hire me and it's suddenly as though
my parents are my colleagues—for eight whole years! Me! What on earth
were they thinking? And it was the most intellectually stimulating setting
I've ever found myself in. Maybe some of the old notions sound completely antiquated now, funny, ludicrous even, dead wrong—but so what?
Can you imagine what today's most cherished academic doctrines are going to look like in thirty or forty years? 'Diversity.' 'Deconstruction.' 'Postmodernism.' 'Queer Studies.' 'Postcolonialism,' for Pete's sake! Gag me

with a silver spoon! Hate Yale? What am I, some sort of belly-crawling in-grate? Why, I even divide my charitable giving between our Homeless Shelter and the Yale Graduate School! How can anyone even begin to imagine that I hate that hallowed spot? I don't hate Yale! I don't! I don't hate it." I draw a breath. I say, "Whew, just listen to me go on. Don't I sound like that suicidal nut case Quentin Compson at the end of *Absalom Absalom*?"

"Let's stop talking for a minute, do you mind?"

"What? Why?"

Gently, Laurel says, "Something's the matter, Ernest. Do you know what it is?"

"What do you mean, 'Something's the matter'?"

"You've not been yourself since we got up this morning."

"How do you mean?" I ask.

"You're completely manic, Ernest. Can't you tell?"

"Oh sweet Jesus. What's today?"

"Friday."

"No, I mean today's date."

"March the eighth," Laurel says. "Two thousand and two."

"I forgot and left my calendar back in Ohio."

"Yes?"

"The day I learned Dad died? Yesterday was its fifty-fourth anniver-sary, and it was today the coroner ruled his death a suicide. And here I am at sixty-three with more sharp edges, still, than a porcupine! If I don't re-member to put a reminder on my calendar it always sneaks up on me and I feel myself going crazy without knowing why. . . . His novel's number one on all the national best-seller lists and the poor suffering deluded bas-tard kills himself, four kids under ten years of age. . . . Whoo!"

"But at least now you know the reason—"

"Yeah, I guess I do. And also what's getting my dander up today. Thanks. Hey, did you know the Yale Department of English, back when I was there, judged Faulkner to be little more than a dumb, uncultured rube? You can just imagine what they must've thought of poor old Scott Fitzgerald, as though he was even on the radar! And that 'simpleton' Hemingway? Not to mention Dad, notoriously well-known Bloomington, Indiana novelist and suicide, universally familiar around the environs of Indiana University whilst I was a student during the late fifties, but

171

nowhere to be seen, not a cipher, not a morsel of him or his big fat book anywhere upon the immaculate landscape of Yale, *sic transit*!"

"Let's go, Ernest. You'll regret it if you miss seeing him."

"My fictive ex-student? Laurel, we must blow this pop stand! Let us book!"

We head back through the tunnel. "Well, hello again!" the woman greets us cheerfully. "How was the ice cream?"

"Great," I say. "Just terrific, actually."

We climb to the main floor with its check-in area and large, ornate cocktail lounge and fountain we are unable to spot anyone who looks sufficiently official, so we climb another flight and go out onto the small circular drive where arriving hotel guests disembark. "He'll be coming in from this direction," says Laurel, pointing toward where the Pinellas Bay Way debouches onto the main drag of St. Pete Beach. A friendly looking man in a crisp summer suit, wire dangling from his left ear, approaches us and says, "I'm afraid you can't wait here. But do you see where that small crowd is forming?" He points toward Bay Way.

"Thank you very much," I say.

"No problem." He places two fingers against one of his eyebrows, a friendly little salute.

We leave the hotel and head over to the indicated spot where fewer than fifty people have congregated on a patch of grass behind a barrier consisting of a single strand of yellow plastic tape stretched at waist level. The area contains a single park bench on which four middle-aged women stand head and shoulders above the crowd. In the street beyond the tape a man in a green summer suit, wire dangling from his left ear, left shoulder noticeably drooping, says, "Ladies, I'm afraid you'll just have to come down off that bench."

"Why?" one of them asks.

"Well, for one thing, because I just said so," the man explains.

All four grudgingly climb down. "Thank you, Ladies," says the man.

Normal traffic appears to flow unimpeded. A garbage truck coming from Bay Way pauses for what seems an inordinate length of time before moving on, and it occurs to me that for all anyone knows the thing could be stuffed like a Thanksgiving turkey full of high explosives.

"Anyone know when our president is due to arrive?" I put the question to no one in particular.

"I'm on my cell," says a woman standing a couple of people over. "My son says the motorcade's just now coming abreast of Eckerd College. Oughta be here in oh ten minutes."

A mob of Harley Davidsons thunders past. A dozen or so thirtyish-looking people on racing bikes streak by. "Do you suppose any of those are with the Secret Service?" Laurel asks.

A van swerves to the curb. The doors open and out pour several smiling adults, male and female, sporting blow-dried hair and depressingly white straight teeth. "Hi!" they say. "Oh, hello! Good to see you! Glad you're here! An honor! Really! So good of you?"

"Who are they?" I ask.

"State politicians," someone explains.

The politicians climb back into the van, which makes a left turn heading toward the Don CeSar.

"I have a strange feeling," Laurel says. "I can't quite describe it, but it's a feeling that something might happen. That we might become a part of History. Do you know what I mean?"

"Yes, I do," I reply, aware that for a few minutes now no traffic has come from the causeway. Suddenly a voice cries out, "Here they come! Here they are!"

A black limousine cruises slowly by, its windows tinted dark, very dark. It makes a slow left turn and vanishes around the corner. "Did anyone see him?" I ask.

"Probably a decoy," someone suggests.

An identical limousine cruises past. I can barely make out the people inside, features obscured. Silhouettes. Then: "Here he comes!" "It's him. It's the president!"

And it is. I see him darkly through the tinted glass, smallish and a little hunched over, thumbs up, smiling, confident, reassuring. I'm thrilled. Star struck. Damn! A chill shivers up my spine and expands like clear slow lightning through the tissues of my mind. I fast-draw from the hip and shoot a picture before his limo turns and is gone.

"Don't you just hate politics?" asks Laurel as the crowd begins to disperse.

"You said it!"

"Let's have lunch."

"At . . . what's the new name?"

"Who cares?" says Laurel. "Now and forevermore, it's 'Zelda's'!"

"You know, that's the best thing anyone has said all day."

Conversation: St. Pete Beach

December 31, 2002

Laurel: Done? Already? I mean you just started. It was a week ago when we decided to do this book project. It was Christmas Eve; we were sitting around having a bottle of white wine, eating our Wendy's Mandarin chicken salad, sliced avocado, and garlic bread.

Ernest: As Willie Nelson says of himself and his fellow country music writers, "Thank God, we're not the ones in charge." [*Laughter.*]

Laurel: What do you mean?

Ernest: That in a sense the piece wrote itself. It didn't, of course. But when the tide decided to come in, I let it. Of course, I've revised and revised. I'm still revising.

Laurel: You were up in your study—I don't know five hours, six hours, two hours—and then you came down and the first draft was finished. I was like, "WHAT!?!"

Ernest: Well, actually. . . .

Laurel: It takes me a week, days, months to write a first draft.

Ernest: I guess this has been roiling around in my head for about a year, and I decided at last to write it, put myself back on the beach heading toward the Don CeSar, and let 'er rip. Though I did not write it in one sitting. You were taking a nap when I worked on the first two or three pages. A test-boring, so to speak. It wasn't 'till the following day that I finished a first draft.

Laurel: Do you usually begin writing by imagining yourself bodily back in the time and space?

Ernest: Yes. But it's not like a daydream at all, more like having a night-dream when you're wide awake. Writing has that night-dream clarity and vividness and heightened sense of reality. And something else—I don't know what the next second or sentence will bring. Somehow it's constant surprise and discovery, even when I'm writing about the past—as though it's impossible to predict both the future *and* the past. Go figure. Anyway, once

I'd written the first two or three pages, I stopped for the night, but had a hard time sleeping, kept getting up, scribbling notes to myself. . . .

Laurel: Does that point to a kind of privilege that you and I have, now? We can get up during the night and write. Historically it's the kind of privilege that male writers have had that women, particularly those with children, have not had.

Ernest: Uh-huh.

Laurel: I certainly have more freedom now that my children are grown. It's a privilege to know I can stay in a space, an uninterrupted space. I need to believe I have that open-endedness during certain phases of my writing.

Ernest: There was one year during my three decades as a university professor when I was able to write full time. Mostly I stole time to write between teaching, grading, seeing students, attending committee meetings. It's a near-death experience to stay up all night writing, then try to teach the following day.

Laurel: So you're really used to "fitting" writing into your day?

Ernest: Yes. That's right.

Laurel: Let's talk about revising. I want to talk about how my reading of the first draft of your St. Pete Beach paper affected my revision, and how mine affected yours. In both of our cases, revising separately, we developed issues of death and dying.

Ernest: Right. There was a lot of death surrounding 9/11 and its aftermath, was there not? And a lot of dread. No need to read one another's pieces to bring that back. . . . I hadn't taken any notes about our time at St. Pete Beach. We had a few snapshots in the album that I looked at before starting to write. And I think that after we read one another's initial drafts we both "threw off all our inhibitions," in the words of that thriller I was reading aloud from last night in bed—

Laurel: Yes!

Ernest: And I allowed some of the more troubling issues to surface in my own revision. The process became a *re-visioning*, a reseeing and deepening of the entire experience.

Laurel: Would you care to say exactly where you revised your narrative?

Ernest: I recognized that the dynamics, the unconscious forces driving me along St. Pete Beach were the same ones that had driven me across Death Valley.

175

Laurel: And, the section I added to my revision was our visit to the Florida Holocaust Museum.

Ernest: In response to something I'd written?

Laurel: Actually, my revision was based on three things. One, the piece was going into a different framework—*Travels with Ernest*—than I originally had in mind; two, I felt that your piece demanded a kind of textual response in mine, a prequel, if you will; and, three, I have a greater willingness to think about the state of the world, now, rather than just feel about it.

Ernest: Plus the Holocaust.

Laurel: Yes, plus the changes in my own spiritual and intellectual life—my greater involvement with Jewish history and with Beth Tikvah Synagogue.

Ernest: For years you've been reluctant to even think about the Holocaust, and now you've opened up to writing about it.

Laurel: [*Sigh. Deep breath.*]

Ernest: Well . . . I thought your account of the Holocaust Museum was spot-on. It was exactly as I remember it. I didn't see anything I'd want to alter, except perhaps include some mention of the photo of that Nazi guillotine they put those poor Jehovah's Witnesses under. For pounding on Hitler's door while he was trying to take a nap.

Laurel: Speaking of witnesses, we were potential witnesses to history being made and witnesses to history not being made during Bush's visit to the Don CeSar.

Ernest: History certainly was not made if one defines it in terms of assassinations, disasters, and wars. The garbage truck contained garbage, not TNT. . . . According to one theory the novel came into being to give voice and memory to ordinary folk. After all, the vast bulk of human history consists of our own "little" lives, but we remained invisible and mute until the novel came along and conferred upon us a presence and a voice. And now historians are at work writing History from the viewpoint of the common folk.

Laurel: And, of course, that's what's going on in the Florida Holocaust Museum, . . .

Ernest: Precisely.

Laurel: People without names are honored and commemorated.

Ernest: And their names are—

Laurel: Being brought forward, but some names, like those of the Armenians, are not there—

Ernest: Yes—

Laurel: Only shadowy, anonymous faces behind lace. The eeriness—

Ernest: And I think that's one thing you and I are doing in these travel essays and conversations: giving voice to personal history as History. Let us now praise not-so-famous men—

Laurel: And women! Well, you're becoming a C. Wright Mills type sociologist.

Ernest: I'm honored.

Laurel: [*Laughter.*]

Ernest: That puts me in extraordinary company.

Laurel: For Mills, the intersection of history and biography is sociology.

Ernest: Good.

Laurel: And that's one of the things we've been doing.

Ernest: Making me an Honorary Sociologist?

Laurel: Thinking about history and biography raises another kind of witnessing. I consider myself an ethnographer who tries to describe factual things—objects I've seen, for example—as accurately as possible. I seem to have rules about my ethnographic writing that I can't fully specify. I seem to have limits about what I allow myself to make up, and what I don't allow myself to make up. I don't allow myself to make up objects that aren't there, for example.

Ernest: One of our local newspaper columnists was scandalized when Annie Dillard breezily informed an audience of aspiring writers that an event she portrayed in one of her autobiographical narratives as having had a profound influence upon her life was, in fact, merely an anecdote she'd overheard somewhere. I once heard J. P. Donleavy say that "writing is turning your worst moments into money." So, what's wrong with co-opting someone else's worst moments if it puts a couple of bucks in your pocket? Maybe writing is also what Mark Harris calls "TEGWAR—The Exciting Game Without Any Rules." I believe that there is a difference between fiction and nonfiction, but is it hard-and-fast? I'm not a historian or reporter, not a photojournalist, let alone a tape recorder like the one we're talking into now, or a photographic plate. Monet didn't paint every leaf and tendril or passing dragonfly to embody a certain truth about water lilies—

Laurel: You're colorblind, Ernest.

Ernest: Lousy comparison, I know. Not to mention presumptuous beyond belief. "Ernest Goes to Art Class" . . . which wouldn't exactly fix the problem. . . .

Laurel: The little ethnographic drama I wrote, "The Case of the Skipped Line," is based on actual field notes. The dialogue reports what people actually said. The power of that drama, I think, is that I did not fabricate the dialogue. Many conversations that I put in my text are pretty close to what was actually said. While I was still sleeping in a crib, my father began training me to have a memory for the spoken word—

Ernest: Coaching you to provide testimony in court on behalf of his arch-criminal clients.

Laurel: So I'm more comfortable with filling in dialogue than I am with recreating settings, objects, and events. Bush was there, we were there: the ethnographer's warrant. But, in truth, I struggle with my limits, my rules, my claims to knowing. My struggle, you see, is not just with how I interface with postmodernist ideas. It's about my belief in the importance of witnessing, intensified through my current engagement with Holocaust literature.

Ernest: Yes, I understand.

Laurel: As a witness to people's lives, I do have research training, some writing skills, and access to publication venues. How can I best use my resources? What limits should I impose on my writing?

Ernest: James Joyce in *Ulysses* tried to make everything factually accurate about Bloomsday, June 16, 1904: what was occurring in the world and in Dublin, what the settings looked like, the precise configuration of the fictional Leopold Bloom's dwelling as it actually existed in Dublin. He believed concrete fact to be imbued with sacredness, even though his people and their story are fiction.

Laurel: Yes.

Ernest: As Molly Bloom would say, and did say! There *is* a sacramental quality to "what actually happens" . . . isn't there?

Laurel: Yes . . . no . . . let me think about that. On another note, let me raise a question about how we appear in each other's narratives. In yours, "Laurel" plays a central role. In mine, "Ernest" is present, but not central. I represent "Ernest" as I perceive of you—an intelligent, sensitive, interesting kind of person. In your text, you represent "Ernest" as—

Ernest: Driven, carried away like Nick Carraway in *Gatsby* . . . pretty much the way I sometimes see myself, alas [*laughter*]—

Laurel: [*Laughter.*]

Ernest: Playing a game of catch-up with the spiritual and material universe. And "Laurel"—well, calm, with true presence of mind, more the detached observer, but caring. And quick. You have the best lines. Me, as a "character"? Well, I'm "Ernest in Captivity," like the Jim Varney character in "Ernest Goes to Jail." When my Uncle Harold heard where I was planning to attend graduate school, he told me about the Swedish kid protesting to the Ivy League recruiter, "I don't vunt to go to Yale!"

Laurel: How to present oneself in one's text is a central issue for me. I don't think of myself as a character in my texts, although I know that I am.

Ernest: I'd like to say, also, that there's "Ernest the Judge" who is also the writer.

Laurel: Right. And, of course, I know the distinctions between writer, narrator, and character.

Ernest: Actually, I don't conceive of my people—in fiction or nonfiction —as "characters." They're *people. We're* people.

Laurel: You're ahead of a lot of ethnographers who don't see their people as people, but as subjects. Or objects.

Ernest: Conceiving of other people merely as an idea in one's head makes for bad writing, bad psychiatry, bad marriages, bad parenting, bad karma—

Laurel: And "bad" autoethnography, too, seeing everybody as objects to be manipulated in texts.

Ernest: "Look at me! Center of the universe!" It's the aroused flea floating down the river on his back and shouting, "Raise the drawbridge!"

Laurel: Which brings me back to my thinking about writing as a sacred activity. Elie Weisel's memoir *And the Sea is Never Full* begins with a story that resonates with me.

Ernest: Let's hear it.

Laurel: The story is about a rabbi in St. Petersburg, Russia, who is in jail. The jailer comes to the rabbi with a question. After Adam ate of the forbidden fruit and fled, God said, "Where are you?" How is it possible, the jailer wanted to know, that God did not know where Adam was? The rabbi answered: It is not that God did not know where Adam was; *Adam* did not know where Adam was.

"To write, to write about oneself, one's past and one's burden of memory," Weisel says, is to ask of oneself the question put to Adam: "Where am I in my life? What am I doing? Where am I going?" Answering that question, for me, means being open, honest, aware of, conscientious, and conscious of myself as writer, narrator, and textual presence, and of my life as lived in relation to others. That, it seems to me, is the central core of writing—whether it be ethnographic or literary, and that is what we are working at in the writing of this book.

Ernest: Amen.

CHAPTER 7

SEDONA, ARIZONA

1989–2002

While sick men shall cast sighs, of sweet health all despairing,
While blind men's eyes shall thirst after daylight, draughts of daylight,
While lepers are, dancers in dismal limb-dance,
As long as men are mortal and God merciful,
So long to this sweet spot,
Here to this holy well shall pilgrimages be.

—Gerard Manley Hopkins

Little we see in Nature that is ours.

—William Wordsworth

Call of the Canyon

April 1–15, 2002

Laurel Richardson

"He's either the narrator or the janitor," the boy, sitting on the window ledge at Gate B-18 says, triumphantly pointing to the maintenance man on the stage-like dolly outside the cockpit's door. Which am I? I wonder. Am I a narrator telling a story? Or a janitor cleansing my life? Probably both. Aren't all writers?

We are flying to Phoenix, and from there we'll drive to Sedona. For the past thirteen years we have rented different houses there, usually for a month. My son Josh and his son Akiva will join us tomorrow night for four days.

Our plane lands early. Our luggage arrives in a timely fashion, as does the shuttle to the Advantage Rent-A-Car lot. Only an hour has passed since landing, and we're already on Route 17 driving the two hours north to Sedona in our nifty white Dodge minivan.

"Let's stop at the Forest Service to get our parking passes," I say, as we approach Sedona. "That way we'll be ready to go hiking in the morning. I think they close at 5:00." Parking passes are a requirement put in last year by the Forest Service. Without one you are subject to a whopping fine, and worse—a tow.

"How'd you like to be coming back from our Expired Volcano Trail?" I say.

"You mean Deer Pass?"

"And find our car gone!"

"And two miles uphill to the main road past where the dead cows lie—"

"And the coyotes prowl—"

"And the homeless camp—"

"Where we couldn't hitch a ride, even, because it's against the law."

"And, who knows—if someone did stop for us, it might be the same ones who murdered that young girl."

"Was she really murdered?" I ask. "Raped, too?"

"Both." Ernest answers. "The only violent crime ever recorded in Sedona."

"And it happened last year."

We reach the Forest Service office at 4:25. The sign says they close at 4:30.

"We just made it," I say, thinking to myself "perfect timing."

"Don't worry, I'll help you," the ranger says, returning to her telephone conversation. She's explaining in great detail to her child—husband?— how to "start the baked potatoes."

"Here're your passes, your maps, and your guidebook," she says.

It is now 4:45.

"Let's go to our safety deposit box next," I say. We keep an answering machine, cash, and Sedona ID's in the box.

"The bank lies a piece beyond our rental house," Ernest says, "but yippie-i-a. Let's do it. I think they close at 6:00."

We arrive at the bank at 4:50. It closes at 5:00. I sit on the leather lounge chair, reading a brochure for Bank of America loans, while Ernest, and "our" teller—aged a little—enter the vault. Ernest gets our booty. As we leave, I say out loud, "Perfect timing! All day, we've had perfect timing."

Stepping down to the parking lot, I see a woman in her eighties, backing up her Lincoln Town Car. She doesn't see the small, bandy legged eighty-year-old man walking behind her car. She doesn't feel the car hitting his shoulder. He's banging on the rear window.

"Stop! Stop!" I yell. She looks confused, as she tries to size me up. Am I a danger to her?

"You're running over a man!" I yell.

She brakes.

"I didn't see him. Thank you," she says.

"Thank you," says the frail man. He's no taller than my shoulder, shaky on his legs, toupee a-kilter.

"Your whole life has led up to this moment," Ernest says. "To your saving this old man."

"If that's so, it is worth it." I mean this. "And saving the old woman, too, from the horror of running over a man."

"If I'd been to your left, seen what was happening, yelled at her. . . ," Ernest muses.

"Yes," I say, taking in Ernest's beard, steel-rimmed glasses, and booty bag. "Yes. She'd probably have sped up."

I wonder if we are not always in the right place at the right time, and don't know it. I like thinking about an underlying order and purpose, and how small things matter in big ways. A sparrow's flight in Beirut creating a tidal wave in Bermuda.

Still on Ohio time, we wake up at 7:30, early for us, to sunshine and warmth. Unlike my usual morning behavior, I am in no hurry to get going. I am content to sit, read, and watch the spires of red rocks change colors before my very eyes, just as they had when I was a child and saw them nearly every Sunday afternoon, in the Westerns playing on the movie screen. So many filmed in Sedona! *Call of the Canyon, Broken Arrow, Shotgun, Riders of the Purple Sage, Billy the Kid, Cheyenne, Gunfighters.* Oh, those were the days! Jeff Chandler, John Wayne, Ray Milland, Robert Taylor. Burt Lancaster, Randolph Scott, Dick Powell, Robert Mitchum. Oh, those were the heroes! Jane Wyman, Maureen O'Sullivan, Barbara Stanwyck, Ella Raines, Barbara Bel Geddes, Maureen O'Hara, Hedy Lamarr. Oh, those were the cowgirls!

A consciousness of good and bad, right and wrong, heroism and villainy in the settling of the West, no doubt, was constructed through these movies, but I can't bring it forward. The beauty of the landscape, the love interests, the horses, for me, were the movie—not the plot or the ideology. Even now the "heroes" collapse into each other, in my mind, and arise conjoined as the Consummate Western Hero, bandying a brace of silver pistols, tipping his ten-gallon to Miss Starlet, galloping his white horse over red rock shale, hiding in the massive red rock spires, protecting the settlers, winning, not the West, but the girl, whom he abandons in favor of his horse.

"I think we've got everything," Ernest says, loading the minivan with his backpack, our hiking boots, and maps, while I carry out three extra liters of water.

We're hiking Ernest's favorite "first" hike, a three-hour trip around Courthouse Butte and Bell Rock.

For years we tried to complete the loop, but could never find the passage between Courthouse Butte and Bell Rock. Three years ago, we scrambled up shale and tried again the go-nowhere trailettes. Ahead of us were two young Forest Service rangers doing the same thing.

"Where's the trail?" they asked us.

"We've never been able to find it," we said.

"Well, we're here to improve it," one said.

This year we can find the trail that connects Courthouse Butte and Bell Rock, and so can everyone else—the spandexed-set, mountain bikers, and dogs, on and off leashes.

I pocket a little red sandstone for Ernest, who has been making "wall charms," vertical dangles of found objects, rocks, and enameled tin-snipped figures. At the top of a wall charm is the sun, and then hanging from twisted copper wires come the bird and mammals until at last the eye finds the human form, smiling, alive, belly-buttoned. Everyone who sees them wants one.

We drive up Dry Creek Road to the Enchantment, a spiffy resort edging the Forest Service Land of Boynton Canyon. Yavapai legend holds that Boynton is the place from which all Indian humankind was birthed. They describe it as a birth canal, smooth red canyon walls narrowing into a mysterious darkness. There energy-swirls are so strong that the intuitively sensitive are warned not to journey here until they have exposed themselves to the lesser vortices.

Boynton Canyon is a sacred site—a holy site to visit, not to inhabit. Over a period of centuries, various cliff-dwelling tribes lived in the cliffs and caves surrounding this canyon. Their homes are ruins, now, blending into the scenery, graceful looking sites I like to visit. Recently, Palatki Ruins has been opened to the public. The rock faces there are covered with pictographs. But here in Boynton Canyon, over the centuries, shamans created "medicine wheels," circles of stones marking a sacred space and evoking the earth's energies. Marking the four directions on a circle with meaningful objects creates a sacred center where one's prayers are believed to be in harmony with the earth's healing energies. Contemporary Native Americans still create medicine wheels here. The Forest Service takes them down because, as one Ranger told us, "The wheels are a violation of the separation of church and state."

"We're going to the gift store," Ernest tells the Johnny-on-the-spot guard at the gate of the Enchantment. He gives us a green parking pass. There is ample parking, flat adobe buildings, and a three-hole golf course. We note a new service road and construction vehicles. Supposedly, the local Indians are happy with the Enchantment. Visiting its gift store is a Sedona ritual for us ever since Ernest found and secretly bought for me a handcrafted silver and antelope bone brooch, a modern rendition of a Hopi Kachina. It is my favorite pin,

"This store has changed," Ernest says. "There's absolutely nothing here of any interest."

"Everything's kitschy," I say, surprised, given the spending potential of their clientele. I have a vague memory of ads in magazines for the Enchantment, and I wonder if their ads have generated a more bourgeois guest list. "I want water," I say, feeling the dryness of the high desert, "but I can't find a drinking fountain. Let's try the restaurant."

The hostess brings us each a large plastic water bottle, "Bottled especially for the Enchantment." "No charge," she says.

"I guess we've passed as guests," I say, gulping down the delicious cold water. "Don't throw away my bottle," I tell Ernest, although I'm not sure why. "I'm 'over the hill,'" I say, yawning outrageously, as we begin our drive back down to town. We're at five thousand feet.

"Trying to oxygenate your cells?" Ernest asks.

"And how lucky I am to be 'over the hill,'" I continue. "I don't have to be Sisyphus anymore. I don't have to push a rock up a hill, watch it roll down, and push it up again. I don't have to achieve, accomplish, conquer, push anything."

"Accepting retirement, are you?"

"It is about time for me to embrace it—enjoy it," I say. My mind turns to the seven years that have passed since I took "early retirement" from the sociology department; years in which I have moaned and grieved my loss of status, office, perks, easy professional identity; years in which I have retained some semblance of connection to the academic world through teaching part-time in Cultural Studies, attending conferences, editing journals, publishing research, guiding graduate students, reading obtuse postmodernist theory and . . . STOP! You're making me tired and bored. I say all this to myself, between yawns.

Ernest turns left into the Sedona Public Library parking lot. The larger-than-life bronze statue of Sedona Shnebley—the pioneer woman for whom the town is named—welcomes us with outstretched hand, holding an apple.

"I want some good trash to read," I announce through a yawn.

"Looks like that's not going to happen," says Ernest, reading the notice on the glass-plated door. "The Library is Closed Indefinitely due to a Lack of Operating Funds. Sorry for the Inconvenience."

"Let's take our favorite canyon hike," I announce the next morning. Ernest and I seem to have a natural give-and-take of hike choices in Sedona. We've never argued about which hike to take when. And he is generous about the pace I set, slower than he would naturally go. He anticipates my skittishness on wet rocks by offering his hand, and accepts my decision about when it's time to turn around. "There's no race. There's no destination," he always says. "Plus I've got this thirty-pound pack. . . ."

We drive south on Highway 89A through West Sedona. The Forest Service has been selling off its holdings throughout the area, trading its land for parcels in—who knows godforsaken where. There is no stopping the collusion of government and capitalism here in Sedona. Hundreds of acres have recently been mutilated with roads, sidewalks, faux natural settings and recirculating waterfalls. Trailheads are gone. Half-acre lots barely contain their half-acre houses. What I had considered the choicest viewpoint in all of Sedona has been obliterated by rows of timeshares—an idea new to Sedona.

"Not only are they unsightly," I moan, "they are unseeing!" No timeshare faces the View.

"I can't believe what they've been doing to *our* Sedona." I'm angry. "And, look! They're turning this road into a five-laner!"

"Well, soon we'll be alone together hiking Long Canyon," Ernest says. "Away from the madding crowd—'the pilgrims, still pilgrims, more pilgrims, still more poor pilgrims. . . .'"

"They look pretty damn rich to me!"

"Ah, there are more ways of being poor than you and I can imagine."

To reach Long Canyon we drive up ten miles of paved road, three more on dirt, and hike uphill through scrub for a mile.

"Do you see what I see?" I ask Ernest.

"Yep."

"And hear what I hear?"

"Yep."

Spread beneath the pristine canyon walls, there is now an eighteen-hole golf course. With golfers, electric golf carts, Musak, lights, action, and billboards advertising "Paradise Time Shares."

"Betty," I say on the phone to my best friend who introduced us to Sedona. "Our Sedona isn't our Sedona anymore. We were fortunate to have it when we did. There are even timeshares here."

"And do not ask for whom the time shares," Ernest comments.

Ace Shuttle delivers Josh and Akiva to our door. Their trip has been a horrendously long one of stalled airplanes and missed connections. I am sorry for them, but think that if they had come on the plane with us, we would not have gone to the bank right away, and that poor old man would be dead.

"What do you want to do first?" I ask seven-year-old Akiva. This is his third trip to Sedona, and he knows the lay of the rocks pretty well.

"Climb Cathedral Rock," he says, with a hint of premature triumphalism in his voice. He has not yet reached the summit.

We go in two cars, giving them independence from us, and arrive just in time to take the last two parking spaces in the small Forest Service lot. Josh and Akiva head straight up Cathedral Rock's fault line, while Ernest and I hike at the base, left to the creek, and then right to the valley vista.

"That's Josh and Akiva up there at the top," Ernest says, noting the two blue dots waving at us, as we begin our hike back to our car.

"Can you back out your car, so we can get out?" Ernest asks the woman who is in the process of parking us in.

"You can get out," she counters.

"Well, we can't," I enter the fray. This is a first, I am thinking.

"Back up the car, Pris," her husband, already out of the car, advises her.

"If you back up and let us out, then you can take our space," Ernest sweetly says to the woman, who is now consumed by recalcitrance. "Then someone can park you in."

"That's what I'm afraid of," she says.

"Back up the car, Pris," her husband coaxes. "Back up the car."

She relents, we are released. If we'd been a moment or two later, we'd have been trapped. "Good timing, again," I say.

"I want to go to Rachel's Knoll," I announce when we've all reassembled. One of Rachel's distant relatives deeded her choice Sedona land many years ago, and Rachel—believing she has been entrusted with a sacred gift—has refused to sell the knoll to the pack of growling and panting developers. Instead she has built trails and opened the land to the public as a place of peace and meditation.

"Let's all go," Josh says.

Akiva has taken off his shoes and is walking around a large medicine wheel on the knoll when his face seems to light up. "Take off your shoes," he says. "Come over here. Do you feel something different?"

"You're feeling what people call vortex energy," I say, explaining energy ley lines and medicine wheels. "And, yes I do feel it." Sedona is considered one of the most powerful of earth's electromagnetic spots. The red rocks are iron and basalt. I feel a benign jolt of current through me. My fingers tingle.

Akiva hops and jumps about the knoll. "Here," he says. "Here. Here." He makes himself a small medicine wheel, which he invites us to walk around. I place a red stone in each direction and one in the center. Akiva does, too.

"Airport Mesa, next," Akiva declares, full of pride and wonder. Airport Mesa is a vortex, an easy climb, and offers a wonderful view and lots of cracks and crevasses for Akiva to explore. A woman with her ten-year-old son and an Indian guide come up after us. She puts a Navajo blanket under the lone scrub tree, sits down facing north, closes her eyes and breathes. Josh sits on the edge of the mesa, facing east toward Bell Rock. Akiva and the boy climb in and out of crevasses.

"Come out of there," the Indian guide says, when the boys descend into a deep crack. "Rattlesnake in there. This rattlesnake season."

"I've got my pocketknife," the boy says.

"I've got my pocketknife, too," Akiva says, showing off his black two-incher. "I brought it for getting rattlesnakes. What you do to get a rattlesnake," Akiva continues in his pedagogical voice, "is hold it by its tail and stab its middle."

"Akeeevah!" Josh's voice rises over the mesa, brought back from his reverie. "You never hold a rattlesnake by the tail, because then they know where you are and can get you."

"I want to go on the helicopter," the boy says

"Yeah, and the air balloon," says Akiva.

"Yeah, and scuba diving."

"Yeah, and parasailing."

"But my Dad won't let me," says the boy.

Akiva's silent.

The woman folds up her blanket, and I say, "My grandson enjoyed being with your son."

"Yeah," she says. "Good Timing."

That's my line, I say to myself.

On our last full day in Sedona I suggest to Ernest that we climb Doe Mountain. I'm feeling a little blue about Akiva and Josh's departure from Sedona and wondering if we will all ever be back here together again.

"Are you up to it?" he asks. The last time we climbed Doe Mountain, I needed frequent stops. Once on top and thrashing our way around in the scrub pines, I was afraid we would never find the trailhead. Dusk came, and we came down in a thunderstorm. My boots had no purchase on the rock faces. Ernest held my hand. This year, because my left shoulder is "frozen," my left arm has limited strength and movement.

Years earlier I had lost on Doe Mountain a cherished object—an Evander Preston hand-crafted golden earring that Ernest bought for me in Pass-A-Grille. "These," I had said to him. "I want these." "No," I said, "I don't need a new fancier wedding band." We know where I lost the earring, and on our near yearly pilgrimage we look for it without success and without dismay. *Looking* is the ritual.

"This so-called passable road is even worse than ever," Ernest comments as he jags about potholes large enough to swallow up a javelina.

"And the parking lot is fuller than usual," I say.

189

"And look at that! A wider trail. Switchbacks."

"Looks like some benches along the way, too."

We easily ascend the mountain.

"Ah! How nice!" I say.

We drink from my Enchantment Resort water bottle. "'Drink and be whole again beyond confusion,'" Ernest says.

"That's great, Ernest," I tell him.

"It's Robert Frost," explains Ernest.

Replenished, we walk around the mountaintop. We go to the place where the earring was lost, look, and once again accept its "lostness." We select stones and create a medicine wheel there—the unseen earring, the center. We take in the red rocks, cliffs, canyons, high desert, mesas. I think of the Indians, the settlers, the writers, Sedona, Zane Grey, the spiritual seekers, the movie stars, the developers, the entitled, the poor, the maimed, the retirees, the janitors, the narrators.

Sociologists talk about demographic changes in cities as "invasion-and-succession." Each new immigrant group displaces the one that came before it.

"You know, Ernest," I say. "Something like 'invasion-and-succession' has been happening here in Sedona for centuries. Each new group of 'pilgrims' brings their hopes here."

"To this sweet spot."

"And they leave their traces. Cultural overlay. And we leave ours. The rocks don't change. What changes are the people—peoples—that are drawn to them."

"You're done with Sedona," Ernest says. "Aren't you, Laurel?"

"Yes. . . . It's been perfect timing."

Grandson of Paleface

1995

Ernest Lockridge

"That's Kate Moss," I inform Laurel in a conspiratorial whisper.

"Who is Kate Moss?"

"The Super Model they photograph looking like a heroin-addicted stick of firewood. The Most Famous Model on the Face of the Earth."

"But, Ernest, this girl looks so . . . *healthy*."

"Take my word, honey, it's Kate Moss."

"If you say so. . . ." Laurel knows not to pooh-pooh my celebrity-IDs out of hand. She "learned her lesson" in 1987 when we were crossing the main square in Santa Fe behind a fast-moving black-clad fireplug of a woman wearing a broad-brimmed black hat and gesturing to the retinue swirling like leaves in her wake, and I say, "Laurel, that's Bella Abzug," and Laurel says, "No, it can't be!" and runs ahead and asks, "Are you Bella Abzug?" and Bella Abzug, Feminist Icon and a Founding Mother of the Movement, says, "Of course," dismissively. My radical-feminist wife comes back cowering. "Ernest, she bared her teeth at me."

My unnatural ability to spot faces lurks somewhere in the sub-basement of my tangled genes along with the red-green color-blindness that disqualifies me from becoming, say, an Air Force fighter pilot, yet would place me in the Infantry's front line as a camouflage spotter. Paradoxically my brand of "color-blindness" resides in a *hypersensitivity* to color: RED against a green background so overloads my delicate senses that I may not notice red unless someone happens to say, "Wow, just look at those gorgeous red flowers!"— whereupon Mother Nature barrages my tender little retinae with Her arsenal of blazing mini-flamethrowers. I knew something was not "right" with yours truly one hot bright afternoon on a playground in Manistee, Michigan when I observed my red tricycle slowly . . . becoming a green tricycle . . . then resolving back into a red one. I'm a victim of hardwired neural repression. Now, for me *psychological* repression acts something like this: I recall the "Trauma" in excruciatingly Cinemascopic detail but the spongy blemished little morsel of gray matter preserving the memory is numb, saturated with Novocain.

Where was I . . . ? Oh, okay, late afternoon of Monday, October 2, 1995, and we've pulled onto the Airport-Bluff overlook and climbed out of our rental car. West Sedona lies spread out below us like a Land of Dreams. One other vehicle occupies the overlook, an oversized white van with basalt windows. There's a burly, stern-looking fellow who resembles my high school's vice principal, Mr. Cuddy. There's a slight young fellow with greasy slick-backed hair. He's wearing sunglasses. And Kate Moss, wearing skin-tight short-shorts. They're a mere ten feet from us and Kate Moss blasts us dead-on with the blistering ray-gun of her smile.

But it's the young man in sunglasses who speaks. "Oh, hey! *Hi* there, folks!"

"Uh, hi," I reply.

"Good to see you! Really, really good! Really!"

"Well . . . uh, hey . . . thanks. Me, too."

Abruptly the Super Model and the boy return to the van. Mr. Cuddy slides back the side door. The boy boosts Kate Moss's shockingly callipygian derriere with his palm as she's climbing in, then follows her. Mr. Cuddy slides the door shut and faces us. He stands facing us until Laurel says, "By any chance was that Kate Moss?"

A big grin splits Mr. Cuddy's dour vice-principal's face. "Could be . . . could be. . . ." He turns from us, heading briskly around to the opposite side of the van. A door slams. The engine fires up. The van roars down Airport Road toward West Sedona where we're renting Jane Russell's house during the month of October.

"Ernest, who was the boy accompanying Kate Moss?"

"Not a clue."

"He acted as though *he* were the celebrity."

"Those dern sunglasses. . . . Wait . . . it's coming to me . . . my God! That punk greaseball kid was none other than Johnny Depp!"

"Who?"

"Depp and Moss! Boy oh boy!"

" And Depp is—?"

"The *actor*! You and I saw him in . . . oh, jeez, what was it? That John Waters thing. . . ? *Cry-Baby*! He was the thug on the motorcycle."

"The romantic lead," Laurel says. "I remember now."

"According to the ENQUIRER Johnny Depp registers himself into hotels under various aliases, such as 'Mr. Donkey Penis.'"

"Why, do you suppose?"

"Ask Kate Moss. . . . Wow, wow, wow," I mutter, turning my attention to the View, a textured quilt of green and copper. Ahead of us looms Capitol Butte like the ruins of an ancient pyramid vast beyond imagining. On its eastern flank stands a craggy formation like a hawk-headed sentinel. "Kate Moss . . . Johnny Depp. . . ."

"You seem somehow . . . bereft."

"Frankly, my dear, I feel like a complete idiot! Here I am, at my age, standing in the midst of . . . all this"—I bestir the atmosphere with my arms—"and a couple of teenage minor celebrities get me all starstruck! What is *wrong* with me?"

"Could you have seen them in one of your Sedona Westerns?"

"Wrong generation by fifty or sixty years. Now, if it were Randolph Scott and Barbara Britton—"

"Or Jane Russell?"

"Yeah! Big Jane's impressive frontal developments in that push-up torture-basket of barbed wire Howard Hughes designed. . . . Could he have shot *The Outlaw* here in Sedona?"

"You're asking me?"

"Anyway, if we'd encountered her, or the likes of Bob Steele and Vera Ralston, I'd really be frothing at the mouth—"

Laurel smiles.

"Though if you really want to know the truth I haven't given a damn about Westerns since I was a snot-nosed kid in Bloomington. . . ." Where, on Saturday mornings, I joined the snot-nosed Stampede at the Harris Grande to revel in Westerns. Roy Rogers, Bob Steele, Randolph Scott, Tom Mix, Sunset Carson, Rod Cameron, Johnny Mack Brown, John Wayne, Rex Allen, Tim McCoy, Gary Cooper, Buck Jones, Jimmy Stewart, Buster Crabbe, Ken Maynard, George O'Brien, Tex Ritter, George Montgomery, William Boyd, Harry Carrey, Tim Holt, Gene Autry, Hoot Gibson, Joel McCrea, George Brent, Lash LaRue. Heroes All!

Following Dad's suicide when I was nine Grandpa started squiring me at night to the tumbledown Roxy for Western double features. Nickel admission for kids, twelve cents for adults. "Scuffy, wake me when the shooting starts," and Grandpa commences snoring. And there in the stuffy air stirred by a half-dozen sluggish ceiling fans my soul wafts away from my spindly little self and into the romance landscape of Sedona, Arizona where Westerns are getting filmed by the ton and Bad Guys yield their lives and all their secrets to Good Guys with blazing six-shooters, Justice and Truth merging together in a setting of transcendent natural Beauty.

"Boy, Laurel, know what I just remembered? Driving into Sedona yesterday past Bell Rock, Courthouse Butte, Cathedral Rock, and Coffee Pot, it struck me in a flash that ever since I was a kid Sedona's been one of the big mise-en-scènes for my dreams."

"Why didn't you tell me?"

"Guess I was too caught up in my own movie."

We're on the veranda behind Jane Russell's house savoring our "spectacular view of Coffee Pot" as per the realtor's brochure, and browsing *The Red Rock Gazette*, a mélange of local occurrences, items of historic interest locally, and New Age ads. "'Earth Mother Foundation,'" I read aloud from my half of the paper.

"'Energetic Transformational Astrology,'" Laurel reads from hers.

"'Universal Tarot, Personal Development, and Self-Empowerment.' 'Bio Chakra Therapy.'"

"'Shamanic Healing.' 'Animal Communication and Energy Therapy for Your Pet.'"

"'Religion of the Light and Sound of God.' 'Magic of Massage.'"

"'Immortality Consultation.' 'Love Yourself to Peace.'"

"'Completed Karmas: Write down ten names. Do you want to know if they were with you in past Incarnations?'"

"'Whales and Dolphins Healing the Children.' 'Magical Harp Sessions.'"

"'Crystal Sanctuary, a Transformational Resource Center.' 'Three-Thousand Angels from around the World.'"

"Shall we descend to a mere clothing ad?" Laurel asks.

"Shoot."

"'Whether he draws his gun or a good hand he does it in our clothes.'"

"No doubt the Meanest Man in the World does everything in his clothes."

I'm referring to the grimy figure we encountered only this afternoon in the wall-to-wall tourist strip that constitutes "downtown": Hopi jewelry and pots, paperweight scorpions in polystyrene, Crystal Supermart, Pink Jeep Tours, Vortex Safaris, Navaho Rugs, Red Dirt T-Shirts, Big Chief Tobacco with a life-size wooden Indian guarding the open door. . . . Alongside the Indian slouches a wooden cowpoke chainsawed from the same tree branch, pot-metal six-gun hanging at his side. . . .

Gazing at this somehow . . . weird objet d'art I find myself making eye contact with a pair of living human eyes, but deadly mean, like those of an aroused Diamondback. The filthy rake of his right paw goes down for his Colt Peacemaker. Terror electrifies my spine. I croak out, "Sorry!"

"In a pig's asshole!"

"Ernest?"

I seize Laurel's hand. "Let's get the bejesus out of here!" Making our getaway down the betouristed sidewalk I feel the palm-sized portion of my back that shields my heart tingling audibly. . . .

Now safe and sound on Jane Russell's veranda Laurel muses, "It's magical here in Sedona. I feel more . . . relaxed than I have in years. . . ."

"There's supposed to be something floating in the air called 'negative ions' that lift your mood. Who knows, maybe there's lithium carbonate in the city water. There's this natural spring sacred to the memory of some saint where Gerard Manley Hopkins sampled the water and his depression lifted for a couple of days while he scratched out a poem about it."

"Recite it."

"I can't."

"Of course you can."

"You keep on giving me too much credit. In truth, my memory stinks to the heavens and Hopkins was a manic-depressive. Anyway, as it turns out this sacred spring is absolutely *loaded* with lithium."

"I don't care what's making it happen, I love Sedona. . . . If only your friends didn't tote those guns."

"That's from Jane Russell's dance-hall number in *Son of Paleface*," I say.

Laurel sings her rendition of the movie's theme song.

When she's through I say, "If memory serves the climax occurs when Bob Hope wakes up in a sleeping bag with Trigger and the earth moves."

"Does he spend the rest of the movie recovering from the trauma?" asks Laurel.

"Who, Trigger. . . ? No doubt our poor old Meanest Man in the World had his mangy ass booted all over as a kid," I ruminate. "So nothing's his fault."

"'Intense natural energy emanates from vortices deep beneath the red rocks.'" Laurel's reading *The Red Rock Gazette*. "Maybe it's all true."

"There are more things in heaven and earth than are dreamt of in our philosophy, Laurel."

"Isn't that the truth."

"What is our philosophy, by the way? Postmodernism? Prefuturism? Crystallography?"

"Prior to yesterday, when was the last time you actually saw the Milky Way?"

Last night the Milky Way was rushing like a river of silver light across a heaven glittering with stars. "God knows."

We continue our perusal of the *Gazette* in silence.

Daylight fades . . . fades.

"Boy, Laurel, listen to this. Coffee Pot up there?" I'm pointing toward the hawk-faced red rock formation towering over us.

"Uh-huh?"

"It was once named Horus, after the Egyptian sky god with the head of a falcon. Horus is the son of Osiris, god of the dead, and his sister Isis, goddess of fertility."

"How can you possibly remember all that?"

"It's all here in the local rag. Actually it isn't. Not all of it. So, anyway, some homicidal deity—those old gods were a perverted, sadistic lot—murders Osiris, mangles him to morsels and scatters his pieces across the Nile Valley. So Isis hatches this scheme. First she goes around the countryside collecting her brother's body parts. But when she stitches them back together she discovers, Uh-oh! The piece de résistance—to wit, her brother Osiris's organ of procreation is nowhere to be found. So, she fabricates a prosthetic device—"

"Out of what?"

"Genoa salami from Basha's." Basha's is the supermarket closest to Jane Russell's house. "In Truth, Laurel, Isis expropriates a live fish of some unspecified species, mackerel, catfish, piranha—"

"How inventive of her," says Laurel. "But why not merely adapt, say, a donkey penis?"

"Have you ever actually seen one of those things?"

"Can't say I have."

"It may have been a matter of measurements, but as but a lowly scribe of Clio, Muse of History, I am not allowed to speculate. So, Isis attaches the scaly prosthesis to her brother, who remains dead as a doornail by the way. Then, after consulting *The Kama Sutra*, Isis mounts Osiris. Thus by means of necrophilia, animal sodomy, and incest they conceive their son Horus, now looming right up there, over Jane Russell's house."

"Why go to all that bother?" Laurel asks.

"So Horus can get back at whoever was responsible for his father's death. For revenge, what else?"

"The story's nothing but an insidious Rube Goldberg device," says Laurel.

"Those old deities were our first triple-x movie stars," I say. "I thought you knew."

"I definitely prefer 'Coffee Pot,'" Laurel says.

"It lacks the manic grandeur of 'Horus.'"

"It smacks of domesticity," says Laurel.

"What could be more 'domestic' than Horus, Hamlet, Orestes—"

"*Peaceful* domesticity."

"It's an oxymoron."

"In literature, Ernest."

"And the movies. . . . Well, let us take shelter in Jane Russell's house. It's growing dark."

We enter the living room through sliding glass doors. Jane Russell's house is a spacious Western dwelling with a wood-beamed cathedral ceiling and cavernous fireplace. In truth, she sold off the house a couple of years ago before leaving the area for good.

"Do you sense Jane Russell's presence?" Laurel asks.

"Nope. Not that I haven't been trying very hard."

"Whatever happened to her?"

"Let's see. . . . Ah, yes!" I say. "Jane Russell underwent a sex-change operation and became Elvis."

1996

"What would've happened if the man hadn't called off his dog?" Laurel asks.

It's a hot cloudless mid-October afternoon.

We're sitting off to the side of Broken Arrow Trail and consuming lunch from our backpack—salami, potato chips, cheddar cheese—and gulping root beer from aluminum cans.

I'm wielding my razor-sharp K-Bar Marine Combat Knife to slice things the way Laurel likes them sliced, paper-thin.

About a half-hour ago an unleashed Doberman Pincer charged up to us on the trail and crouched in our path snarling and baring his fangs. "Will you please call off your dog?" I called to the owner, a tall slender

197

man wearing crisp blue jeans and a crisply tailored denim shirt, fifty feet or so ahead of us on the trail and looking on impassively. The dog's within a foot of us now snarling and slobbering to beat the band.

"Can't you see what's happening?" I call out.

"He's harmless around most people." The owner barely raises his voice.

Unsheathing the K-Bar I tell him, "He'll be completely harmless if you do not call him off at once."

Now I answer Laurel, "If he hadn't called his dog off? How well do you like raw meat?"

"No thank you."

"Goldang, dawgmeat washes down real nice an' easy with that there Sarsparilla, Podner!"

I'm relieved nothing happened. After becoming nauseated whilst skinning and gutting the rabbits I shot with Uncle Tommy—my mother's elder sister's husband who for a year or so played at being my surrogate father—I ascended to the moral high ground of allowing other men to slay and dress my meat. But . . . let's say I "neutralized" the Doberman without suffering a miserable death, I'd then have had to deal with the man.

Even with the sun beating down I'm shivering.

"Did you see *Broken Arrow* with your grandfather, Ernest?"

The eponymous *Broken Arrow* was shot on this site. The trail features a kaleidoscopic array of red rock vistas that I absorbed from the Silver Screen forty-seven years ago. "Don't recall. I saw the movie in 1950, and Grandpa didn't kick the bucket for another couple of years. . . ."

"Wasn't *Broken Arrow* violent for its time?" asks Laurel.

"Only if you count Jeff Chandler without his shirt on," I tell her.

"Too bad about your grandfather, Ernest."

I wipe both sides of the K-Bar's coal-black blade against my shorts and ram the knife back into its sheath. "It was a fucking tragedy."

"You looked . . . mean back there, facing down that beast."

"Never mess around with a boy called 'Ernest,'" I say. "He's meaner than any mere boy called 'Sue.'"

"Oh, I know," Laurel agrees.

"Evil begets evil," I quip.

"What malignant force would cause dogs to be the recurring motif of this vacation?" Laurel asks. We're lounging on the second-floor balcony of our rental house on Brewer Road, having just returned from Basha's Super-market following a contretemps in its parking lot. Jane Russell's house be-ing not for rent, we've settled for this brand-new three-story stucco dwelling whose "spectacular views" are marred by a chaotic array of power lines, and by a succession of trucks rumbling to and from home-construction sites fur-ther up the hill.

Our rental home's stocked with virginal leather-upholstered furniture that we're breaking in. On tables and floor stand white leather "sculptures" of Native Americans in feather headdresses, the price tags hanging from them. The prices are astronomical. The house was built for a pair of high-powered yuppies residing in Phoenix who according to the rental agent have yet to spend the night here. We've employed the motor-powered dumbwaiter in the squeaky-clean garage to ferry groceries up a floor to our state-of-the-culinary-arts scullery, and now we're taking it easy on a pair of brand-new plush patio loungers, rehashing our most recent ordeal.

"Hey look, Laurel, what if Snoopy Rock up there"—I'm pointing up, northeast, at the formation that's visible in full from our luxurious balcony—"was once-upon-a-time Anubis? We know how they try to tame these for-mations by dumbing down their names."

"Coffee Pot instead of Horus."

"Right. So Anubis is the jackal-headed Egyptian god of—"

"Cease and desist, Ernest!"

"You asked me the question."

"Sorry, honey. Dog Lady's more than enough awfulness for a single day."

"Whatever Laurel doesn't want, Laurel doesn't get."

Earlier today whilst edging on foot around a battered van illegally parked in Basha's fire lane I'm waylaid by Cerberus, the three-headed death-dog of the *Inferno*, snarling and snapping at my throat from an open side-window of the van. A matter of millimeters, and Dante's monster ca-nine could rip away my life.

"Ernest!" Laurel calls out. "You're all right?"

"Miraculously."

The sticker on the van's twisted rear bumper says: PROTECTED BY ANGELS.

A bedraggled woman ambles over from the pure-water dispenser. "Don't you know no better than to get close to someone's van?"

The thwarted trio of German shepherds are snarling up a storm.

"Those your dogs?" I ask her.

"What if they are?"

"Well, for one thing they nearly ripped out my throat."

"Would-a served you right, asshole."

"What if someone in the future isn't quite as fortunate as my husband?" Laurel asks the woman.

"Serve *them* right. It's why I got them dogs."

"I see that you believe in angels," Laurel says.

"What if I do?"

"Then why do you need dogs?"

Safe and secure on our balcony I say, "The poor creature—"

"Which 'creature'?"

"Dog Lady. Someone or other's been beating her silly since childhood."

"Which justifies everything these days . . . Ernest?"

"Yuh?"

"Take a look up there at Snoopy Rock, would you please? A good look?"

"'Kay."

"Are you looking?"

"Uh-huh."

"See Snoopy on his back? There's his nose . . . and over there are his feet."

"Yeah?"

"So he can't ever have been named for some ghoulish Egyptian god with the head of a jackal."

"Guess not."

October 24, 1996. My son-in-law phones from San Francisco to say my daughter's just given birth to a nine-pound seven-ounce boy, mother and son doing fine. My first grandchild.

They're giving him a name from his father's side of the family, the same name the Dog Pound assigned to the cat we recently adopted.

1997

Thanks to the Tech-Bubble our stock-portfolios are performing so robustly that we're indulging in a spot of house hunting. Vacation home?

Second home? Retirement home coupled with a permanent move to Sedona?

I'm not exactly panting for ownership of two houses simultaneously—two houses whose roofs will eventually leak, water heaters burst, basements flood, air conditioners fail during the hottest afternoon of the year.

But the prospect of owning a piece of Sedona carries a hot Cathectic charge for me. To revert back into the Universe of Arrested Childhood I'd need only step outside. Or be wheeled. Or goggle rheumy-eyed through my plate-glass picture window toward Coffee Pot, Bell Rock, Boynton Canyon, Doe Mountain, Snoopy Rock, Capitol Butte, Cathedral Rock. What better Clipper Ship on which to make my Last Voyage than a Second-Childhood Home custom-tailored to my infantile fantasies?

We're escorted inside a split-level whose back yard is a Cliff Wall and whose front view is a Strip Mall.

There's a "highly affordable ranch with cathedral ceiling" that's a double-width trailer in a trailer park.

We're ushered inside a number of virgin Western-style houses built on spec in the developments sprouting up around Sedona. Going for a half-million each they're shoulder to shoulder like old chums. We listen to the arguing next door.

Under pressure from developers the federal government's selling off the National Forest. Public trailheads transmute into private property overnight. NO TRESPASSING signs abound.

A walled-in compound in Oak Creek Village south of Sedona resembles the compound in *The Godfather*. A Sedona man with Mafia ties is blown to smithereens in his Cadillac in Phoenix.

Black tour-helicopters buzz the trails during our hikes. The raucous Red Rock Bi-Plane scours the sky around the clock making a forced landing on Dry Creek Road after running out of gas, decapitating the tourists in the rumble seat.

In the galleries Sedona Art Works have been turned out on Assembly Lines by Lasers.

Traffic's insane. Our robed and be-turbaned Holy Man strolling back and forth along Route 89A has vanished into thin air.

We're in the living room of our rental house on Rodeo Drive watching a rented video of *Stay Away Joe*, a 1968 marvel starring Elvis.

"Jeez, honey, look!" I say. "That guy has got to be Jane Russell!"

"Look at what, Ernest?"

"His *face*, for Pete's sake! Or *her* face."

"Oh, their *faces*. . . . Now I see. Elvis and Jane Russell could be brother and sister. . . . Or mother and son. . . ."

"Of course their faces. What else did you think?"

"Elvis does have rather large . . . breasts."

We're watching Sedona movies until we pig out, having brain-damaged ourselves thus far with *Johnny Guitar, Desert Fury, Gun Fury, Texas Trail, Leave Her to Heaven, National Lampoon's Vacation, The Last Wagon*—and *Albuquerque* with Catherine Craig, formerly Catherine Feltus who attended Bloomington High School with my mom and dad prior to becoming an obscure starlet and marrying Robert Preston. Catherine Feltus/Craig executes bad-guy Sidney Blackmer by shooting him through the forehead with a tiny pearl-handled revolver that looks just like the one with which my Grandma Lockridge frightened off an intruder in Shawnee, Oklahoma Territory, 1903. As a teenager in Bloomington, Indiana I mounted the miniscule five-shooter on my bedroom wall and purchased one hundred .32 rim-fire rounds for it from Smaltz's Hardware. Mr. Smaltz put the bullets in a brown paper bag for me.

The very next day I shot one hundred of my B. H. S. classmates through their pointy heads.

Don't you wish.

Jane Russell's house on Corral Road is less than a block from where we're staying. It's not for rent and not for sale. So we've settled into a sybaritic dwelling constructed on the template of a Pompeian villa. There's a central courtyard whose elaborate Water Feature daily attracts a writhing mass of bright-colored snakes. The East-Indian owners' taste runs to sculptures of severed hands and peeled-away faces that we've stowed in drawers for safe-keeping, making a schema to remind us where to replace them moments prior to our departure.

In *Stay Away Joe*, Jane Russell/Elvis Presley plays a devil-may-care Native American Don Juan called "Joe" who mounts a hutch or two's worth of Playboy Bunnies in a tumbledown West Sedona shack she/he occupies with a borscht-circuit comedian made to resemble a Native

American Shaman. The Shaman gives off Sayings: "Injun Brave heap love squaw's heap tasty red meat!"

He makes jokes. "What did Brave ask mermaid? 'How?'"

After an unconscionable expenditure of our lives *Stay Away Joe* bumps and grinds into the Credits and I say, "That is the most abominable movie I've seen."

"Worse than *Raintree County*?"

"Yup."

"Which takes some doing, I gather."

"Did you know, Laurel, that Leslie Fiedler called *Raintree County* a 'Western'? Not the movie, the novel. Fiedler opines it in *Love and Death in the American Novel*."

"Do you recall his reasoning?" Laurel asks.

"Nope."

"Isn't Fiedler's book somewhere up in your study?"

I don't answer.

"When we get back let's—" she begins.

"Use the goddamn thing for target practice," I tell her.

Friday, October 24. My daughter and son-in-law are in Sedona with my grandson to celebrate his first birthday. He's good-looking like his parents. And smart. And bursting with enthusiasm for life.

"Oh boy, Popop!"

I'm tootling "Happy Birthday" on my clarinet.

"Wow!"

A burly truck crunches noisily up Rodeo Drive.

"Ohhh, truck! Truck!" he cries.

He'll hold two things at the same time, one in each hand—two balls, two teddy bears, two balloons, two candy canes. His parents adore him. So do I. So does Laurel. He's having a wonderful childhood. A safe one, too.

We're celebrating his birthday on the concrete deck of the Enchantment Resort. There's a cake with *two* candles because my grandson wants it that way. Boynton Canyon's on naked display, dazzling in the noonday sun. My grandson's holding two silver spoons, one in each hand. "Oh wow, Popop!"

"Still house-hunting, Dad?"

"Nope."

"We'd buy Jane Russell's house in a second," says Laurel.

1998–2002

We're at the vegetarian Thai restaurant on Route 89A.

The proprietors, a husband-wife team, are engaged in snarling at one another. He's a tall stringy doe-eyed professorial or aging-hippy-type Caucasoid. She's the sole Thai woman I've seen who is not at the least pretty.

There's one other customer in the restaurant. He's alone at a window table with his back to the window, holding oversized-looking chopsticks and staring into a bowl of rice. He's jockey-sized and unnaturally handsome, features like some fragile porcelain doll's. "Laurel, can you see that tiny little man?" I whisper.

"He's not microscopic, Ernest."

"Know who it is?"

"You're about to tell me, aren't you."

"Richard Gere."

"Oh, Ernest, he can't be!" Laurel's a big fan of motion picture Superstar Richard Gere. "It's simply not possible!"

"Do it you-self, lazy stupid!" snarls the Thai wife.

"But, Ernest, this one's so *tiny*!"

"Yeah, practically a midget," I say.

"And up there on the screen with all those big actresses he looks perfectly . . . regular!" Laurel says.

"Movies deal in illusion, Laurel. And what's wrong all of a sudden with being short?"

"Not one thing," says Laurel. "Shorty."

"Alan Ladd was only about four inches tall, and look what they managed to do with *him*," I say, keeping my voice down.

"What?" asks Laurel.

"Well, for example in *Shane* they made him look nearly half the height of Jack Palance, whereas in reality Alan Ladd came up only to his anklebone."

"How wonderful being famous must feel," Laurel muses. "Knowing people recognize you and regard you in such a positive, complimentary fashion."

"Do you think Mr. Pint-Sized over there registers himself into hotels as 'Mr. Donkey Penis'?" I ask.

"I'll go over and ask him," Laurel says. "Sounds like a terrific conversation-opener."

"Remember Bella Abzug," I caution her.

"It might improve things around here if you could speak the English language for a change," the restaurant's male proprietor tells his wife.

"Go an' fuck you-self, dumbbum!" his wife says back over her shoulder, abandoning a plate of noodles in front of Laurel. She drops a second platter in front of me and stomps off.

"The very sort of thing I've just been talking about," the husband informs the ceiling.

We wield our chopsticks.

"How's yours?" I ask.

"Dreadful."

The Superstar pushes back his chair and rises to the standing-height of John Keats, about that of an average ten-year-old boy. Not glancing at any of us he leaves the restaurant and heads out into the night. Laurel makes a movement to follow. "Maybe I should find out—"

"Giddy-yap, honey. He's mounting his Shetland pony."

This time it's the husband who approaches our table. "May I help you folks? Dessert? Herbal tea?"

"No thank you," says Laurel. "Wasn't that Richard Gere?"

"Personally, I wouldn't even know him if I saw him. The famous, the obscure—here in Sedona it's all one and the same to us."

"Boy could I use an ice-cold beer right now," I sigh.

"The restaurant serves no alcoholic beverages, sir."

"I was merely giving voice to a fleeting thought."

"And how were your dinners?"

"Simply fabulous," I enthuse. "Don't even think of changing a thing."

"We always try to do our best," says the man, surveying the empty tables. He returns to where his wife is clattering pots and pans in the sink.

"And to think that once-upon-a-time I wanted to be famous," I muse. "To emulate my father. . . . People who had a childhood like Dad's either flatten out and give up, or they become superachievers. That was Dad's trajectory. Highest undergraduate grade-average ever recorded at Indiana University, President of this, Vice-President of that, Valedictorian, Phi

Beta Kappa, Harvard grad school, Grand First Prize in Indiana's Short-Hand Competition. . . . He took dictation from his father, a fast-talker," I add by way of explanation.

"And you don't necessarily become—?"

"One in four, supposedly, or one in eight—I forget. Anyway, it's not the Bite of the Vampire."

"And weren't there four characteristics—?"

"I read about them somewhere and the light bulb went on in my head. Yeah . . . the ones who're like comets do have four things in common. First, no other major problems, no physical disabilities, social maladjustments, health problems, and Dad was this healthy, incredibly handsome guy. Second, somebody who deeply loves and takes an interest in you, and Grandma fulfilled that role to a T. Third, high intelligence. And fourth, a Quest, some blazing Future Goal which in Dad's case was to write the Single Greatest Work of Literature ever."

"Greater than *Hamlet? The Odyssey? Paradise Lost? Ulysses?*"

"Sheer megalomania, but hey, it kept him going," I say. "Until the day arrives when he's achieved his ultimate personal best, only to wake up and know at last that no matter how great his success he will always and ever remain nothing more than this repulsive cockroach in human form."

"The suicide note you discovered on his desk—" says Laurel.

"'As for the miracle of being—it is of course a miracle, but it is not necessarily a good miracle. Some lives are fortunate, and some which seem fortunate become involved in agony, and who shall say whether this is through their fault or not? No one blames the child of less than ten for the errors of his personality, but link by link he is bound to the grown man.'"

"'Not necessarily a good miracle.' My God."

"I'm just glad he didn't do his wife and kids the favor of murdering us while we slept."

"Can you not recognize the obvious fact that they need their check?" the husband inquires of his wife.

"You stick it where no sun don't shine, Mister Smartpants!" his wife advises him.

"'There is nothing nobler or more admirable than when two people who see eye to eye keep house as man and wife, confounding their enemies and delighting their friends,'" I say. "Guess who wrote it."

"Amy Vanderbilt?"

"Homer."

"Be sure to alert me if you spot him," says Laurel.

Grandpa's on his back snoring up a storm in his coffin. He's lying in state here in Sedona's Cathedral of the Red Rock. The tall windows give the mourners a panorama of Sedona's natural splendor rivaling Cinemascope.

"Ah, Ernie. . . ?" It's Walter Merdle, beside me in the last pew. Walter serves as senator in the Indiana Legislature where he chairs the committee that funds Grandpa's Hoosier Historical Institute. Under Grandpa's tutelage Walter wrote his novel *The Warble of Fleetfoot*, wherein the Native American hero and heroine turn out to be White Europeans kidnapped from their cribs and raised by Savages. Walter modeled his oeuvre on Grandpa's own unpublished novel *Black Snake and White Rose*. Like Grandpa, Walter broad-mindedly considers the Red Man to be the White Man's equal—except, naturally, at the very highest levels, Tecumseh being no match for Napoleon or General Custer. Because he *is* White, Merdle's hero Fleetfoot faces a limitless future at the conclusion of *Warble*.

Soft, pale, heavyset, wearing horn-rimmed glasses, Walter says, "So, Ernie, what did you think of my little *Warble*?"

"May I be candid?"

"It's your show, Ernie."

"Your novel is terminally malignant. Mind you, I biopsied it in only a few spots."

"So you lacked the courage and stamina to peruse the whole magilla?"

"One need not eat the entire ox to know that it is tough. You're an idiot."

"I'll have you know, young man, that I am a Circuit Court Judge!"

It's true. Walter Merdle combines the roles of novelist and jurist, in the glorious tradition of Henry Fielding, and of Grandpa, who served as magistrate in the Oklahoma Territories and more than once had Jim Thorpe pitched into the clink for public intoxication.

"So there's no Justice, what else is new?" I grumble.

"But did you also know, Ernie, that your grandfather judges his son, your father's *Raintree County* as inferior to my own humble little *Warble*?" In fact, *The Warble of Fleetfoot* consumes nearly nine hundred pages worth of solid wood pulp.

"Grandpa already told me. Actually, Walter, I was only kidding around. In my expert opinion *The Warble of Fleetfoot*'s a bona fide world-beater. Don't ever think of altering even a word of it."

"Ha ha. For a moment there, Ernie, you really had me going."

"*War and Peace* doesn't hold a candle to *The Warble of Fleetfoot*. And as for works of lesser merit such as Plato's *Republic*, *Gulliver's Travels*, and the egregiously overrated *Hamlet*—fer-*git* 'em!"

"Ernie, I see that you've come into a House of the Lord packing heat."

"This is also the Wild West, Walter," I rejoinder, looking to see who's not here. Where are Grandma and Dad's elder sister Aunt Lillian? Where's Dad's eldest brother who drowned right after completing high school? Where's Dad's alcoholic elder brother? Where's Dad?

I recognize a baker's dozen of the spinster schoolteachers who lionized Grandpa sufficiently to trail behind his stocky little figure during his summer Site Recitals. "*Upon this site!*" Thus would Grandpa launch into his orations, standing on the actual Battlefield of Fallen Timbers, or Tippecanoe. . . .

I spot 'Sieur La Salle wearing a bedraggled periwig, and George Rogers Clark in mud-splattered buckskin—subjects of Grandpa's biographies for boys. Grandpa idolized Heroes who commanded little bands of men in the Wilderness.

"Uh, Walter?"

"Ernie?"

"What can you tell me about those seedy-looking characters lining the front pew?"

"Why, that's the Sedona chapter of NAMBLA."

"What?"

"North American Man-Boy Love Association, Ernie. I'd better go join them. After all, they picked up my train fare."

Now solemn organ music wafts across the air. A little fat man rises from the front pew and walks over to Grandpa's coffin. He's familiar-looking. . . .

Peter Lorre! Wow! Contemplating the reclining bust of Grandpa, the squat little movie actor arches his eyebrows. His lips commence a sardonic writhing. "Oh come now, Bela," says Peter Lorre in his Peter Lorre voice, cross between a simper and a hiss. "Surely you are only pretending."

Now I'm approaching Grandpa's open coffin. Reaching for the Colt Peacemaker dangling at my hip I say, "Wake up, Grandpa."

I'm awake. Laurel's beside me in a house we're renting on Airport Road. She knows the story. When I wake up on the feather mattress in the Sun Room I pretend to be asleep but it never works. There are always Grandpa's tiny alert eyes gleaming like cockroaches. "Awake, Scuffy? Come over into Grandpa's bed." His bare feet pinion my ankles beneath the comforter. I struggle, fighting off his paws. He's a garbage pail of feces and waterlogged cigarette butts. "Don't you know what real men do in the woods, Scuffy? You're not one of those sissy little girls, are you?"

My mother looks stricken. "You'd better be telling the truth, Ernest, is all I have to say."

"I won't go into Grandpa's bed. Not even one more time."

"What am I going to do now?" She worships the ground my grandfather walks on. "I suppose I'd better call your grandmother."

Grandma and Aunt Lillian arrive at our Stull Avenue home following supper. "Might be a good idea if Mother and I spoke with Ernest in private," says Aunt Lillian, my father's older sister who weighs four hundred pounds and is a Monroe County social worker. Aunt Lillian resides with Grandma and Grandpa at Murmuring Maples, Dad's boyhood home on High Street here in Bloomington. She and Grandma have shared the master bedroom ever since the day Grandma discovered herself to be pregnant with my father, her last child. Grandpa sleeps in Dad's tiny boyhood room called the Sun Room due to all the windows. Grandpa shared the room with Dad until after Dad's high school graduation.

"Would the front room be all right for this?" my mother asks.

"Come along, Ernest." Aunt Lillian edges sideways through the doorway into the front room. "Coming, Mother?"

Aunt Lillian shuts the three of us in together. She and Grandma occupy the couch. I sit facing them in a straight-backed chair. "Now, Ernest," Aunt Lillian begins. "Why don't you talk about Dad, I mean your grandfather."

I talk.

"And this started how long ago?" asks Aunt Lillian.

"After Dad died." I was nine when he committed suicide. Now I'm ten. "It's when I stay overnight at your house, and you make me sleep in the Sun Room."

"Does Dad touch you on your penis?"

"Oh, Lillian!"

"Please, Mother. Allow me to get to the bottom of this in my own fashion."

"Only when I can't keep both of his hands away at the same time."

"And what about placing your hand on *his* penis?"

"I won't touch it!"

"And what about your . . . bottom?"

"Grandpa holds me down on my back."

Grandma squirms and sighs on the couch.

"Now, Ernest, did Dad, I mean your grandfather ever have you take his penis in your mouth?"

"No!"

Who could even think of such a thing?

"Thank the Lord!" Grandma puts in.

"Think hard now. Does your grandfather ever push his penis inside your bottom?"

"What?"

"Surely by now you've observed how dogs—"

"Lillian!"

"No!" I cry out.

"Never?"

"Not ever!"

"Or persuade you to push your own penis inside him in . . . that particular manner?"

I'm growing sick to my stomach. There's a danger of vomiting up my mother's pot roast and carrots. "No!"

"Thank the Lord!" sighs Grandma.

"Mother? Any questions for Ernest?"

"No, Lillian."

"I have just one more question. Ernest?"

"Yes, Aunt Lillian."

"Why have you decided to come forward with this?"

"Because Grandpa told me that he doesn't have forever."

"Well, that about covers it." Aunt Lillian hoists her bulk up off the couch. "Mother and I will have a little talk with Dad. Right, Mother?"

"Do I have to get in bed with Grandpa any more?" I ask them.

"No, most assuredly you do not. Come along, Mother."

"All right, Lillian."

We exit into the hall where my mother is waiting with stricken eyes.

"Ernest is going to be fine," Aunt Lillian assures her.

"I have always had only the highest regard for Ernest's grandfather."

"Well, that's not to say Dad doesn't have his little peccadilloes. All men do. At least that's been *our* experience, isn't that right Mother?"

"I need to go, Lillian."

"I need to know what this is all about," my mother says.

"Let me put it like this," Aunt Lillian says. "I don't mean to accuse Ernest of making a mountain out of a molehill but it's nothing that cannot be dealt with within the confines of the family."

"Is Ernest telling the truth?" my mother asks.

"I'm not well, Lillian," Grandma says.

"Some things are best swept under the rug, and this is most definitely one of them," Aunt Lillian says.

"Does Ernest require punishment?" my mother asks.

"Don't anyone even *dare* punish this child!" Grandma cries out.

"Now, Mother, calm down," Aunt Lillian says. "Becoming hysterical isn't going to help a thing. Come along. We're finished here."

My stepson Josh and his son Akiva visit us in Sedona. Akiva's six. I'm his "Pa Pa." Josh is a master-mechanic. He's a wonderful father to Akiva.

When I saw Akiva for the first time, the day following his home birth, I experienced an overwhelming sense of déjà vu. "I *know* that child," I told Laurel. "I've seen him before. And there's something else, too. He's going to be incredibly smart."

"How can you tell?"

"A knack I have, something in the genes. Trust me."

Josh is an expert rock climber. He and Akiva are scaling clear to the top of Cathedral Rock. They're so far above us that I make them out as a pair of tiny blue dots against the red cliff wall. It comforts me, knowing that they're both utterly safe.

I'm on the couch in our living room, here in Worthington, Ohio, leafing through our Sedona photo albums. Here are some things we have no pictures of:

Kate Moss

Johnny Depp

211

CHAPTER 7

Mr. Cuddy
Jane Russell
Or, Elvis
The Meanest Man in the World
The Doberman Pincer
Cerberus
Dog Lady
Richard Gere
A Vortex
The Milky Way
My Dream

I scout several video rentals in and around Columbus, Ohio for the Sedona Westerns that I've not yet seen, but the clerks all tell the same story.

"Naw. Sorry, Mister. Couple, three years back we got rid of our Westerns."

And I return home feeling bereft, like F. Scott Fitzgerald's Dick Diver in *Tender Is the Night* when he cries out, after his father's burial, "Good-by, my father—good-by, all my fathers."

HAPPY TRAIL—THE MOVIE
Worthington, Ohio

Meanwhile, back at the ranch. . . .

—Anonymous

Happy Trail—The Movie

May 8, 2003

Ernest Lockridge and Laurel Richardson

Opening Shot. The Great American Kitchen in Middle America. Ernest and Laurel seated at their round table. No need to describe them: their casting precedes the script by decades. Across the table lie scattered AAA triptiks to exotic Des Moines, Iowa. Also manuscript pages of Travels with Ernest. *The Great American Back Yard, visible through the French Doors, requires urgent mowing. Solid walls of green—leather-leaf viburnum, rhododendron, mock orange, pea berry, arbor vitae, dogwood, redbud, crabapple, peony, maple, lilac, and a plethora of weeds and weed-tree saplings—create a Natural Fortress. Bird feeders ring the yard like sentinels. Finches bejewel the thistle-feeder. There's a sponge-ware birdbath manufactured in Zanesville, Ohio. A sundial that came down from Ernest's great-grandfather rests on a pedestal of mortared limestone shards. "Grow old with me, the best is yet to be," says the sundial. "I record only the sunlight." It's a sun-drenched morning. Ernest turns on the Radio Shack tape recorder, bought on Sale in 1996 for $26.60.*

ERNEST:

Our story's a farrago of close calls. Death Valley, Shenandoah, Diamond Mountain. Near-death experiences we've not written about. That fall I took at the Lew Wallace Memorial in Crawfordsville, Indiana dislocating my shoulder—

LAUREL:

Ouch! Yes.

ERNEST:

Remember dependable old Roy at the climax of those great grainy movies, riding Trigger at full gallop to save Dale Evans?

LAUREL:

I'm still in love with Trigger.

ERNEST:

Hell, the last time I was on a horse he tried to devour one of my legs.

LAUREL:

Horses are vegetarian, Ernest.

ERNEST:

My mount was expressing utter contempt for his rider's lack of horsepersonship. So anyway, our Ernest is none other than the *Anti-Roy* who leads the heroine into peril. He's the saloon owner, the bad guy who's on the verge of dropping shapely Dale down the mine shaft if sharpshooting Roy fails to arrive in the nick of time.

LAUREL:

You're giving yourself too much credit, Ernest. You don't do these things on purpose, do you?

ERNEST:

So I'll simply come across in my own book as the worst damn travel guide since . . . help me out here, honey. . . .

LAUREL:

Moses.

ERNEST:

Right. What say we open a travel bureau, TRAVELS WITH ERNEST, and advertise ourselves using Robert Frost's line about "a guide to lead you who only has at heart your getting lost"? Good thing I spent my professional life leading folks astray through poems, novels, and the like. At least the pitfalls there don't actually *kill* people.

LAUREL:

On our trip to Death Valley this last April, we didn't attempt anything near so ambitious as crossing the valley on foot. We couldn't even find the place where we thought we had tried to cross a decade ago. So, you know, you can't cross the same valley twice.

ERNEST:

You can't go home again.

LAUREL:

You can't step twice into the same valley.

ERNEST AND LAUREL:

Into the same graben.

ERNEST:

Damn good thing, too. If I'd found the spot, I'd have had us walk it again. And who knows what might've happened? Let it not be said that experience has ever been my guide.

LAUREL:

So, we've gotten lost—not on purpose. But part of me thinks everything happens for a purpose. (*Coughs.*) I can't stand my voice. Got to go take a Claritin.

There's a metallic thud against plate glass out on the Sun Porch adjoining the kitchen.

ERNEST:

What the devil—?

LAUREL:

Wait. . . .

A flustered fallen sparrow rises from the grass, ruffles its feathers, cocks its tiny head, and takes off into the clear spring air.

ERNEST:

Thank God. . . .

LAUREL:

Ernest, don't you think the symbolism is becoming a wee bit overly . . . fortuitous?

ERNEST:

Who are we, mere mortals, to question the workings of a Higher Power? Now, where were we before God interrupted the conversation?

LAUREL:

In our accounts of our travels, then, one of the motifs is that we got lost out there in the real world. In the world of "action." But there's something else about "lost" that intrigues you. Yes?

ERNEST:

Just that the writing of this book, itself, has represented a traveling into unknown, uncharted territory. Have we "gotten lost" in the process? Or, what have we lost, if anything, and what have we found? For instance, as I wrote I more and more found myself exploring the "in here" along with the "out there," something I had no intention of doing when we initiated this project. Quite the contrary, in fact. I'm accustomed in my writing, especially my fictional writing, to decking myself out in camouflage. So this is new to me, traveling through the world, and *openly* through myself.

LAUREL:

So, would you change your mind then and say you weren't such a bad guide?

ERNEST AND LAUREL:

(*Laughing.*)

ERNEST:

I wouldn't go *that* far.

LAUREL:

Learning about yourself?

ERNEST:

Most of what I've "learned" about myself isn't exactly welcome knowledge.

A strange knocking begins in the living room.

ERNEST:

(*begins to rise*). What the holy hell—?

The knocking ceases. Then starts up again.

LAUREL:

A-ha! *That's* the noise!

ERNEST:

What is?

LAUREL:

Mimi's trying to pry the ping-pong ball out of her cat maze toy.

ERNEST:

Glad it's not the sky falling in.

LAUREL:

Don't you wish all mysteries were so easy to solve?

ERNEST:

Where were we?

LAUREL:

That we do get lost—in a good way—in our writing.

ERNEST:

So . . . in the end I decided, what the hell! I'd go the whole hog and expose this . . . thing that's lain festering and misunderstood for well over fifty years now. And not merely to serve up some nasty little tidbit regarding the trivial "mystery of myself," but to solve a "public mystery," something still floating "out there" that might interest a few doddering survivors from the 1940s who recall big fat best-sellers like *Raintree County.*

LAUREL:

And wonder why your Dad committed suicide.

ERNEST:

I regard my little revelations as a kind of public service (*laughing*) to Our Common Culture.

LAUREL:

Let's just get lost in this conversation!

ERNEST:

But not to the extent that it bears a hideous resemblance to *My Dinner with Andre.*

Doorbell rings.

LAUREL:

The Appraiser.

ERNEST:
Twelve noon, by golly. Right on time.

Ernest turns the tape recorder off. Laurel and Ernest go through the living room to the front door. They open the door and find two young men wearing bill-backward baseball caps standing on the brick stoop. They are not The Appraiser.

YOUNG MAN:
We're from Dan the Gutterman. You called—
ERNEST:
By all means, go to it!
YOUNG MAN:
(*crestfallen*). Don't do it?
ERNEST:
Sorry. No, I meant *do* it, guys. Go ahead! All those maple seeds're growing into a National Forest up there. And, yeah, snake out the drain-lines to the street.
YOUNG MEN:
Yes Sir!

Laurel and Ernest return to The Great American Kitchen and resume their seats at the round table. Ernest turns the tape recorder back on.

ERNEST:
Whew! Okay. Now why don't *you* go to it?
LAUREL:
Okay. What surprised me about my last narrative for this book was that I wrote myself back into Sociology 101. And, I couldn't let it go. I tried writing it out of my text, but it wouldn't go away. So, there it is. "Invasion-and-Succession." Although I don't have a secret past or a public figure of a father to contend with, I do have a deep sense of loss—still—from my personal experience as a three-year-old with what the sociologist calls "invasion-and-succession. . . ."

Fade out of The Great American Kitchen. Pan onto Lake Park Avenue on Chicago's South Side, 1940. A row of mansions line the street. On the left is a general store. Pan slowly past Mansion One, and past Mansion Two—which has a gravel front lot and a mangy boxer chained to a post, to Mansion Three. It is gray stone. Hold. Pan inside. Mansion Three is semipartitioned. Laurel's mother's family—Orthodox Jews from Russia—occupy the small partitioned-off section; Laurel and her immediate family occupy the rest of the mansion. Three-year-old Laurel is in her grandparents' kosher kitchen. The doorway is ajar.

GRAMMA:
Gelt le Leah. (*She hands Laurel two pennies.*)
LAUREL:
At dank, Bubba.

Gramma leans down waiting for Laurel to kiss her cheek.

AUNT CEIL:
Eich ben Schlopen Maedala. (*Smiling, she cups Laurel's hand and puts a little golden ring with a big glass topaz on her middle finger.*)
LAUREL:
Danka, Tanta Ceil. (*Laurel twists the ring on her finger and smiles.*)
JAMPA:
Mook, mook, kindela. (*Smiling, Jampa hands Laurel a glass of milk. Kisses her on the top of her head.*)
AUNT CEIL AND LAUREL:
(*singing together*). Aleph-baez, Aleph-baez.

A voice yells from beyond the doorway.

MOTHER:
Enough already! Stop talking Yiddish! We're Americans now.
FATHER:
It's okay, Rose. Maybe I'll learn some Yiddish, too. It might help me with my political career. (*Hearty laugh.*) Or with the notorious Jewish criminals I've chosen to defend. Laurel (*heartily*), come on back here. I've bought something for you.

Fade out. Fade in on the sidewalk. Laurel's there with a new red trike. Her father—a tall, handsome Irishman wearing a dark pinstripe suit and a Dobbs hat—places her on the trike's seat.

CHAPTER 8

FATHER:
Have fun on your own little red trike. Just for you. Yours. Not your brother's or your sister's. Not a hand-me-down. New and just for you!

Laurel's father goes back into the house. Laurel rides her trike to and from the corner store. The boxer is in the gravel lot, chained to his post. He looks at Laurel with the whites of his eyes showing, and his muscles showing, not hidden with furriness, and the thing between his legs showing, too. He growls at her and snaps. Each time she passes she looks at him with fear and hatred.

LAUREL:
You bad dog! Traife Hund! Traife Hund!

Laurel parks her trike by Mansion One and enters. Mansion One is partitioned into twelve apartments. African-American adults and children are in the hallways. There is happy music, giggling, and banter. Laurel knocks on a door and an eight-year-old African American boy invites her in. Several sets of bunk beds are in the room, as are several African American children and a baby. Laurel climbs onto a bunk and The Boy joins her.

LAUREL:
Does the baby drink choc-late milk?
THE BOY:
No. She drink white milk juss like yo'll.
LAUREL:
We're going to move.
THE BOY:
When?
LAUREL:
I don't know. But we are.

The Boy scrambles down from the bunk and rummages inside a small crate that holds his clothes and possessions. The Boy hands Laurel a small crystal ball—a marble purie.

THE BOY:
Heah, take this.

LAUREL:

Danka. You're nice, kinehora.

THE BOY:

So're yo'll. Kine-ho-ra?

LAUREL:

Stops the evil eye, Gramma says.

Laurel is holding the purie in her ring hand riding her trike past The Boxer, who is looking at her with wet hungry eyes. A stringy-haired, freckled, ten-year-old girl wearing a hand-me-down outsized cotton dress is in the gravel lot.

LAUREL:

Bad Hund! Traife Hund!

THE GIRL:

(*yells at Laurel*). "Ne-gra lovah! Ne-gra lovah."

LAUREL:

Iknorant! Traife! Iknorant traife!

Laurel's trike spills her onto the gravel. The purie rolls too close to The Boxer for Laurel to retrieve it. Bits of gravel stick to her skinned forearms, which she pats. She starts to cry and runs for home.

MOTHER:

Why are you crying? Where is your trike?

LAUREL:

Her Dog bit me. (*Points to scrapes on forearm.*) Here.

FATHER:

I'd better call the police.

Fade out. Fade in on the gravel lot. The Girl is there holding her father's red-speckled hand in one of her hands and Laurel's purie in the other. Her father's hair is red and his face is red—just like hers. He is wearing a sleeveless undershirt. The Boxer and Laurel eye each other. Two policemen arrive with guns.

FATHER:

The police are going to shoot our neighbor's boxer for attacking you. Do you know what it means when a dog gets shot?

LAUREL:

It hurts him.

FATHER:

It kills him. That means the dog will never hurt you again. But we should never kill just to kill. All animals have a right to live. Do you understand?

LAUREL:

(*hesitantly—then more forcefully*). Ye—ss.

FATHER:

Well. . . .

LAUREL:

(*howling like a dog; camera angle such that viewers at first think it is The Dog*). Ai-Ai-Ai!

FATHER:

The boxer didn't attack you, did he?

LAUREL:

(*soulfully, shaking her head*). No.

Father pulls some bills out of his pants pocket, which he folds into the police officers' hands.

FATHER:

Top of the day, Gents. Thanks for coming.

Fade out. Fade in. A moving truck appears in front of the family's mansion.

LAUREL:

Are we really moving? Where's Gramma? Jampa?

FATHER:

They're not coming with us. We will not see them for a while.

LAUREL:

(*crying hysterically, breathless*). Zie gezint. Zie gezint, zie gezint, zie gezint.

MOTHER:

In American it's "God be with you!" Say it.

LAUREL:

(*screaming*). Zie gezint!

Fade out. Fade in. The moving truck is filled, as is the car. Laurel is riding backward in the back of the car. She sees her tricycle, handlebars askew, lying on the sidewalk by the gravel yard.

LAUREL:

My trike!

FATHER:

There was no room for it. And soon you'll be old enough for a bicycle.

LAUREL:

(*crying*). No fair!

The camera follows Laurel's eyes through the car's rear window. The Boy is running to get the trike. The Girl unchains her dog. Fade out.
Fade back to The Great American Kitchen.

LAUREL:

So, I was surprised that the writing ended with sociological ideas. I kept trying to bring it to a spiritual plane—hope and prayers and blessings—but the sociological truths just kept coming back for me. . . . The changing human history of Sedona in which I experience my own life.

ERNEST:

You've been trying to get away from sociology only to discover that you can't. It's an ingrained habit of mind. But why even want to escape such central aspects of ourselves? Aren't there some old habits we should be . . . maintaining on life support?

LAUREL:

Sociology for me, literature for you?

ERNEST:

In writing these stories I find I'm still deeply involved in the appreciation and love of literature, and even—God help me—teaching it. You can't force yourself to retire, I guess. After writing up my Peter Lorre dream I imagined myself back teaching one of my so-called "creative writing" classes using my dream to illustrate how fiction resembles the night-dream where connections "happen" because the neurons, the whole intricate organic package of the brain, itself, is so tightly wrapped. Dad, you know, assigned primacy to dreaming over being awake, but that's another story.

LAUREL:

Or yet another part of the same story. Was your Peter Lorre dream a bona fide night-dream, by the way?

ERNEST:

Yup. Shortly before coming to Sedona I happened to catch Peter Lorre as a child-murderer in *M.*, and my sleeping brain "recalled" that story or urban legend about Lorre contemplating Bela Lugosi—Dracula!—in his casket and coming out with his famous wisecrack.

LAUREL:

(*rising up from her chair and flapping her arms, mimicking Bela Lugosi*). I ham halmost a Gahd!

ERNEST:

The Bride of Dracula, eh? Bela Lugosi, but also Bella Abzug. How nice for us writers that these connections happen, eh?

LAUREL:

Maybe because we have a deeply ingrained core vision—a perspective, our way of knowing and organizing the world. So deep that it affects us without conscious effort. And lets our writing move us in new directions. In this book, you've moved into a more personal realm. And, I've moved more into literary nonfiction. And we've both loved the process.

ERNEST:

Yes.

LAUREL:

I've liked our negotiations over what will be in the book, too. I had originally written the negative parts of my Sedona narrative for another purpose—a book I have in mind about "resisting retirement." And I didn't want to include it in this book.

ERNEST:

But I had an overpowering feeling of something I wanted to get out. At the time only God knew what. But I told you my feelings—

LAUREL:

Once I knew them, I relented.

ERNEST:

And I wrote about Sedona.

LAUREL:

And I revised my piece. I'm glad I did. But what is fascinating to me is that I revised mine to foreshadow yours. To set yours up, and it set me up, too. I'd never before been the first act in a stand-up—

ERNEST:

Routine.

The phone rings.

LAUREL:

Maybe that's The Appraiser.

The phone rings again. Ernest checks the caller ID.

ERNEST:

It's Botox Bob.

He hands the cordless phone to Laurel.

LAUREL:

Who?

ERNEST:

Your dermatologist's office is calling.

LAUREL:

Why, I've never even thought of—Yes, this is she . . . thanks for the reminder . . . bye. . . . Botox? My God, Ernest!

ERNEST:

Hey, I'm thinking of having the wrinkles taken out of my—

LAUREL:

We're on record here!

ERNEST:

Okay, where were we? So yes . . . collaboration took on a whole other meaning for you, eh?

LAUREL:

Yes, it did. What about you? Anything . . . different?

ERNEST:

Can't say I've ever really collaborated before, unless one counts Occupied France during World War Two.

LAUREL:

Oh, Ernest, get real!

ERNEST:

Jawohl! I'd never written creative nonfiction prior to this, at least not intentionally. And indeed the whole issue of "intentionality" has taken on new meanings for us both, I think. All these trips . . . and it was never our intention at the time to use them as writing fodder.

LAUREL:

Of course not.

ERNEST:

So it really is fascinating to me that we recently embarked on two trips—Bermuda and Death Valley again—with the explicit intention of writing about them. And now we don't want to do it. Why not?

LAUREL:

(*large breath, opens her mouth to speak*).

ERNEST:

And let me just throw in another thought before it slips into a Black Hole. I have never in my life written narrative on assignment. Never been a reporter. Never written a creative piece on assignment, even as a college student because I never took a creative writing class, though I've taught 'em up the kazoo. And that's it! The mere notion of traveling somewhere to write about it cramps, or strangles, my style because it stifles my freedom. For me, narrative writing may be the closest I've come to a pristine sense of Freedom. . . . Boy am I a spoiled brat!

A whirring, roaring noise from outside becomes audible. It grows gradually louder.

LAUREL:

If I'd go somewhere with the idea of doing an ethnography, I'd be taking notes and collecting materials in the field. But I don't want to do that, because I want to enjoy what I'm doing for itself. I don't want to be—your favorite phrase—"a participant-observer," removed from the experience when I've gone for the experience.

ERNEST:

To be a participant-observer means you're not really *in* the experience, you're *outside* it the way a—

LAUREL:

A journalist.

ERNEST:

Or all those guys with cameras around their necks like dog collars as if to announce, "Look, I'm not really present in my life, I'm here to photograph whatever's outside me." Once upon a time I carried a notebook to jot down observations, things I overheard. "The Novelist"—twelve steps removed from life. Well, screw that. I went cold turkey. No notebook. Nothing. Or, whatever's inside my skull when I'm there facing the blank screen. I'm gifted with an extraordinary memory—

LAUREL:

(*getting testy*). Look, I have a good memory, Ernest, maybe not the same as yours—

ERNEST:

For things I'd just as soon forget, thanks.

LAUREL:

Oh. Okay. I used to like the participant-observer role, because it gave me something to do in situations where I was bored or uncomfortable or tired of being with people.

ERNEST:

We're introverts, all right. Both of us.

LAUREL:

But, I don't like doing that anymore. I want to be engaged in the world I'm in—not dispassionate about it.

ERNEST:

We've not traveled anywhere with the idea of getting into trouble so we can write about it—pushing an envelope so something dramatic might happen. No need to, really. My sheer ineptitude as a travel guide comes to our rescue as "travel writers," in terms of creating difficulties.

LAUREL:

The motor scooter this time around in Bermuda, for example—

ERNEST:

We went to rent one, the way we'd rented a moped our first time on the island twenty-four years ago. But this time I couldn't get the hang of the thing. I'm riding around in wobbly circles on the tarmac and the rental guy keeps saying, "It's a disaster, it's going to be a disaster." And he had it exactly right. If we'd gone and rented the thing anyway I can guarantee there'd have been something dramatic to write about—if one of us had managed to walk away from the wreckage. Instead, we bought a seven-day bus pass and had ourselves a safe and secure, and undramatic good old time.

LAUREL:

About Bermuda—I have some other feelings, too. . . .

Laurel's soliloquy.

LAUREL:

We went to Bermuda first in March 1979. You and I had been together since September of 1978. We'd been together for six months. Yes. We'd been living together for six months. We had my impossible teenage sons. You had your children. We had some of your friends opposed to our relationship. I had students who thought I had stopped being a feminist because we were living together. You had no money. You had the old broken-down Ford with the bad brakes. You did have a job. A full-professor in the Department of English. A penniless full professor. You were struggling with the moral issues of leaving your wife, but yet the preservation of your own life had already become such that you had to leave. If you were dead, the children would have had nothing. So the moral decision was to leave. I paid for the trip to Bermuda. It was my idea. I wanted to know how it was for you and me to be together in a space not complexified by my family, your family, my friends, your friends. I wanted to see how we were together—just us— for a week or ten days. And, we had a wonderful time. Yes. The weather was horrendous. We had the storm—the near hurricane—blowing out the windows in our hotel's main dining room. We rode on the motor scooter. We ate well. We had a great time. And to me that was a turning point in our relationship. It was never a question of whether we cared or loved each other—love is not enough—it was "Will this work? Can we be with each other? Is this a possible permanent lifelong relationship?" It was that turning point that I felt. And because it was such an important time, it feels too private to write about and to share with the world. I can't write about something this central, important, and private. . . .

LAUREL:

When I compare our First Bermuda Experience with the second one, although we had a fine time with each other we didn't much like Bermuda this time around—

ERNEST:

It had changed.

LAUREL:

And I didn't want the negativity of my feelings about Bermuda—it's still beautiful to look at—

ERNEST:

And my photos of this trip were the best I ever took—

LAUREL:

Yes. But, I don't want my negative reactions to the "new Bermuda" to affect my memories and construction of the "old Bermuda" that solidified our relationship.

ERNEST:

There's something distinctly *non*literary about our first trip to Bermuda, back in 1979. Think of, say, Hemingway's "Short Happy Life of Frances Macomber" or "The Snows of Kilimanjaro." A couple are "getting away from it all"—away from toxic outside influences—in an effort to bring their relationship back to health, only to discover that the relationship *is* the pathology. Isolated in a test tube or Petri dish the relationship becomes a full-blown disease. For us, being alone together had precisely the opposite effect.

Heavy buzzing noise . . . becoming louder and louder over their heads. The guttermen are cleaning out the gutters, and roto-rootering to the street. The racket resembles a helicopter landing on the roof.

ERNEST:

For me the high point of our 2003 return was the pilgrimage we made to Holiday Inn where we stayed in 1979.

LAUREL:

The hotel's still there, though it's been derelict and abandoned for the past fifteen years.

ERNEST:
We made a pilgrimage up the high hill to pay homage to the Holy Site.
LAUREL:
And took snapshots of our room.
ERNEST:
Its balcony.
LAUREL:
And I wanted to be Juliet up there, but the sign said, "NO ENTRY."
ERNEST:
(*hearty laughter*). And the tennis courts were still there. . . .

The buzzing noise lessens. Fade out.

Fade in. The scene shifts to 1979—the tennis courts, Holiday Inn, Bermuda. Ernest and Laurel are playing tennis. Ernest is on a second serve. Over a dozen Bermudan men have gathered behind the fence. They stand there silently, looking at Laurel. And who would blame them? She leaves her side of the court, walks over to Ernest and whispers in his ear.

LAUREL:
Ernest?
ERNEST:
Uh-huh?
LAUREL:
I know why Lolita always missed her second serve. Do you?
ERNEST:
No. Why?
LAUREL:
(*walking back*). Try to figure it out. (*Teasing.*) Maybe I'll tell you later on this evening.

Ernest sends his second serve into the net. Fade out.
Fade to The Great American Kitchen.

LAUREL:
And it was there that I got my only point ever off of you!
ERNEST:
Tennis point.

LAUREL:

Well, of course.

ERNEST:

Playing *mind* tennis!

LAUREL:

The only way I could get a point. That tennis in Bermuda was a little scary wasn't it?

ERNEST:

All those guys gathering to stare at you on the court. A huge crowd had formed by the time we decided we'd better bag it up. That didn't happen on our second trip.

Buzzing noise resumes outside.

LAUREL:

Honey, I'm twenty-four years older!

ERNEST:

And we didn't play tennis. We did, however, make a return trip to Death Valley with the notion in mind of wrapping up this book by having its bottom half-shell our initial trip to Death Valley, with our most recent one closing the nut-case and sealing it neatly shut.

LAUREL:

Binding us in a nutshell.

ERNEST:

And now we've decided against that.

LAUREL:

It's a more open-ended project now. Let's hope that's a virtue. . . .

The guttermen are working the rear of the house now. The noise grows more intense.

LAUREL:

And let's hope we're getting *them* on tape. Geez! Shut up there!

ERNEST:

Did I already mention the guys with cameras?

LAUREL:

Yes. But what about these gutter-suckers?

CHAPTER 8

ERNEST:

Well, for one thing they're turning my brain to mush. It's churlish to complain, though. There they are up there risking life and limb to improve the environment—

LAUREL:

By cutting down the National Forest?

ERNEST:

(*his voice rising*). And what are we doing for the Earth?

LAUREL:

(*almost shouting*). Waiting for The Appraiser?

The noise reaches a deafening level. Then suddenly it stops. Dead silence.

ERNEST:

What did you say just now?

LAUREL:

Waiting for The Appraiser.

ERNEST:

Which reminds me of something else I wanted us to talk about, and that's our pop-culture titles coupled with our high-culture epigraphs.

LAUREL:

Which one is *Waiting for Godot?* High culture or low?

ERNEST:

Both. Long before I became "educated" in the great high-culture works of Shakespeare, Milton—not to mention William H. Burroughs and Samuel Beckett—I was educating myself in great works of literature starring Randolph Scott, John Wayne, Roy Rogers, you know, the whole magnificent universe of literature created by Edgar Rice Burroughs and writers of the same kidney such as Zane Grey and Frank L. Baum. Didn't what's-his-name, the Cowardly Lion in *The Wizard of Oz* . . . *Bert Lahr*! . . . create the role of Estragon in *Waiting for Godot?* And now it all fits together or somehow goes together and certainly is all part and parcel of yours truly. I mean, those childhood organ-transplants took! Hell, honey, the John Wayne movies during the English-speaking world's Golden Age of Literature were written by *Shakespeare*!

There comes a strident banging on the front door.

LAUREL:

That's The Appraiser.

Ernest turns off the tape recorder. Laurel remains in the kitchen as he goes to the front door and opens it. A gutterman is standing on the stoop.

YOUNG MAN:

(*handing Ernest the bill*). We've finished up here, sir.

ERNEST:

Hey, thanks a whole lot. (*He glances at the bill, removes a checkbook from the desk in the living room and, bending over, scrawls out a check with the checkbook against his knee. He tears out the check and hands it to the young man.*) There you go. And, hey, thanks again, I mean it.

YOUNG MAN:

Any time, sir. Just give a call.

Ernest shuts the door. He returns to the kitchen and seats himself at the table.

ERNEST:

Job well done.

LAUREL:

You inspected their work?

ERNEST:

I meant, job over with and finished. Let's see whether we can finish up here before The Appraiser arrives.

LAUREL:

So. . . . It delights me that we have chosen pop-culture referents for our papers and for the title of our book, *Travels with Ernest*—with its nod to *Travels with Charlie*—

ERNEST:

John Steinbeck and his mutt. Right?

LAUREL:

Right.

ERNEST:

And Martha Gellhorn's *Travels with Myself and Another*. She was Hemingway's third wife and "Another," though never named, is none other than Hemingway, himself. So, a euphemistic version of *our* title.

CHAPTER 8

LAUREL:

And to the Ernest movies—

ERNEST:

Which conferred much-needed dignity upon the world's most popular male name.

LAUREL:

I think of our book as a True Romance—which sounds like a paradox, even an oxymoron. But our True Romance incorporates both sociology and the humanities.

ERNEST:

By all means, let's pay homage to the old pop "True Romance" magazines—

LAUREL:

And to the ancient literary genre, the Romance—

ERNEST:

Where heroes have mysterious adventures and affairs of the heart—

LAUREL:

In locations remote from common life.

ERNEST:

Extravagant adventures. *The Odyssey. Arabian Nights. Orlando Furioso. The Faerie Queene, The Alexandria Quartet . . . Travels with Ernest!*

LAUREL:

And, what about our epigraphs from High Culture?

ERNEST:

Prince Hal, Jack Worthing, and Tarzan form a continuity. Me Ernest, you Laurel! Might as easily separate the alphabet from alphabet soup as separate the "high" from the "low" in our grand farrago of a Culture. Wilde, hey wot?

LAUREL:

I'll drink to that. (*Laurel lifts her Enchantment Resort water bottle.*)

ERNEST:

Let me just retrieve my Irish pub glass. (*Rises from the table and goes to the cupboard, opening it.*) Here we are. (*Removes the glass, filling it with water from the filtered tap, holding the glass high.*) Skoal! Those old Vikings sure had one terrific idea, quaffing their toasts from a human skull!

LAUREL:

To life!

Ernest and Laurel touch containers and drink.

ERNEST:

You said something once. . . . That it seemed to you that my narratives form an independent narrative. I forget how you put it. . . .

LAUREL:

Your meta-narrative starts with a mystery. You are beside yourself on March 7th trying to get yourself maybe killed walking across Death Valley.

ERNEST:

And ends with a little "revelation" regarding The Great American Suicide. . . .

The poor S.O.B. Yes. . . . This didn't just "happen," you know. Somewhere along the way I put in a wake-up call to the young novelist slumbering still inside my skull.

LAUREL:

And I guess my sociologist stayed awake, too. I weave cultural themes and motifs in and out of my pieces. And identity issues. The Jewish Irish Princess. Who am I? Who will I be? Like cultural traces left in Sedona, the traces of myself are still in my Self.

ERNEST:

There are an infinite number of ways and means for leaving some vestige of our lives on the geography and history of the earth before we die and become dust again. Our little book models one of them, perhaps . . . or many different ways.

LAUREL:

We've talked about our work as physical, intellectual, and emotional travel. I know I've cried through the writing of many of the stories. I've put some things to rest and new things have come forward that are surprising me. I'm feeling more and more that I need time to myself to do some solo writing. So, one thing that's happened here is that rather than us becoming more like each other through this process, I think we've become more individual, more independent. I feel clearer.

ERNEST:

Go on.

LAUREL:

When we first got together some umpteen years ago, I wanted to write a mystery novel with you.

ERNEST:

Ah, that.

LAUREL:

I no longer have any need to do it. That's off the table now. I feel clearer now in my own style, my own form, my own vision. I think our marriage has been strengthened through this process of collaboration.

ERNEST:

Which allows each of us an independent voice.

LAUREL:

And a chance to share our life experiences. To write, to put our trail on the ground.

ERNEST:

We're walking along together here.

LAUREL:

Right.

ERNEST:

It's not as though you're taking the road less traveled by and I'm taking the road not taken.

ERNEST AND LAUREL:

(*Laughter.*)

LAUREL:

The uninterrupted life is not worth living. Life is what happens when you're making plans. . . . Is that tape recorder still running?

ERNEST:

Uh-oh.

LAUREL:

What's wrong?

ERNEST:

I forgot to turn the thing back on.

LAUREL:

When did you turn it off?

ERNEST:

I think the last time one of the gutter guys banged at the front door. A half-hour ago?

LAUREL:

What were we talking about then?

ERNEST:

I don't remember.

LAUREL:

(*soothingly*). It'll be on the tape.

ERNEST:

Unless the tape recorder was malfunctioning.

LAUREL:

(*with certainty*). Ethnographers are used to that. It always happens. Tape recorders don't work. I always tell my students not to trust the machinery— to listen and take notes.

ERNEST:

Did you do that while we were talking?

LAUREL:

No, but between our two wonderful memories we can surely recreate what was lost thirty minutes ago.

ERNEST:

Honey, I'm exhausted. Boy do I wish old Roy Rogers would come riding to our rescue now. And not that damned Appraiser, who's—what?— over an hour late? I'm sick of waiting.

LAUREL:

Ernest, I have an idea. Let's do something different.

ERNEST:

Start taking Geritol?

LAUREL:

What about casting this conversation as a play?

ERNEST:

The play's the thing. Andy Hardy rides again!

LAUREL:

Laurel and Hardy!

ERNEST:

Heigh-ho, heigh-ho, it's back to work we go!

LAUREL:

Wait! Let's do it as a *movie*! A movie script!

Ernest picks up the tape recorder and examines it.

ERNEST:

Save that thought!

APPENDIX: HOW THIS BOOK WAS MADE

Carolyn Ellis (coeditor): How did you happen to write this book?

Laurel: Christmas Eve 2002, Ernest and I were sitting at our kitchen table, drinking a little wine and talking about the year that was nearly past and the one to come. I was weighing three writing projects and trying to decide which one to focus on during 2003. Ernest listened to my litany of "this one . . . but" and "that one . . . but" and "yet that one . . . but." He took me out of my slushiness by suggesting that we work together on a book, named that night, *Travels with Ernest*.

I am a sociologist/ethnographer. Ernest is a novelist. Sociologists are accustomed to collaborative projects; novelists are not. Even before we were married, I wanted to write with him; he was resistant—even after marriage. In 1999, though, we found a method for collaborating that was comfortable and intriguing for both of us. In twenty-six words, this was that collaborative process: we traveled; she saw; he saw; she writes; he writes; she reads his; he reads hers; they talk; he tapes; she transcribes; they vette; they publish. Each of our voices and the collaboration is honored. Because we had already presented at conferences and published two collaborative "travel" pieces—Beirut and Russia—we knew the project was eminently "doable."

Ernest: I had many things I wanted to write about. The collaborative format and structure of the travel pieces were an opportunity to express what I have wanted to express for a number of years.

Laurel: I realized that the three projects I was weighing focused on my future—and I couldn't adequately deal with them until I'd cleared up some issues from my past. *Travels* was thus constructed in our minds, that Christmas Eve, as a route through our separate and shared memories, a journey that could release our energies and bring us more fully into the present. We didn't know that the writing would so deeply renew who we are as individuals and as partners.

Ernest: Less than six months after deciding to write the book, we delivered the manuscript to AltaMira Press.

Laurel: I have never written so quickly in my life.

Arthur Bochner (coeditor): Did you faithfully adhere to your collaborating method throughout the writing of the book?

Laurel: No, we didn't.

Ernest: Go on, Laurel. It's your favorite bailiwick.

Laurel: Happy to do so. In the Beirut and Russia pieces our focus was on how ethnographic and fictional perspectives differ or overlap. Thinking about issues of observer reliability, validity, and "truth" (with a small "t") is why we chose to write separate accounts and not read or talk about them until we were having our taped conversation. We were engaged in a kind of "double-blind" science experiment.

I was also interested in replacing the idea of "triangulating"—looking at material from three rigid, fixed points in order to demonstrate "validity"—with the idea of "crystallization" (Richardson 2000). Crystals are prisms, which reflect externalities and refract within themselves, creating different colors, patterns, arrays, casting off in different directions. What we see depends upon our angle of vision.

Ernest: But as we worked on *Travels*, our interests widened and deepened.

Laurel: Yes. We no longer felt a primary focus of the book was "reliability" and "validity"; rather, we wanted to provide narrative models of how similar experiences can be shaped through different points of view—disciplinary grounding, gender, sensibilities, biographies, spiritual and emotional longings. We strove to move beyond the methodological questions into the literary/ethnographic demonstrations. The travels, thus, were geographical and emotional, relational, and symbolic.

Ernest: Then, as the book developed we began reading one another's drafts and became much more interactive around the writing of the narratives. Although we used literary techniques, we continued to write "true" accounts: we did go on these travels; these things did happen to us; we do feel what we say we feel.

Carolyn: What can you tell us about the writing of the narratives themselves?

Laurel: Both Ernest and I believe in writing as a method of discovery (Richardson 2000). We write to find things out—to make sense of things. We wanted to tell the story of our travels, but we wanted to do more than that; we wanted to make sense of our life experiences, put them in some kind of order. We set no parameters—no limits—to where our writing might take us.

Each of my narratives presented themselves as different problems I wanted to solve or a genre I wanted to explore. For example, "Laurel in Arabia"—written as a letter to my best friend—allowed me to discover how the intimacy of the epistolary form could be tweaked into a narrative account of interest to people other than my best friend.

The Ireland piece—"All in the Family"—was the first time I had constructed a narrative from looking at photos. Writing the piece required that I be patient with my emotional states because I was—to my surprise—recovering my father's place in my life. Once I knew what the piece was about—family—I heightened those narrative elements in the rewriting. The Copenhagen narrative—"Lost in the Space"—raised ethical and emotional issues, and I resisted writing it. How could I protect my hosts in Copenhagen? Should I be writing this narrative at all? Why was I so bothered? I made a writerly decision to keep the long preamble to the actual travel in the text as a narrative device for showing the reader "Hey, I am scared to go there. Scared to write this."

The Sedona piece—"Call of the Canyon"—presented another set of writing problems. I was challenged to let go of how I had framed the piece (for another venue) and then challenged to incorporate into my narrative material that would foreshadow and set up Ernest's narrative. Although I had resisted all of this, it turned out to be a Godsend for through that writing I discovered how deep my love still is for the sociological way of knowing and telling about the world.

Ernest: Somewhere into the writing of the book, I realized that I wanted the narratives to add up to a larger novelistic narrative, and I began shaping them with that desire in mind. "Death Valley Day,"—the first narrative in the book, although not the first one written—sets the problem: What is going on with Ernest? In the last narrative, "Grandson of

Paleface," I give the reader the answer. I complete the story I've wanted to write for much of my life.

Laurel: One more thing. I am a poet who likes subtext, metaphor, repetition, and body-engaging rhythms in my writing. So, in the rewriting—once I had discovered my emotionally "true" topic—I enhanced the literary markers.

Art: How did you construct the conversations?

Laurel: Ernest and I have spent twenty-five years talking to each other about matters large and small, intellectual, emotional, and spiritual. We have established interaction patterns and conversational conventions that allow us to interrupt each other—or allow one of us to go on at length. I tend to be more linear in my talking; Ernest can riff. Both of us value humor, word play, and imagistic thinking. We routinely eat three meals together every day. We talk a lot. I say all of this about our conversational habits to situate the "Conversations" in our lives, and to set forth the idea that the "Conversations" are "real" and "true"—in the sense that they represent/reflect our interactive strategies and desires. They are not contrived. Rather, they are a kind of "naturalistic sociology" exemplifying our shared "ethno-linguism," a la Edward Rose . . . and (to quote Thurber's *Golux*) "not a mere device."

Ernest: When you overhear a conversation, you're drawn into the topic, have ideas, and want to enter—put in your own two cents' worth. That's our intention . . . our invitation to our readers to enter our conversation—

Laurel: Or create new ones about their lives and work.

Carolyn: C'mon, now, I'm a "methods junkie," what's the nitty-gritty?

Laurel: Okay. We come to the kitchen table, sometimes with scribbled notes, prepared to converse, each of us having read the other's piece. "Prepared" is too slight a word. Eager is more like it, because we have not talked about what the writing/reading has evoked in us. We decide who will start the conversation; turn on the tape recorder, and talk.

Using my ancient Dictaphone machine, I do all the transcribing, an activity at which I am experienced and which I enjoy. (Sometimes, I even get into the "flow.") Just as I do when I transcribe any tape, I retain the pauses, overlaps, ahs and ums, laughs, volume, tone, and repetitions of the conversation. My goal is to preserve as nearly as possible the content and the interactional style of the conversational event.

The first written conversations (Beirut and Russia) were published almost verbatim because (as the reader probably remembers), I was interested in issues of "validity," "reliability," and "true" renditions. Later conversations we vetted and edited, more and more severely, until we found ourselves bending the barrier between the "oral" transcribed conversation and "addenda"—thoughts added to the transcript, as we engaged anew in dialogue with our text and ourselves. That is, the conversation invited *us* back in again.

Typically, after transcribing—no longer attached to the issue of "exactitude"—I would do a first draft, vetting my voice, deleting chatter, mindless repetitions, false starts and dullisms, but without altering Ernest's transcribed speech. I would sometimes add a new thought, hit the enter key, and bold type "ERNEST?" asking him to respond *in writing* to my thought. Then I would deliver a hard copy and disc to him.

Ernest: I would then edit my parts and respond to Laurel's probes. Occasionally, too, I would add new material and ask her to respond in writing.

Laurel: Each conversation went through multiple revisions, as we tried to enhance the readability and deepen our understandings. So, these published conversations themselves exemplify crossing over literary and sociological divides.

Carolyn: Hmm. This sounds similar to what Art and I do when we co-construct a narrative.

Laurel: Similar, yes. But one difference, I think, is that you and Art are striving for a unified text—while Ernest and I are most concerned about opening up the text.

Carolyn: Well, what about the construction of the movie script?

Laurel: The last travel section in the book is about Sedona. We settled at the table to have our routine taped conversation, but it felt disjointed, forced, and interrupted by doorbells, guttermen, cats, etc. We wanted (1) to explicate the Sedona narratives, (2) explain why we chose not to write about the trips we had purposefully taken that spring for inclusion in the book, and (3) bring closure to the book. Well, guess what? We were trying to do too much for the form—the conversation; what we wanted to accomplish exceeded the limits of a naturalistic conversation, which had been our template. We had to either reduce the content or find another form that could contain it.

At the end of the conversation, Ernest and I were horsing around with puns and movie stars and it occurred to me that we could use the Sedona conversation as a basis for a movie script. So, when I transcribed it, I kept in all the house noises, interruptions, and asides. Thinking the conversation could be recast following movie conventions, I proposed the soliloquy and flashbacks.

Ernest: When I first read the transcript, I was crestfallen. Unlike the other conversations, this one seemed unsalvageable. But Laurel had proposed the movie script idea and I thought, "Let me try." I downloaded the movie script of *The Usual Suspects* from the Internet so I could see how to format a script. I set the scene, introduced the characters, moved content around, directed fade-ins and fade-outs, and incorporated the cat, the guttermen, the phone calls, and The Appraiser.

Laurel: Then I rewrote the narrative of my earliest childhood memories (Richardson 2002) as a flashback scene. That writing challenge echoed one I gave my qualitative seminars—shaping material into different formats. For the flashback scene to work in the movie script, I had to cut out the secondary and tertiary themes of the narrative. Those themes were lost, but the primary one was intensified.

Ernest: Because movie script conventions permit time to stand still during flashbacks, the format was complex enough to contain the disparate goals we had in mind. And to add new ones, such as bringing Laurel's childhood—the roots of her sociological perspective—into the text.

Laurel: We also discovered that the book was a love story—a subtitle we wanted to use, but were persuaded not to—a story of two people who love each other, their work, and their lives.

Ernest: We liked that we had broken the book's format—moving it and us into a new space, modeling again our desire for open, inviting texts. We had found, to quote ourselves, a "Happy Trail" and we took it.

Laurel: Ernest was the chief writer of the script. He redacted, edited, rearranged, wrote in laugh lines and gave literary nuances to off-stage characters, such as The Appraiser. I credit him as first author of the script. Giving credit where credit is due is for me an ethical issue.

Art: So, that's it?

Laurel: Not completely, no. I like to get feedback from others on how my work *sounds*, so I read my work out loud—to my Memoir Writing

Group, Women's Poetry Workshop, and to my friend, Betty Kirschner. Not only do I get their feedback, I get their support.

Carolyn: I'm interested in how you handled discord. While traveling? While writing?

Laurel: We are good travel companions in that—generally—we agree on where we want to go, what we want to see, and how we want to get there. We both have similar "body comfort" needs and we try to have those met. Because I am the pickier (and the more easily fatigued) one, I tend to make the travel arrangements. Sometimes, in fact, traveling has been a way to escape the professional and extended family stresses of being home. We have the same attitude toward our writing together . . . and we have found a process that works. When we disagree, we tend to take a "time-out"—not trying to force a decision down the other's throat. Usually, after a spell, we can find a common ground.

Ernest: [*pause*] Yep.

Art: Any further thoughts?

Ernest: Yes. What we really like about the collaborative method we display in our text is that it is a method open to everyone—

Laurel: Indeed, I think of it as a "writing-strategy" that breaches established hierarchies such as those between the researcher and the researched, the student and teacher, the scientist and the humanist.

Ernest: No one's voice need be filtered through another person's sieve.

Laurel: And another thing, too. Students in my writing classes often talk about how lonely they get when they are writing. I hope we have given them some strategies for abating that loneliness.

Carolyn: So, where has your text taken you?

Laurel: Gratitude is the first word that comes to mind. I am grateful to have had the experiences I have had. Grateful for the writing format and process. Grateful for the existence of the Ethnographic Alternative series. The next thought is one I always have about my work, the desire that it find its audience.

Right now, I want to finish the little details associated with the publishing of a book, clean off my desk, and clean up my computer files. Then, I want to avoid, if I can, the "postpartum" ennui that sets in when I finish a major project. I'll try to reduce my blues through fulfilling other writing commitments, writing memoir to share with my Memoir Writing Group, and spending time with friends and family, and traveling—to

Shreveport to see my siblings and their spouses, to London to see some theater, and later to Japan to see my granddaughter, Shana. Ernest and I are talking about going to France and Mali, sometime in the foreseeable future, to visit Ernest's daughter and her family. And, then there's Sedona.

This writing project has changed how I feel about myself in the world, my marriage, and my family. Soon, I hope, I will be ready to take on one of the solo projects focused on my future that I had in mind before this project began. Which project I am not sure, but I am sure it will benefit from having gestated, waited, until I had made more sense of my past.

Ernest: I feel terrific. I feel I have a new lease on my writing-life. I don't plan to write fiction, but I will continue to write creative nonfiction. But there's a whole lot more to living than just writing about it. For now, I'm putting finishing touches on "Laurel Plaza," a small brick patio behind the Great American Garage, making Wall Charms, taking care of grand-kids, and playing jazz sax with the South Street Band right here in Worthington, Ohio.

References

Richardson, Laurel. 2000.
"Writing: A Method of Inquiry." In *Handbook of Qualitative Research*, 2nd ed., eds. N. K. Denzin and Y. S. Lincoln, 923–949. Thousand Oaks, Calif.: Sage.

———. 2002.
"Writing Sociology." *Cultural Studies/Critical Methodology* 2, no. 3: 415–423.

INDEX

ABOUT THE AUTHORS

Laurel Richardson is professor emerita of sociology and visiting professor of cultural studies at The Ohio State University. She completed her undergraduate work at the University of Chicago, and earned her PhD at the University of Colorado. She is the author of five books, among them *The New Other Woman*, which has been reprinted in six languages, and *Fields of Play: Constructing an Academic Life*, which has been honored with the SSSI Cooley Award. She is coeditor of the best-selling women's studies anthology *Feminist Frontiers*, now in its sixth edition. She has published widely in professional journals on qualitative methods, sociology of knowledge, and gender, as well as in literary journals. Her article "Writing: A Method of Discovery" is the most widely cited qualitative article. She has been honored for her teaching, contributions to research, service, and affirmative action. She is also a poet.

Ernest Lockridge is professor emeritus of English and creative writing at The Ohio State University. Prior to his appointment at Ohio State, he was a faculty member of the English department at Yale University, where he also earned his PhD. He spent a year as a fellow at the Center for Advanced Studies at the University of Illinois, Champagne. He is the author of three published novels; one of which, *Prince Elmo's Fire*, was a Book-of-the-Month Club selection. He is editor of *Twentieth-Century Interpretations of the Great Gatsby* (reprinted twenty times), and author of other works of literary criticism. While at Ohio State he received the Alumni Distinguished Teaching Award, Ohio State's highest and most coveted award for teaching. He is a jazz musician.

Laurel Richardson and Ernest Lockridge, married to each other, live in Worthington, Ohio. They also travel.

CREDITS

Pages 3, 190, 214: Excerpts from "Directive" from *The Poetry of Robert Frost*, edited by Edward Connery Lathem. New York: Holt, Rinehart, and Winston, 1947 [© 1969 by Henry Holt and Company, © 1975 by Lelsley Frost Ballantine]. Reprinted with permission by Henry Holt and Company, LLC.

Pages 127–48: Laurel Richardson and Ernest Lockridge, "Out of Russia." *Qualitative Inquiry* 7, no. 6 (2001): 90–109, © 2001 by Sage Publications. This chapter was originally published as "Out of Russia," reprinted by permission of Sage Publications, Inc., as chapter 5, "Petrozavodsk."

Page 181: Excerpts from "St. Winefred's Well," from *The Poems of Gerard Manley Hopkins*, edited by N. H. Mackenzie and W. H. Gardner. Oxford: Oxford University Press, 1967. Reprinted by permission of The Society of Jesus in the United States.